Financial Guide to Life

Managing, Saving, Investing, and Spending
Your Money

John Kimball

John Kimball
Silver Spring, Maryland
www.FinancialGuideToLife.com

Cover Design by Annoula Argiropoulou - www.annoulacovers.com
Book Layout © 2016 BookDesignTemplates.com

Financial Guide to Life / John Kimball. -- 1st ed.

Print Edition ISBN
ISBN-13: 978-1546744306
ISBN-10: 1546744304

Kindle Edition ISBN
.

Dedication to Sandra
Without whom little else would be possible

Compound interest is the most powerful force
in the universe.

— ATTRIBUTED TO ALBERT EINSTEIN

Contents

Introduction

Why Didn't Somebody Tell Me
This Sooner?!

Your financial future begins now. Are you going to let it control you, or are you going to take control of it? Don't just let your finances drift along, live from paycheck to paycheck, or wait for a lucky break. No matter what your financial situation, there are plenty of things you can do now to make your financial future brighter and the sooner you start, the better off you will be.

Planning now to ensure a better future seems obvious, but too often, it's hard to actually do. Lack of money, knowledge, time, or incentive lets the opportunity of *planning* slip away until a sudden need bangs at your door. The aim of this book is to provide you the knowledge and tools to better prepare for and manage life's many financial decisions. Some things we have little control over and some a lot. Some people will have to work harder or smarter than others to get results. Regardless, it is possible to control your financial future and achieve your financial goals. This book may or may not make you wealthy, but it can certainly help bring you more financial security. It will pay for itself many times over with any of its tips for saving and spending wisely.

I will be discussing sound financial principles and practical tips that will improve your financial future and give you peace of mind along life's financial journey. I will discuss them in detail as they apply to various stages along that journey. But they are more than just general goals; I will be providing you detailed tips for putting them into practice with sections on managing, saving, investing, and spending your money wisely.

I especially recommend this book to all young people, because the earlier you can start practicing sound financial principles, the better your future will be. Therefore, I start at the beginning when young people are just out of school and ready to start their own path along life's financial journey. These are the financial issues I wish someone had explained to me when I was just starting, fresh out of college with a Master's Degree. Many times when researching and writing this financial guide to life, I cried out, "Why didn't someone tell me that sooner? I want a do over!" While I am a certified financial education instructor, the basis of this book is what I have learned thru forty years of facing the same financial decisions as you, first with mistakes and trial and error, then extensive research and study with what actually works in real life.

It's never too late to get control of your finances and there is always room for improvement. I hope that no matter which stage of life you are in, you can benefit from these financial principles, tips, explanations, hard-learned wisdom, and advice to be more successful in your financial future.

I think there are three parts to managing your money:

- **Psychology** – getting and maintaining the *will power* to do what you know you should and the *won't power* for avoiding what you know you shouldn't.
- **Knowledge** – the information and principles you need to make decisions and take action to improve your financial security.
- **Tools** – resources and aids that will make it easier to maintain your will power and apply your knowledge.

Being financially successful involves both knowledge and psychology. You need the knowledge of how to be successful and the will to do it. Plenty of financial authors and seminar instructors focus on the psychological factors of getting you to follow thru with financial advice. I think it's easier to want to do something when you know how, so this book concentrates primarily on the specific knowledge and steps you should take to be financially successful. Moreover, any task is easier with the right tools, so I will concentrate on providing you the practical knowledge you need and the tools that will make everything else easier.

In particular, I try to bring, I think, an unprecedented effort to link to a growing wealth of internet tools, calculators, comparison aids, databases, and resources that will supplement the knowledge in this book and make it easier to manage your money. Of course the day this book goes to print, a bunch of links will become obsolete. That is an annoyance, but hardly fatal. Usually the resource will still be on the linked website, but moved to a different URL. Just go to the website and do a search for the moved webpage, or use your favorite web search engine. If still a no-go, I usually list several similar resources. I likely will also update the links periodically on the book's related website: www.financialguidetolife.com .

The *Financial Guide to Life* necessarily covers many topics along life's financial journey from starting out, thru marriage and kids, saving and investing, buying stuff, and on to retirement. So some chapters you won't need right away. Keep the book very close by on your bookshelf and pull it out as you need it. Nonetheless, I recommend you at least skim any chapters you skip right now so you will have a sneak preview of coming attractions and can plan accordingly. I even suggest you reread it periodically to gleam new information, improve understanding, and reinforce will power. No really, I'm not just saying that to prevent you from giving your copy of this book to your son so he doesn't have to buy his own copy.

You will soon notice that I repeat things throughout the book. That's partly because one of the few phrases I remember from my Latin class is, "repetitio est mater studiorum" (repetition is the mother of study) and partly so when you reread one particular chapter, you won't have to jump back and forth to other chapters as much.

I hope this book is your next step to financial security and peace of mind – perhaps all the way to the millionaire club.

John Kimball
www.FinancialGuideToLife.com

Part One

Introduction to Part One – Managing Your Money

There are many aspects to managing your money and it affects so many things in our lives, yet few of us get any formal training. Too often, we learn from trial and error, which can be costly, not just in money, but also to our financial future, peace of mind, and relationships. However, there are many financial principles we can apply to managing our money and the earlier we learn and apply them, the better our futures are likely to be. In Part One, we are going to start reviewing sound financial principles that should improve our financial security, peace of mind, and future. Of course, not everyone's situation is the same or unchanging, so we will discuss several life stages and situations to see how to apply sound financial principles to managing your money.

Chapter One

Starting Out

- Get settled with a job, place to live, and perhaps a car.
- Start paying off your debts, student loans, and credit cards.
- Begin saving for emergencies and retirement.
- Enjoy peace of mind that comes from financial security.

The period when you graduate from school, are young and single, and are just starting out can be both scary and exhilarating. It will never be quite like this again, so get off to a good start. Don't just wait for things to happen and hope for the best; instead, ensure your financial future by understanding sound financial principles and knowing how to make them happen.

Get settled with a job, a place to live, and perhaps a car

Employment

Your first priority is getting a job since your income is the starting point for all other financial calculations. There are plenty of school, book, and web resources available for creating a resume and looking for a job. If you know a dream job, go for it, but chances are you will need to be flexible and willing to try different things. Temporary jobs give you experience, income, and time to look further. Taking an entry-level job to "get your foot in the door" can lead to other opportunities within or outside an organization.

I took a nondescript job just to get my foot inside an organization so I could look around for something else and, to my surprise, I liked it, was promoted quickly, branched out into other areas, and stayed thirty years. I never got my dream job (until I started writing non-fiction books), but really liked the job I ended up with in the information technology field. That computer job didn't exist when I graduated from college before PCs were invented.

Technology and jobs are changing even faster now, so be prepared to move around, try different things, and learn new skills. Consider a variety of jobs and careers whether you are young and starting out or experienced and looking for a new start. Don't be afraid to change jobs. Some people say to start looking for a new job as soon as you get your current one. This may be an exaggeration, but it pays to know your options, enhance your skills, and look for opportunities. This could be the easiest way to give yourself a raise. A Wharton study found that outside hires are paid 18% more for the same job than internal staff promoted from within.

You may also need to consider your priorities when choosing a career, a particular job, or a time to move on. Certain jobs may lead to some combination of good money, benefits, useful experience, or high job satisfaction. Each person must decide what is most important to them at any given time. Some jobs provide none, so move on; others provide all four, so make sure you excel and hang on to it. Don't overlook good benefits, which sometimes may be even better than a good salary. This website will help you calculate the worth of a company's benefits for easier comparison: http://calcxml.com/calculators/total-compensation.

Don't overlook a career in the military or public service with the local, state, or Federal governments. Your pay may be lower than the equivalent job in the private sector, but it is offset with a variety of benefits commonly offered by large organizations including leave, pension plans, a variety of insurance, and student loan forgiveness. Don't overlook less tangible benefits. Some organizations like the military and public sector jobs have published salary scales so you don't have to grovel for equal salaries and raises like Dagwood Bumstead in the comics.

After you have some experience, keep your options open for starting your own business. There is nothing like being your own boss – as long as you are a good boss. On the one hand, nearly half of small businesses fail within five years. On the other hand, it can be a good road to wealth, or at least a decent living doing something you like. It's much easier taking a chance on your own business before you have to worry about a mortgage and children.

When you do land that job, your starting salary might be negotiable. Don't be shy about handling this important issue. Accepting a low offer at the beginning of your career could lead to a lifetime of lower earnings as raises, benefits, bonuses, and future offers may be based upon this low foundation. Ladies, this is one reason why women may have lower salaries than men, because women are less likely to bargain at this critical moment. Be the first to get your starting number on the table to begin negotiations. Try to find out what salaries are at the company or job position. Research salaries at these websites:

- http://www.glassdoor.com/index.htm
- http://www.payscale.com/
- http://salary.com/

Try to hold out for the recruiter's second offer. Perhaps point out that you have a large student loan that you are anxious to pay off or want to get off to a "responsible financial start". Can the business do better to help you meet these goals? Don't consider these points as embarrassing, but rather show that you want to be responsible, which is one of the things recruiters are looking for.

No matter what job you have or what level you have it; it is important to do your best, build a good reputation and references, be seen helping the organization meet its goals, and be dependable. This is the best way to get ahead, earn bonuses, or even keep your job during bad times. When I was a manager, I discovered that most people considered themselves *above* average, which isn't a bad thing. But what I was looking for were employees whom I could depend upon to always handle a wide variety of matters, do them very well, be results-oriented, and work to meet the organization's goals creatively. Always remember that your reputation is one of your most important assets and that it is easy to harm and harder to repair.

A Place to Live

Getting that first paycheck is sweet. You see more money than you ever have before. But alas, you soon discover that it never seems to go as far as you would wish. (WARNING: This problem does NOT necessarily disappear even when your paycheck grows bigger.) There are even more demands on your paycheck than on your time, and the biggest one is a place to live. While you are looking for employment, you are probably living with your parents. Sometimes, this may continue for a time even after you are employed so you can have more money to pay off debts or save for a goal. If so, be prepared to make it temporary, pay a token rent, pay your own bills and expenses, help with chores, and use that time wisely to prepare for your independence. If you expect parents to pay for your apartment for more than a very, very, very short time, know that doing so may be harming their capability to pay off their debts and prepare for retirement. If they aren't financially prepared for retirement – are you going to support them?

Sooner or later, you will be out on your own, even perhaps to a new city. Since housing is your biggest expense, consider getting a roommate, a smaller apartment, or looking in affordable neighborhoods. The less you spend on housing, the more you will have for your other priorities. You may have had a roommate in a college dorm and you can probably do so now as well. But there is more at stake now, so you should have a discussion about splitting expenses, chores, and space. Making sure the other person has a job and habits you can live with in advance, makes the year lease much easier to live with. Consider the "Splitwise" app (https://www.splitwise.com/) to make it simple to keep track of who has paid which expense and who owes whom at the end of the month.

Owning an automobile

If you don't already have a car and determine that you can afford one and really need one, (okay or just want one); then see the chapter on buying a car. But if you can get to work and shopping without one for a while, you could save a lot of money that could go towards debts and saving. In addition to car payments, consider the cost of ownership including insurance, gas, parking, repairs, and maintenance. Also, consider one of the several "car-sharing" companies that let you rent a car by the hour, day, or month for occasional needs. Twice, I even had a fantasy come true when I lived in a location where I could walk to work which was great.

Start paying off your debts, student loans, and credit cards

After you are settled with employment, a place to live, freedom, and money to spend; it's an exciting time, but don't get carried away. It's probably going to be a while before you can live the same life style as your parents. Do NOT use credit cards to rush that goal. That will only make your financial security worse. Using credit cards may seem to enhance your today, but it will worsen your tomorrow. Plan to live a frugal lifestyle for a while as in your student days. See later chapters to learn to budget, save, and spend frugally. If your income is from commissions or other variable sources, then learn to live on your worst year's income. Anything above that, devote to paying debts, increasing emergency funds, and savings goals.

Your next priority is to get control of your debts which may mean student loans, a balance on your credit card, or a car payment.

Student loans

You may not have thought much about all those mounting student loans when you were acquiring them, but now they are coming due. In 2016, the average student loan debt topped $30,000. The level of student loan debt has now passed credit card debt in America and is only exceeded by our level of mortgage debt. First, review where you stand and what your options are. Start with these websites to get information about potential options:

- www.ibrinfo.org
- www.Salliemae.com
- www.loanconsolidation.ed.gov
- www.studentaid.gov
- www.finaid.org

There are many types of private and government student loans. You may have a variety of student loans from a variety of sources at a variety of different rates. If you are unsure about what you have, you may be able to look up your loan information at this government website: http://www.nslds.ed.gov/nslds_SA/ . See about consolidating your loans into one loan with one payment at one fixed rate. Consider the tradeoff of stretching out the length of the loan to ten or twenty years. Note, however, that a longer term means a lower monthly payment, but also longer debt and more interest over the life of the loan. Graduated payment loans are another option, allowing lower payments initially and increasing every two years, or income based loans that increase as your income does.

Government backed loans may have several attractive features including deferring repayment until you get a job (up to three years), basing the level of your payments upon the level of your salary (Income based repayment – see www.ibrinfo.org), and even for-giving the remainder of your loan after twenty-five years or working in a public service or non-profit job for ten years. Check to see if you can get a reduced rate by signing up for automatic payments from your checking account. Don't think about defaulting on your government student loans as they can garnish your wages, grab your tax refunds, and reduce any government benefits -- and there is no time limit or statute of limitations. On the other hand, it is much easier getting some type of relief when you really need it. One relief plan is called "Pay As You Earn" and bases your payments upon your salary and family size. It can forgive the unpaid balance after twenty years. There are plenty of requirements, so review your options here: www.studentaid.gov .

Private student loans account for about 15% of student loan debt. You might be able to consolidate and refinance these. Review possibilities at a student loan comparison site such as: http://www.simpletuition.com/. Sallie Mae is the largest private lender. If you face financial difficulties and have tried the usual repayment options, Sallie Mae may work with you to provide some means of relief based upon your ability to repay includ-ing interest-only payments, reduced monthly payments, extended payment schedules, and even temporary rate reductions.

If you have difficulties working with any of your student loan lenders, you may wish to contact the Consumer Financial Protection Bureau (CFPB). This new government agency was created as part of the reforms stemming from the 2008 financial crisis and includes an ombudsman and consumer affairs specialists to hear consumer complaints. The biggest complaint they hear about student loans relate to negotiating relief when people face unemployment or financial difficulties. You can contact the CFPB at their website: www.consumerfinance.gov.

There are many programs where you can get government loan forgiveness or partial repayment in return for service. These could be particularly attractive to graduates with large loans, trouble finding a job, or an interest in public service or certain careers such as in education or health. Review these programs for details: Teach for America, Peace Corp, AmeriCorp, federal Health and Human Services for health related fields, federal government service, military, and various state and municipal governments.

The important point is to put student loans on auto pilot. See if you can get the monthly payment to an amount that is relative to your income and have the monthly payment automatically deducted from your checking account. Ensure you make pay-ments on time, but if you face difficulties, be persistent in trying to work out relief with your lender. Note that up to $2500 in student loan interest may be tax deductible (2013 adjusted gross income less than $75,000 for singles, $150,000 if married). It likely will take a long time to pay off student loans, but you may have other things to worry about.

Credit cards

In order to borrow money, you usually need a good credit history of borrowing and paying back debts on time. So how can you get that first loan to start your good credit? Somewhat surprisingly, credit card companies have begun aggressive marketing among college students who have no credit history. Presumably, the companies are counting on Mom and Dad to cover any potential losses. Too often, young adults don't have the knowledge, experience, and maturity to start down the right financial road, and credit cards can be an easy trap for debt. Ending your college career with credit card debt can be a tall burden on top of student loan debts, lack of a job, getting a security deposit for a an apartment, or dream of buying a car.

Yet, might be smart to get one of those easily available student credit cards while still a senior. Ironically, after you graduate, the old credit rules apply and it may suddenly be difficult to get a credit card because the companies suddenly want to see a good credit history of paying back debts. If you have trouble getting your first non-student loan, try these tips. The easiest credit cards to get are usually from retailers such as department stores or from the bank where you have a checking account. In fact, your bank may have a program to help people establish credit. One program is called a "secured credit card" where you deposit money equal to the credit limit on your credit card. The credit limits on your newly acquired credit card may be very low, but pay it on time and hopefully in full. After six months or so of reliably paying on time, you may be able to ask for an increase in your credit limit or apply for a regular credit card.

Once you have bills, especially credit cards, you should make every possible effort to pay them on time. This is how you establish good credit which makes getting future loans easier and cheaper. Late payments lead to a lower credit rating from one of the companies that score your credit history. Low credit scores make future loans harder to get and rates higher and thus more expensive. This is one of the most important rules everyone needs to learn very early in their financial lives. See Chapter 25, on *"Credit Ratings"* for more detailed information about the importance of your credit score and how your actions affect it.

An alternative to credit cards is a "prepaid card" in which you load it up with a certain amount of money, then use it as a credit card, withdrawals from ATMs, or even bill paying in lieu of checks. Prepaid cards may be useful for people without checking accounts, people who can't get credit cards, teens learning financial management, and anyone who wants an easy way to control their spending. Some people use it instead of a checking account as you may be able to directly deposit checks in the account and pay bills online. It's certainly better than using a check-cashing store. Prepaid debit cards may be an easy way to control spending since, unlike credit cards, you can't run up debt. You can only spend the amount you put on the card. Consider using your checking account for recurring expenses and filling a prepaid card with an amount you have left over for all other spending. This can help you remember the difference between "needs" and "wants" and spend accordingly.

Note that many prepaid cards are notorious for high fees, so as usual, compare carefully and choose one that does not allow overdrafts or charge high fees for maintenance, ATM withdrawals, or inactivity. Compare these features: fees, ATM network convenient to you, methods to reload funds, mobile app to check balances, text alerts for low balances, web access to statements, and bill paying.

Review options here and don't forget your credit union:
- http://www.nerdwallet.com/prepaid/
- http://www.bankrate.com/credit-cards.aspx

Begin saving for emergencies and retirement

It is critical to get control of your debts, but even before they are paid in full, you need to start saving. You may have specific things for which you are saving (car, house, wedding, trip, etc.), but there are two more you probably haven't thought of that are even more important: an emergency fund and retirement.

Start an Emergency Fund

Everyone should try to keep an emergency fund equal to 3-6 months' worth of expenses. If your earnings fluctuate or your job isn't secure, then aim for 6-8 months. You never know when a financial pot hole will loom, but I know with certainly that an emergency will arise sooner or later. Without an emergency fund, what will you do with a sudden security deposit, car repair, medical emergency, appliance repair bill, water-logged smartphone, job layoff, or other emergency? The great recession was not the first time that many people lost their jobs, even ones they had had for a long time. Having an emergency fund to handle life's unexpected pot holes without going into debt leads to financial security and peace of mind. Even if you have credit cards to pay off, still aim for at least a 1-2 month emergency fund to cover a sudden security deposit, repair bill, or medical emergency. It is a common debate whether to pay off credit cards or create an emergency fund first. It may seem dubious to sit on a low paying emergency fund while paying high rate credit cards. Nevertheless, too often paying on credit cards becomes normal and getting around to an emergency fund never seems to happen. Having at least a minimal emergency fund contributes to financial security, flexibility, and peace of mind while you are working towards other goals.

Saving for Retirement

No, I'm not kidding. Saving for retirement is one of the last things a young adult wants to think about, but starting early is one of the most important "financial secrets" you should know. Contrary to popular belief, Social Security *will* still be around when you are ready to retire, but it will *NOT* cover all the retirement expenses you need. Many in the baby-boomer generation had supplemental pensions, but those are rapidly disappearing in all but the largest organizations such as corporations and governments. Therefore, YOU are responsible for your retirement. YOU will determine how comfortable your retirement will be. YOU will determine how likely your future self comes back in a time machine and slaps your younger self around.

So why start saving for something 30-40 years away? Because the longer you delay the start of your saving, the more you will have to save in the future. Saving just $50 per week could make you a millionaire in 44 years (assuming your money grows at 8% per year). But, if you wait even *six* years to begin saving, then you will need to save almost twice as much per year to reach the same level. Here, procrastination is very expensive.

The key point for now is to do your future self a huge favor and start saving for retirement as soon as you get your first full-time job. This is vital to do even while paying off your debts and even if your savings plans start small, say $50 a week or pay period each for both your emergency and retirement funds, depending upon your salary. The easiest way to do this is to have your savings deductions automatically transferred to a retirement account from your checking account or paycheck.

Enjoy peace of mind that comes from financial security

How can you have peace of mind when you have to pay debts, start several savings plans, pay bills, and still live your life? You can't buy peace of mind, but you sure can get your finances to help achieve it. Peace of mind comes from having control of your finances rather than worrying from paycheck to paycheck. It will probably be difficult for your paycheck to meet all your needs and wants, so it's critical to establish **priorities**. Use these tips as a guide.

- Put your major expenses on autopilot. Pay your major bills automatically from your checking account (rent or mortgage, student loan, car payment, utilities, retirement savings, and emergency savings). Consider your savings goals as essential expenses. Many companies will let you set up automatic payments from your checking account. For others, use your bank's online banking features to setup automatic payments for any payment that doesn't change each month. Putting your essentials on autopilot means you will pay on time and be less likely to let luxuries gobble up money needed for essentials. Ensure that you have money in your account when the bills are due. Have some kind of overdraft protection on your checking account for those instances when the bill is larger than you expected or your planning is off.
- Learn to live within your means. Adjust your spending so it is less than your income. Track spending for at least a month, make adjustments as needed, and reward yourself when possible. It is important to know where you money is going, so make a list including those little expenses for coffee, soda, dry cleaning, eating out etc. But this doesn't have to be an onerous task: use a spreadsheet, notebook, or smartphone; estimate, round off, use broad categories, be honest, and do it for at least a month. I cover budgeting in more detail in Chapter 7, but for now, web savvy, young adults can be pointed to finance tracking sites like www.Mint.com or www.smartaboutmoney.org.

Smartphone users may value the growing list of money management apps such as "Mint", "Quicken Money Management", CoinKeeper, or "Pageonce".

- Start funding your retirement. This is an early priority because the longer you wait, the more you will have to save later. Start with something, even if it's only $50 - $100 per pay period. See the chapter on *Saving for Retirement*.

- Start an emergency fund for at least 3-6 months expenses. No one expects emergencies, but everyone gets one eventually. Knowing you can handle it financially makes it much easier to sleep at night.

- Pay off credit cards. Don't pay interest for the next year on those shoes or that pizza. Pay more than the monthly minimum. Put any extra money you get towards paying off credit card debt, which is likely to have the highest interest rate of any debt you have. Reach the point where you pay off the balance in full every month. This is one of the greatest feelings of accomplishment you can have and it makes all the rest of your finances much, much easier.

- Save for any of your personal goals such as a car, home, wedding, travel etc. Note that traveling now before you have a family is much easier and less costly, and there is a great big, exciting world out there to see.

- Enjoy the rest. If you don't have anything left over, go back thru your list of spending and prioritize it. Look for ways to economize. See the chapters on *Budgeting* and *Spending* for suggestions. When you have money left over, then you are on the road to financial security and peace of mind which are priceless.

Living within your means by spending less than you earn
is the foundation of financial security.

Once you have identified your priorities and have a plan to meet them, everything else becomes easier. Nonetheless, there are plenty of other challenges awaiting you on life's financial journey. Before we proceed further, note these last items to add more peace of mind.

Accidents and illness can happen at any time and health care can be one of the most expensive emergencies you ever face. In fact, more bankruptcies result from healthcare costs than any other reason. Be ready for it and always have some kind of health coverage. If you don't have health insurance thru your employer, then one of the best features of the new "Affordable Card Act" health care law is the provision allowing children to remain on their parent's health insurance until age 26. When you need insurance on your own, the most affordable options are thru your employer – if you are fortunate to have it offered. Review your options at: http://www.ehealthinsurance.com/ . Young adults are famous for assuming nothing will happen to them, but you should still get the peace of mind of knowing that if a sudden accident happens, your health care is covered and your finances will not be devastated. Don't worry about life insurance until you have people depending upon you.

Be inspired and become more knowledgeable about your financial options by reading more about them. Reading this book (and others) is a fantastic step, but also consider subscribing to a financial magazine (paper or digital) that enlightens you every month about some new aspect of your financial security. My favorites are *Money* and *Kiplingers* magazines that cover a wide variety of practical, need to know information that will help enhance your financial future.

Summary

- To get ahead at whatever job you have: excel, be dependable, and help your customers, boss, and organization meet their goals.
- Your reputation is one of your most important assets – remember that it is easy to harm and hard to repair.
- Living within your means by spending less than you earn is the foundation of financial security.
- Using credit card debt may seem to enhance your today, but it will worsen your tomorrow.
- Put your major expenses, debts, and savings on auto-pilot – automatically deducted from your bank account.
- Start paying debts, creating an emergency fund, and saving for retirement from day one of your independent financial journey.

Chapter Two

Life Stages

- Following sound financial principles at any stage of life
- Enjoying peak earning years
- Saving, planning, and dreaming of retirement
- Simplifying your finances

Following sound financial principles at any stage of life

Regardless of your income level, if you started down your financial journey well, then you have some peace of mind from living within your means, putting your fixed bills and savings on autopilot, paying off debts, having an emergency fund of three to six months, saving for retirement, spending wisely, and setting priorities for enjoying your money that is left.

Life is not about money of course, but so many things in life do affect your finances, and your finances do affect so many other things in your life. As you move into midlife, life can get more complicated. People may start to worry more about how well your job is going, losing health insurance, dealing with debt, maintaining your house, saving enough, family issues, and whether you will have enough money for retirement. Following sound financial principles early makes it easier to deal with all of these related issues, but it is never too late to start.

Like so many goals, sound financial principles are easier to read about than do. If you did not get off to a good start in your twenties, it is never too late, but the longer you wait, the harder it gets. You should still be following the same financial values throughout your life that I discussed earlier. The financial values don't change much as you get older, but they may get harder if you add a family into the budget, hit financial potholes, or get off to a poor start. If you haven't saved much for retirement by your thirties, you now have to save twice as much as you would have by starting in your twenties. And if you don't save much in your thirties, then you will have to save twice as much again in your forties. See the chapter on *Saving for Retirement.* If you have credit card debt, then you need to redouble your efforts to live within your means and start paying it down. See the chapters on *Budgets, Spending Wisely,* and *Debt.*

Waiting for that big raise, bonus, or break is rarely the answer. At some point, you discover that as your income rises, so does your spending. Just make sure that a portion of that raise and bonus goes towards savings and debt – before you ever have a chance to get used to spending it. This is known as "paying yourself first."

Enjoy peak earning years

We will cover those huge financial changes, marriage and children, in the next chapters, but for now let's continue surveying how sound financial principles should stay with you throughout all stages of your life. At some point, you enter your peak earning years and your financial state and habits become stable, whether comfortably or just getting by. Eventually, the kids do actually leave home - even if they boomerang back for a time. You can stop saving for college. Some people can stop worrying about their job as much. Then you may have more options. Some people consider moving to a less expensive or more fun place, reentering the work force or switching to a more interesting job, volunteering, trading in the minivan, vacationing with more options, or rewarding themselves with mid-life splurges. Remember periodically to review whether you still need life insurance to cover debts, update your will and designated beneficiaries, rebalance your investment allocations, review your insurance options, and re-double your retirement savings efforts. Note that at age 50, you are allowed to contribute extra, tax-free retirement savings to your 401(k) and IRA retirement accounts -- do it.

Saving, planning, and dreaming of retirement

In your fifties, it's okay to start dreaming about retirement, researching your eligibility, computing your benefits, calculating the amount of income you need to retire, and yes – redoubling your retirement savings. See the chapter on *Retirement,* but for now note that the "full" retirement age for Social Security is sliding to age 67 for new retirees, while you can retire as early as age 62 with reduced benefits. Many government and corporate pensions can begin at different ages. You will be eligible for Medicare at age 65. The longer you work, the greater your retirement benefits and savings, and the later you will start using them up.

Whether your retirement years are golden depend largely on the decisions you have made, or not, since the day you began full time employment. In 2013, the Social Security Administration website reported that Social Security is the major source of income for most of the elderly:

- Nine out of ten individuals age 65 and older receive Social Security benefits.
- Social Security benefits represent about 39% of the income of the elderly.
- Among elderly Social Security beneficiaries, 53% of married couples and 74% of unmarried persons receive 50% or more of their income from Social Security.
- Among elderly Social Security beneficiaries, 23% of married couples and about 46% of unmarried persons rely on Social Security for 90% or more of their income.

Regardless of your salary or Social Security benefits, it's clear that Social Security will only cover a portion of your retirement income and, with traditional pensions rapidly disappearing; your savings will have to cover the rest. Do yourself a huge favor and start saving for retirement with your first full time job, increase your savings rate with every raise, and take advantage of the "over age 50 catchup" to save even more during your peak earnings years. Even in retirement, the same sound financial principles apply that we have repeatedly discussed, but see the chapter on *Retirement* for special financial considerations while in retirement.

Simplifying your finances

This is often one of the most popular New Year's resolutions. Here are some suggestions.

- Pay as many of your bills as possible with autopay on your credit card to get rewards (but ensure you pay off the credit card), thru the biller's website, or with your bank's online bill service.
- Put as many of your savings goals as possible on autopay with direct routing of savings amounts to relevant savings and investment accounts.
- Consolidate multiple retirement, banking, and brokerage accounts. You may want to keep multiple savings accounts for multiple savings goals.
- Develop a plan to get out of debt.
- Put all tax records into an accordion folder as you receive them.
- Review your budget for needs, savings, debt pay offs, and wants. Put your leftover disposable income on a pre-paid debit card. When the card is empty, your discretionary spending is done for the month.
- Diversify your investments, but also keep them simple by avoiding having too many to manage and rebalance. The simplest investments are index funds, ETFs, balanced funds, and target date funds.

Summary

- Following the financial principles we discuss will make your finances more secure throughout all life's stages.
- The earlier you begin, the easier it will be to deal with life's financial complications, but you can begin at any time.
- Whether your retirement years are golden depend largely on the decisions you have made, or not, since the day you began full time employment.

Chapter Three

Marriage

- Before checklist
- After checklist
- Options for combining finances
- Apply financial principles, but with more coordination
- Financial issues for couples

By now, you should not be surprised that the same sound financial principles apply to marriages and other life partnership as all of our other life stages. The challenges are both magnified and lessened because now we have a partner to help and coordinate with. Finances can be easier because we can get help from a partner, and two really can live more cheaply together than alone. Different people approach money differently. Coordination can be even trickier when we remember that opposites can attract in relationships. So let's focus on financial issues that are unique to marriages and other close relationships that involve living together.

Before checklist

Discussion and coordination begin even before the wedding – especially before the wedding. Discussing your finances and goals before getting married may seem hard, but will lead to fewer problems and surprises later. Here is a checklist to discuss and coordinate before getting married. Plan a nice dinner in and bring this checklist to discuss (share it in advance to reflect on).

- Discuss your financial goals; for example, debt, children, home, saving, travel, etc. Be specific on near term goals and, as always, be flexible.
- Review your joint financial state, income, debts, and savings. Do not keep debts hidden; future surprises yield more mistrust than frank discussions.
- Know each other's credit rating so if there are problems you know how to handle them. (See the chapter on *Credit Ratings.*)
- Decide how to merge financial assets and accounts.
- Agree who will pay the bills and balance the checkbook - one person, both alternating, or splitting responsibilities - but remember that both need to know where you stand financially regardless of who actually pays the bills.
- Determine if you need a pre-nuptial agreement because one partner brings substantial assets to the marriage.

Collaborating on the wedding can give useful insights as to how the partners manage money and can coordinate when married.

After checklist

After the wedding, there are even more financial issues to take care of to ensure you start down the financial road successfully. It is better to do as many as possible at the beginning when bliss makes compromise and working together the easiest. Here are financial issues to review early if not completely before the wedding.

- Update designations of beneficiary for insurance, retirement accounts, and other benefits.
- Change your tax withholdings to married.
- If you change your name, file form *SS-5* with the Social Security Administration.
- Compare health insurance benefits and determine which one to continue as a family plan. You often have 30 days to change plans after marriage.
- Combine your auto insurance coverage.

- Review your life insurance to insure it's sufficient to cover combined debts. Life insurance for both spouses is important to cover expenses and lost earnings should one die. It should be big enough to cover all your debts, projected college expenses, and lost earnings. Adjust it regularly when life or financial events happen.
- Set up a "tax folder" and drop in any tax related bills, notices, statements, etc.
- Review your will or get a new one. This is especially important after the birth of a child. If your situations are simple, you can start with will making software or websites.
- Designate a drawer or file to put copies of all important financial documents, statements, account numbers, and passwords. This makes it easier to manage them, but is invaluable if one spouse becomes incapacitated, goes overseas, or dies.
- Each should have a "power of attorney" to act on the other's behalf if one becomes incapacitated.
- Set up automatic savings funds for your highest priority goals.
- Decide upon a dollar value above which both partners must agree upon a purchase.
- Develop an initial accounting or budget comparing your income with your expenses, goals, savings, and wants.
- Open or merge bank, savings, and investment accounts, but keep separate retirement accounts.
- Do not combine student loans, which would be difficult to untangle if necessary.

Options for combining your finances

One of the most important decisions any couple must decide is how to merge their finances and how they are going to handle the bill paying. It is important for financial harmony for each partner to have access to money for which they don't have to answer questions, but, as always, the personal spending must be in harmony with the family's priorities and does not bust the budget.

Each partner should have personal money to spend
and a method to ensure that it does not bust the family budget.

There are basically three options:
1. Merge separate accounts into one.
2. Keep separate accounts and each person is responsible for paying specific bills.
3. Each person keeps a separate account for their own spending, but most of the income goes into a joint family account that is used to pay family bills.

Merge Separate Accounts into One

This may be the most traditional method. It is still important that each spouse must have freedom to spend personal money without recriminations, but without busting the budget. Regardless of who pays the bills, each partner must still stay informed about the family finances and know what their personal spending level can be without breaking the budget. Agree upon a dollar amount over which both must agree upon a purchase. Use online banking so each can review the bank balance any time. The challenge is that without meticulous budgeting or some tool to track your spending, it is difficult for each person to know how their spending is affecting the family's finances. A tool that enables each partner to manage and track their individual spending is separate credit or prepaid debit cards with a low credit limit consistent with the family budget. This could enable each to better monitor and limit their individual spending. Even if you merge all your accounts and finances, it's still a good idea for each partner to retain a credit card in their own name to continue their separate credit history if needed.

Keep Separate Accounts

This is probably the most common method among unmarried couples living together. Assign the biggest bills to the partner with the biggest income. But, it can be inflexible for handling savings goals, bills that vary widely from month to month, and unplanned bills. Family spending should still be discussed, coordinated, and harmonious with the household budget. Each person keeps a separate account for their own spending, but most of the income goes into a joint family account that is used to pay family bills.

With this method, you must start by calculating the family budget needs including savings goals. A reasonable left over amount could be divided into the two separate accounts for each spouse's individual spending. This puts the family budget first while making it easier for each partner to manage their own spending without breaking the family budget. It can also enable each to better monitor their combined ATM, debit card, credit card, and checking purchases in one personal account.

Whatever method you agree upon can be changed, but it is essential that each partner have personal money to spend and a method to ensure that it does not bust the family budget. This protects the family's financial security and better ensures marital harmony.

Apply financial principles, but with more coordination

As in all other life stages, financial bliss in marriage comes from the same sound financial values we have discussed: knowing how to live within your means, putting your fixed bills and savings on autopilot, paying off debts, having an emergency fund of three to six months, saving for retirement, spending wisely, and having set priorities for enjoying your money that is left. However, marriage means having a partner in trying to meet those goals. Sometimes this may make it harder, other times easier. But at all times, it means you now have to coordinate the family's finances with your partner. Financial harmony leads to marital bliss as much as anything else including you know what. Financial harmony comes from more discussion, coordination, and compromise. This means discuss money issues openly and regularly, understand the family's finances regardless of who has primary responsibility for it, compromise from both, discuss goals, agree on a financial plan, and work together. Additionally, I have discovered that discussion must be accompanied by plans and tools to ensure success.

Financial Issues for Couples

Yes, all this financial bliss is easier said than done, but the effort is well worth it. It's not just your finances that are at stake, it's also your marriage. Financial issues are the leading cause of divorce, and divorce can devastate both parties' finances. Stress over financial issues can make other problems worse. Both partners should give full attention to this issue. Financial tensions and issues will inevitably arise so here are some suggestions for dealing with the most common.

Like most marital problems, keeping silent to avoid arguments is not the best way to solve issues. Silence can lead to resentment and surprises. Mutually satisfactory solutions come from discussion, understanding, compromise, and coordination. Discussion does not mean criticizing in public or yelling. Frequent discussion and joint understanding of the family's full financial status leads to fewer surprises, better adherence to common goals, a smoother transition when one partner goes or passes away, and better decisions when pooling expertise. This does not need to include details about personal indulgences that are within an agreed upon budget.

The reverse of keeping a stony silence is repeated fighting over money which is not uncommon in marriages. Common problems include one or both spouses spending too much, spenders marrying savers, and disagreement on how much risk to take in investments. Left unresolved, financial issues could lead to other problems and even divorce. Warning signs include repeated arguments over the same thing, weekly arguments, inability to agree, unresolved issues, other issues being negatively affected, and worsening finances. Paid counseling may be useful to get unbiased, professional assistance (nfcc.org, napfa.org, aamft.org, or financialtherapyassociation.org), but try these first:

- Get honest data by each partner tracking their spending for a month. (Use a notebook, spreadsheet, or online tool like www.mint.com .)
- Agree on a budget. (See the chapter on *Budgeting*.)
- Agree upon a dollar amount that exceeding requires mutual consent to spend.
- Never go into debt without mutual agreement.
- Don't criticize small indulgences or spending within an agreed upon limit.
- Compromise on goals and agree on specific steps to achieve them.
- Convert nagging and fighting into a monthly meeting to review financial issues.
- One person may pay the bills, but collaboration is needed on knowing the family's financial status, credit card amounts, debts, and investments.
- Over-spending can arise from many reasons. A big one is ignorance of how the over-spending is harming both short and long-term family financial needs and goals. Do the bills together for a couple of months and then have the over-spender do them for at least several months longer. Figuring out how to make ends meet can be a real eye-opener.

- If it is the family's saving goals that are threatened by over-spending, remember to "pay yourself first" by transferring your savings directly into designated savings/investment accounts with automatic transfers before savings can be invaded by over-spending.
- Automate agreed upon solutions such as direct transfers of funds, bills, debts, or various savings accounts to meet specific goals.
- Consider giving each partner a credit card or prepaid debit card with a fixed limit for which they can use and monitor their own spending for both necessities like gas and indulgences like fashions and golf clubs. The card's low credit limit should cap personal spending for that month and not interfere with common expenses and goals. With a "prepaid" card, you can load it up with a certain amount each month and use it as a credit card or withdrawals from ATMs. This is a great way to control spending, but compare cards carefully to avoid any that allow overdrafts and big fees. Either method should make it easier to control spending and meet the common budget.
- If you disagree on investment decision, for example amount of risk, then divide the investment funds into separate amounts for different investment philosophies. This is the perfect area where partners can lead to a better team as one partner may moderate the other's risk and the other partner can limit one's over-caution.
- Compromise as much as possible, agree to disagree when necessary.

Not all marital financial issues involve disagreements. Let's close with two remaining issues couples should know when combining households. Married couples retain separate credit ratings based upon their prior credit history, but now will be affected by any continuing separate accounts as well as new joint accounts. Joint credit, loans, or accounts are reported to the credit rating agencies in both names. Any loans that both sign for will have both credit ratings considered and the worst one is likely to be given more weight. When only one person applies or signs for credit, only that person's credit rating will be used. A creditor can't force both people to sign or co-sign a loan unless both incomes are needed to qualify for the loan.

Know what will happen if the other spouse dies including the will, life insurance, health insurance, survivor pensions, retirement accounts, property, investment accounts, debts, and all financial account information. You should keep most of this information available in one place, folder, or desk drawer. Each of you should also have a living will that specifies your wishes in case you are incapacitated and your spouse needs to make medical decisions on your behalf. Married couples should have the same motto as the Boy Scouts: "Be prepared".

Summary

- Discuss and coordinate financial issues and goals before and after the wedding.
- Compromise on goals and agree on specific steps to achieve them.
- Each partner should have personal money to spend and a method to ensure that it does not bust the family budget.
- Agree upon a dollar amount that exceeding requires mutual consent to spend.
- Never go into debt without mutual agreement.
- Don't criticize small indulgences or spending within an agreed upon limit.
- Regardless of who has primary responsibility for bill-paying, both partners must understand the family's finances and budget.
- Financial harmony leads to marital bliss as much as anything else and comes from more discussion, coordination, and compromise.
- Stress over financial issues can make other problems worse, so this is an area that both partners should give full attention to.

Chapter Four

Children

- Financial impact of children
- Checklist of things to do when a child arrives
- Teaching sound financial values

Financial impact of children

Few things impact a family's finances more than children. In 2016, the Department of Agriculture estimated the lifetime cost of raising a child is over $270,000 until he or she leaves the nest – not counting college. Thankfully, we can pay it on an installment plan over a couple of decades.

The first decision is whether one parent will stay at home with the children and for how long. A Gallup survey in 2012 found that more than 60% of mothers with children under the age of 18 were working. There will be financial consequences either way.

If the family decides that one parent should stay home, you will be learning about "doing more with less". If it's expected to be short-term, then some sacrifices will be necessary; if it's going to be long-term, then we are talking about life style changes. It's even more important that you review your budget to ensure it will work financially. Identify your minimum level of expenses, add in new expenses for the newest family member, include a little wiggle room money, and compare to your expected income. It's okay to hope for, but don't count on that upcoming raise and remember that raises get eaten up faster than they come. Start saving money from that second paycheck as soon as you decide to go the one-paycheck route. That savings, when it's easy, will be invaluable later when it's tougher. Reduce expenses. Some will be easy such as lower commuting, clothes, and lunch costs. Trade luxuries and vacations for increased parental satisfaction. Trade shopping malls and boutiques for discount stores, yard sales, and even thrift shops. Try hard to avoid new debt until there is certainty about re-entering the job market in the medium term future.

Carefully review the saving tips provided in the section *"Spending Wisely"*. At some point, consider the work-at-home opportunities described in the section, *"Debt resolution > Increasing Income"*. If you are not ready to re-enter the job market when the children start school, consider part-time jobs in the mornings or weekends.

Whether the mother or stay-at-home dad goes back to work soon or later, you'll have more child expenses and the first is also the largest (until college). Considering how little day care workers are paid, it's still surprising how big a percentage day care expenses take from that second income – and even more for single parents. Let me pass along two notes. First, be prepared for a long search as many jurisdictions impose limits on the number of babies and infants a day care provider can accept. Second, let me recommend that when a child reaches school age, you look for an after school activity that combines looking after your child with an interesting focus such as karate centers, dance studios, or other fun activity. This teaches a skill or art, more than just baby-sitting with TV or computer games. My boys were able to earn their black belt in karate by the time their day care days were over and the karate center set aside time for homework.

In some states, annual day care expenses can be higher than in-state tuition and you don't have years to save up for it The good news is that you might be eligible for two tax breaks to help offset the cost of day care. One is called the "Child Care Credit" which reduces your taxes when you file and is based upon the amount you spend on day care and your gross adjusted income. The second is called a "flexible spending account" and is offered by some employers. Under this plan, you elect to set aside some of your salary to go to a flexible spending account for day care (similar to ones for health care). There are some restrictions, but the benefit is that any amount up to $5000 you contribute to the flex plan reduces your gross adjusted income at tax time and therefore the tax your owe. When you start a family, there are many such tax perks, such as these that come with lots of restrictions, so I recommend trying tax software at least once to become aware of which ones you may be eligible for.

Checklist of things to do when a child arrives

- Get your child a Social Security number at the hospital or at your local SSA office.
- Update your will and name a guardian. How do you want your stuff divided up and who should take care of your minor children? Lawyers can do simple wills for $300 – $500. Do it yourself for under $100 here:
  - http://www.nolo.com/
  - http://www.legalzoom.com/
- Review your designations of beneficiaries.
- Review your life insurance coverage so it covers your debts, college expenses, and loss of your income. Many people say the simple rule is 8-10 times your income. The good news is that it is relatively cheap for young adults, either thru your employer or basic "term" life insurance. "Whole" life insurance cost more and is more complicated, but returns savings in the future. Get it for a fixed term, perhaps long enough to pay off the mortgage or get the children thru college.
  - http://money.cnn.com/magazines/moneymag/money101/lesson20/index.htm - Learn more about life insurance.
  - http://www.lifehappens.org/life-insurance-needs-calculator/ - Life insurance needs calculator.
  - http://www.insure.com/ - Get quotes from many life insurance companies without the hassle of pushy sales people.
- Add a deduction to your tax withholdings.
- Review your health benefits coverage for a good family plan. Children need different benefits than adults.

- Don't delay in saving for college. Even $50-$100 per month adds up quickly if you start soon enough. Waiting until later means saving more to catch up. See the chapter on *Saving for College.*
- When you start paying for day care, check to see if your employer offers a flexible spending account for day care. If yes, you can get a tax break from the money you divert to this account and use it to pay for day care.
- Start an investment account when born and contribute to it each birthday. Example: Start with $1000 and contribute $100 on each birthday. At age 22, they will have almost $10,000 at 7% compounded annually to help pay off student loans, buy a decent used car, have a wedding, or get settled.

Teaching sound financial values

Few school systems teach personal finance although plenty of resources are available for parents, kids, and teachers:
- http://jumpstart.org/
- http://www.360financialliteracy.org/
- http://www.councilforeconed.org/
- http://ja.org/
- http://www.nefe.org/
- http://www.kidsmoney.org/

This means it is up to the parents. Parents have so many things to teach children and sound money management skills should be among them. How to handle money wisely is one of the most important things children need to know, both while they are growing up and getting ready to be young adults. Too often, explicit teaching of financial values is overlooked, but they learn a lot by observation and how they are treated financially.

Children are ready to learn different things at different ages. Even at young ages, they can learn that it takes money that you get from working to buy things, there is never enough money to buy all we want, and we can't get everything we desire. For youngsters, using real coins and play money is a great way to practice counting, adding, and subtracting.

As they get older, they need real money to learn real skills. Children need to learn similar financial values as those we are discussing for adults of any age: the difference between wants and needs, handling bills and savings, and how to save, spend, and manage their financial resources for short-term gratification and long-term goals. They need to learn how to live within their limited means, save towards a goal, and shop for bargains.

At first, this means an allowance, probably after they start school, can count, and see what money can buy. A commonly suggested amount is around half their age. As they save money, some should go into a savings account. As teens, new financial skills may include allowances that buy gas or clothes, part-time jobs, or pre-paid debit cards. The goal is when they leave home, they have the foundation for managing their own money wisely. An allowance is one of the earliest and most important ways for children to learn and practice real money management skills. So an allowance is both a practical method for children to buy their own stuff and a learning tool. Getting a part-time job is even better for learning hands-on money management skills before going off on their own.

Here is my experience with allowances. We started allowances when the kids were in early elementary school and old enough to know what money was for and how to count it. They also had chores to do over and above cleaning up their own messes and putting their own clean clothes away, but I tried to emphasize that their allowance was not "pay" for doing chores. Everyone does certain family chores because there are chores to do and they are part of the family. Their allowance is unrelated to chores, but is given so that they have their own money to buy their own stuff that they want that we aren't going to buy for them. This was a hard concept to grasp, perhaps partly because now and then they could get an increase by taking on extra responsibilities, such as mowing the grass or being bribed to practice the trumpet. Other parents link allowances explicitly as pay for chores, but they still need to make clear that some responsibilities are due because they are a member of the family or because they need to accept personal responsibility. As our children got older, their allowance increased, but so did the types of things they now had to buy for themselves.

We also used an allowance to enforce certain concepts from the beginning. We explicitly divided their weekly allowance into three parts: one dollar was put into their "savings envelope", one dollar was for their choice of charities (usually church), and the rest for their other uses. On the one hand this was enforced saving, but on the other they learned that before you get your spending money, you first set aside your savings and other priorities.

While still in elementary school, we took them to the local bank and opened savings accounts for them to transfer periodically from their savings envelopes to their savings account. They could and did add other funds they saved or received as gifts. For a while, I gleefully showed them their quarterly savings account statements showing how their money was increasing with compound interest. But then interest rates plunged to negligible amounts, their account statements started reporting their whopping 7 cents of compounded interest, and I quietly started throwing their statements away before they could see how little they were earning for all their savings. Nonetheless, they do enjoy knowing that they have reserve funds in a bank for safekeeping and seeing it grow is gratifying.

Children's money skills are different and inevitably, you will notice that some spend or save more, just as adults do. Regardless of which category your children are in, keep working on their sound financial values as they grow. Other values children can learn at any age include that money is limited for both the family and themselves and that both the family and they need to establish priorities with their needs and wants. Each can set goals and save towards meeting it whether it is the family for a vacation or themselves for a new toy, computer game, or smartphone. At times, you may encourage the goal by matching funds or sharing expenses.

Remember that these values are learned not only by handling their allowances, but also by the family financial matters including how readily or not parents buy them stuff they want more than they need. Family discussions are useful about the family financial state, how much things cost, how leaving the lights on cost money, how their friends' families' financial state may be better or worse than our own, how to shop for bargains, and the necessity to save for goals.

Kids, like all of us, want things, but they haven't yet learned that money is harder to earn than it is to spend. They should not see you as an unlimited bank. Have them choose between multiple wants. Teach them to be thrifty, wait for sales, compare prices, wait for used games, get books from the library, and make hard choices. Help them save for a big purchase. Explain why you can't buy something for them and don't give in to whining. When family finances or the economy is bad, explain what this means for both the family's and children's spending. Set limits early and don't be afraid to repeat NO. Giving kids too much is not only expensive, it also inhibits them learning sound financial values later in life. Ensure both parents are using the same game plan and not being played off against each other.

Whenever the boys needed a new smartphone, I matched a portion and they paid a portion so they had a financial stake in being responsible for their phone and learning the necessity of keeping an emergency fund to handle unexpected necessities. I also gave them the choice of getting a *new* phone that was *average* or a *good* phone that was *used* so they could see tradeoffs and make hard money choices.

There is much debate about when a young adult should get a debit or credit card. On the one hand numerous studies show that people spend less when they pay in cash rather than a card. On the other hand, online spending requires a credit or debit card. It is increasingly common for college students to get credit cards even without a job and leave college with more than $2000 in credit card debt. Before they leave the nest, teens should know how to manage a checking account, debit card, and even a credit card. This includes how easy it is to get into debt and how hard to get out, especially by only paying the minimum amount due. You can show this with many calculators on the internet, or by handling a card when parents can watch. If you do opt for a teen's credit card, go for a small credit limit of a few hundred dollars, discuss how it should be paid, and avoid the consequences of hitting the credit limit. A side benefit is that the child will also start to build their credit rating so that when they have income they will better be able to get a card of their own. Another option may be to add your child as a designated user on one of your cards. This allows you to monitor their use and teach the sound principles for using it.

Another choice may be a prepaid debit or credit card in which the parent can load up a card with a specific amount. Then the teen can use as a credit card or withdraw money at an ATM without the risk of running up debt. The downside is that these cards may have big fees for activation, maintenance, ATMs, and even inactivity. Compare these carefully and avoid any that allow overdrafts for another big fee. In addition to using prepaid cards for the convenience, use the opportunity to budget, check balances on a phone app, check ATM fees, and review the monthly statements. It's even better when they have a part-time job to help pay the bill when that monthly statement arrives. Learning sound money management skills before leaving home can be one of the most useful life skills a parent can pass on. Everyone will get a better start on their own if they know how to live within their means, learn to budget, pay yourself first by setting aside savings automatically, and avoiding credit card debt.

Summary

- If one parent is going to stay home after the birth of a child, practice in advance living on one salary and making the necessary life-style changes.
- Whenever a life event changes your financial situation, review the checklist of financial items you may need to update.
- Sound money management skills are among the most important life skills parents can teach. These skills are rarely taught anywhere but home.
- At young ages, children can learn that it takes money that you get from working to buy things, there is never enough money to buy all we want, and we can't buy everything we desire.
- Children need to learn similar financial values as those we are discussing for adults of any age: difference between wants and needs, handling bills and savings, and how to save, spend, and manage their financial resources for short-term gratification and long-term goals,. They need to learn how to live within their limited means, save towards a goal, and shop for bargains.
- An allowance is one of the earliest and most important ways for children to learn and practice real money management skills.
- Children can also learn from the parents' financial behavior and family's financial circumstances. For example, when family finances are bad, explain what this means for both the family's and children's spending.
- When children leave home, they should have the foundation for managing their own money wisely.

Chapter Five

Women's Special Financial Issues

- Earnings
- Investments
- Marriage
- Retirement savings
- Retirement
- Widowhood

This chapter covers the special circumstances women face that may affect their finances. These special circumstances may include marriage, being out of the work force for child rearing, widowhood, and on average living longer than men. All women need to be informed about the full range of financial issues. Nearly all women will need to be financially independent at some point in their life when starting out, divorced, widowed, or having never married.

Earnings

Two circumstances that may particularly affect women's finances include, on average, living longer and earning less than men. One illuminating statistic is that college educated women may earn several hundred thousand dollars less than a college educated man over her lifetime according to the *Women's Institute For A Secure Retirement*. (Their website has good resources: http://www.wiserwomen.org/). Two reasons, among many, why women tend to earn less than men include being out of the workforce for child rearing and not being as successful in salary negotiations. If you are going to stay home and still want income or experience, consider working part-time, working at home, exploring flex-time opportunities, or working as a freelancer. (For work-at-home and freelance opportunities, see http://www.reviewopedia.com/work-at-home-jobs.htm and http://www.upwork.com .)

Studies show that women are less likely to initiate salary discussions than men and get less when they do. If you work for one of those organizations that don't have standard salary rates and raises for every job, then know that you must be prepared to look out for your interests and don't depend upon someone else to look out for you. A Carnegie Mellon study found that only 7% of women MBAs negotiated their first salary (vs 57% of men) and women got $4000 less on average. Ensure that you get the equal salary from the beginning. That first salary may set the baseline for most of your future raises and bonuses, even if you change jobs.

Be prepared for a negotiation, know what your job is worth, and ensure that you are seen as a valuable employee. It's helpful if you have an idea what the general salaries in your organization are, but if not, get average salary information here: www.payscale.com and www.salary.com. Ask men in the organization for advice on what salary or raise you should aim for and there is a good chance that they will tell you what they make or what they have heard a colleague makes. At the same time, be realistic about your bargaining position and act accordingly; how strongly will the organization want to get or keep you? Practice out loud the night before and jot down a few notes about what you are going to say for their potential offers. Tell them if you have a competing offer. Don't be shy about explaining how you are worth the higher amount to the organization. Be prepared to go for only a few rounds of back and forth. Sometimes it may be worthwhile for each side to think about the bottom line overnight if they can't agree at the session. Don't equate negotiating with conflict. In addition to getting the salary you want, it may earn you the reputation of being tough which may provide other intangible benefits later.

Be ready to get the next raise you are worth. Ensure that your performance throughout the year can be counted upon to advance the bottom line of the organization (and the boss). Finally, remember that women have been among the best hagglers in markets and bazaars since the beginning of business.

Women earning lower salaries than men have more implications than the immediate cash flow issues. It also means lower retirement income later, based upon lower 401(k) contributions and Social Security benefits. You may not have much control of SSA benefits, but you do with retirement savings. While the common suggestion is to save 10-15% percent of your income for retirement, women should consider saving more to be better prepared for a longer retirement.

Investing

Women need to be just as involved and knowledgeable about investing as all the other aspects of money management, whether it's helping with the family's investments or their own retirement accounts and savings. Studies show that women are often better investors than men and it's believed that one reason is that women trade less often and are more "buy and hold" investors. Women may be less likely to like risk when investing which can lead them to do more research, listen to fewer "hot tips", or avoid sticking with losers too long. On the other hand, fear of risk can lead many women to invest too conservatively and miss some of the gains from stocks.

Surveys and studies have revealed differences in investing between men and women which reinforce the idea that they make a good team when discussing family investments. Women may reduce men's risky bets, and men may lessen women's preference for paltry returns on bonds and CD's. Thus, spouses discussing family investments can actually improve investing results.

Marriage

When people marry, they still maintain a separate credit rating. This will now be affected by accounts that are maintained separately as well as co-signed together. When married women choose to apply for credit, they can do so under their maiden and/or married name. Having a strong credit rating is not only important for getting joint or separate credit while married, but may be needed again if the marriage ends.

Once children arrive, women and their families have extra decisions to make starting with whether to continue work or stay at home. Few decisions have as many personal, professional, family, and financial consequences. Each family's goals, priorities, and circumstances will be different. But either way, In addition to the impact on the family, it will affect the woman's future wage levels, professional development, job advancement, and retirement savings. This is one cause of women tending to earn less over their lifetime and having lower retirement incomes.

Retirement savings

Earning less and living longer has particular implications for retirement. On average, women live more than five years longer than men, which means that they need retirement income to last longer. Additionally, they are more likely to be living alone at some time in their retirement. This makes preparing for their own retirement income even more important. In preparing, some women may face more hurdles. They may be in and out of the work force more often contributing to lower lifetime earnings and less likely to be vested in company pension plans. Women especially need to be reminded to resist the temptation to keep too much of their retirement savings in cautious investments when retirement is still distant. Over time, too cautious investments tend to lead to lower returns and less money, or even worse, does not keep up with inflation and so actually loses buying power. Women should be investing more heavily in stocks than cautious investments in their peak earning years so they can have a better chance of saving enough to last thru a longer retirement. (See the chapters on *Saving for Retirement* and *Investing.*)

But all is not negative. Working moms can count up to a year off for child rearing without incurring a break in accruing company retirement benefits. Even stay-at-home moms can plan for their retirement regardless of how distant that day may seem. Working spouses can open Individual Retirement Accounts (IRAs) for both themselves and their stay-at-home partners, and these spousal IRAs have fewer of the restrictions that limit IRAs for upper income earners. This applies to both traditional and Roth IRAs. See the section *"Saving for Retirement"*.

Retirement

Plan for your own retirement, start saving early, save extra, and don't avoid all risk (that is stocks) that tends over time to grow more. Know what benefits you are due from your husband's retirement benefits. Widow(er)s may be due a survivor benefit from their partner's pension. This pays a survivor pension after the partner's death, but results in a lower pension while alive. If pensions offer survivor benefits, they usually enable the pensioner to choose to elect it or not and often the spouse must agree in writing if it is given up. Remember that, on average, women live five years longer than men and compare the age difference between the partner due the pension and the spouse potentially due a survivor pension. Usually, only give up the survivor pension if the spouse due the retirement pension is significantly younger and more likely to outlive the person potentially due the survivor pension. Sometimes, couples agree to forego the survivor pension and replace it with life insurance, but consider that the survivor is giving up guaranteed income for life in lieu of a pot of money that will need to be managed to last for an unknown period of time.

Social Security may pay spouses at age 60 if the other spouse was eligible. Spouses can generally choose the higher Social Security benefit between their own or their spouse's. You are even eligible for SSA benefits from an ex-spouse if you are over age 62, unmarried, and were married at least ten years. This is true even if your ex is still working, as long as you have been divorced at least two years. For more information on Social Security, see the chapter on *"Retirement"*. Remember that eligibility rules can change, so review when your eligibility nears.

Widowhood

Statistically, women live longer than men, are younger than their husbands, and are thus more likely to outlive their husbands. Two-thirds of women age 75-84 are on their own. Be prepared.

- Know the location of important documents and all account information.
- Have a list of whom to contact for important benefits, pensions, and insurance.

- Nursing homes have twice as many women as men, so consider "long-term care insurance" to help pay for nursing homes and some in-home assistance. Premiums can be expensive, but not as much if you get it before age 50.
- Do a new budget to compare your new income and expense levels.
- Update your will and beneficiaries.
- If you are getting a pension that was reduced to provide a survivor benefit for your husband, send in a death certificate and have the reduction ended.
- Do not feel pressured to make big financial decisions soon after your husband's death, such as what to do with the life insurance.
- Don't fall for scams that prey upon the elderly with plans that are too good to be true or you don't understand. Wait before signing up. Get a second opinion even if you need to hire a professional.
- Do remember that paying off debts is usually a wise choice.
- Note that you still need to plan for your investments to last for the rest of your life, which may still require some stocks in your investments. At age 70, a woman can still expect to live on average another 16+ years. See SSA's life expectancy calculator for any age:
  http://www.socialsecurity.gov/OACT/population/longevity.html
- If you are living alone, have a support network to help you. Add a trusted maid, plumber, and a handyman to your contacts list. If you own a house, you may already have a lawn service. If the children have moved several states away, get a network of friends, church members, club members, professionals, etc.
- Consider using trusted professionals including a financial advisor, tax preparer, or attorney to get advice from. They may be expensive, but doing certain financial things without them can be even worse as we age.

Summary

- Nearly all women will need to be financially independent at some point in their life when starting out, divorced, widowed, or having never married. Be prepared.
- Two circumstances that particularly affect women's finances include, on average, living longer and earning less than men. Know what steps you can take to deal with your circumstances.

- If you are going to stay home and still want income or experience, consider working part-time, working at home, exploring flex time opportunities, or working as a freelancer.
- If you are working for an organization that does not have published pay scales, then be prepared for a salary negotiation, know what your job is worth, and ensure that you are seen as a valuable employee. Don't equate negotiating with conflict.
- Studies show that women are often better investors than men by avoiding risky investing behaviors, but also have a tendency to invest too cautiously. Don't miss the long-term higher returns from stocks that you will need in planning for a longer retirement.
- Since women on average live longer and tend to be younger than their husbands, you should plan for your own retirement, start saving early, save extra, avoid investing too cautiously, and know what benefits you are due from your own and husband's, pensions, Social Security, and insurance.
- Don't be pressured to sign away your survivor benefits if you are younger than your husband.
- Be financially prepared for widowhood.

Part Two

Introduction to Part Two - Saving

In Section One, we reviewed how sound financial principles apply throughout various stages in a person's life. The most important principles are to live within your means and save early for short and long-term goals. Saving should not be something that may happen if there is any money left over, something that you will get to in the future when you have a chance, or something you promise yourself after the next raise. Saving is not a wish for the future -- your future depends upon saving now. You need to take charge of your own future by planning for it now. No one else is going to do this for you. This means setting goals, making plans, and prioritizing savings equal to any of your other "needs" and ahead of your "wants".

In this Section Two, we will discuss specifics on how to save money – save towards your goals and spend less money. Chapters will cover how and where to save money, budgeting, and special considerations for two types of savings goals, college and retirement.

Chapter Six

How to Save

- Saving goals
- Saving principles
- Saving tips
- Saving psychology

Saving goals

Many things in life are expensive and for those things we can borrow money, save for it, or a combination of both. There are many things to save for, so you should set and prioritize your goals. Discussing priorities is even more important if you are part of a couple. Goals may be a new gadget, automobile, house, vacation, wedding, or myriad other things, but don't forget your essential long-term goals like college for the kids and retirement for you.

With so many savings goals, how do you prioritize? People's circumstance will be different and even change, but consider these priorities.

1. **Retirement** - You should start saving something for retirement from your very first full-time paycheck. If you have a 401(k) or 403(b) that your company matches, then contribute at least enough to get that matching amount; don't let that free money get away. Increase the percentage with each raise. The amount you have to save for retirement is

daunting, but manageable if you start early. Do this even against competing goals and needs. The money you save early compounds most and best. See Part Two, Chapter 5 - *Saving for Retirement.*

2. **Credit Cards** - Pay off credit cards as quickly as you can. *ALWAYS* pay more than the minimum. Paying 10-20% interest makes meeting all your other goals much more difficult. When this goal is met, shift your payment to your next goal. See *Part Four – Credit Cards.*

3. **Emergency Fund** - Another essential savings goal should be establishing an emergency fund. Having an emergency fund gives you peace of mind when times are good and can be a lifesaver when times are bad. An emergency fund enables you to handle sudden big expenses, such as a security deposit, car repair, medical emergency, or a new appliance without going into debt or a panic. It is even more important when you lose your job, especially when the economy is bad. The standard advice is for everyone to save three to six months of living expenses in an easily available emergency fund such as a savings account, but you should adjust this to your circumstances. Go for a shorter period if you need the money to pay off high interest debts such as credit cards or could live off a spouse's salary for a period. Aim for a longer period, even up to a year, if your job security is shaky or you depend upon commissions. Do save at least something in an emergency fund even while paying debt and saving for other goals; everyone has an emergency eventually. Start setting aside at least something for an emergency fund with your first paycheck, even a small amount. It may take a while to save 3-6 months expenses, but peace of mind comes immediately from knowing you are at least partly prepared for emergencies. You may decide to postpone this goal until after the credit cards are paid off, but I still suggest saving at least 1-2 month's expenses depending upon your circumstances. When this goal is met, move the payments to your next goal, celebrate, and sleep better at night. Don't spend all of your new savings! Some people can use a home equity line of credit or credit card as their emergency fund. This doesn't give the same peace of mind and financial security, but does free money for other priority uses.

4. **College Fund** – As soon as a child is born, start a college fund. You may shift the amount up or down over the years as other needs compete, but always save something each month – as early as possible. The money you save early compounds longest and best. See Part Two, Chapter 4 - *Saving for College"* for more details.

5. **Wants** – The first four goals are NECESSITIES. After those are your next priority for something you WANT like a car, home, vacation, etc. Even if you move up the priority of a WANT goal, you should still be making at least minimum savings towards your NECESSITY goals.

Savings principles

At any stage of life, it's far too easy to let your money flow out faster than it's coming in. Thankfully, there are many ways to help solve this common problem. Most people have fewer ways to increase the money coming in, so let's focus on controlling the money going out.

There are two types of saving you should be doing. We have discussed the importance of saving for a goal such as a home, college, or retirement. You are better able to do this type of saving when you also do the second, which is saving money instead of spending it. Note that it is much easier to save (not spend) money than it is to try to earn more. While our thoughts may obsess with how to earn more or pay less in taxes, it would be much more fruitful to concentrate on how to *save* more, since this is an area that we have much more control over. It's also easier to *save* more than *earn* more when we consider that saving $10.00 is equivalent to earning around $12.50 when you add about a quarter more for income and Social Security taxes. Too often saving is easier said than done, but don't worry, I have plenty of tips to help you out.

Pay Yourself First

You have plenty of people you need to pay with your paycheck and sometimes it seems there are no end to the bills, but don't forget the most important person you need to pay – YOU and the savings goals you have prioritized. With so many competing bills, how do you make sure you are paid, too? "Pay yourself first" which is a phrase from George Classen in his *"The Richest Man in Babylon"*. This means set aside money for your savings goals first BEFORE you have a chance to spend it. Before you get your paycheck, taxes and perhaps health benefits have already been deducted. Now set aside for your savings goals so you will know how much you have left over to spend on the other things you need and want. Don't determine what you can save after you have paid all your bills -- determine what you can afford to spend after you have set aside for your savings goals. If spending comes first, you will never have much left for savings -- if savings come first, you will soon learn to adjust your spending to fit the income that is left. How do you know how much to save? From a budget, which we will come to shortly.

Auto Pay

The easiest way to ensure you pay yourself first is to move your savings into a separate account automatically, before you ever get a chance to see or spend it in your checking account. Your paycheck should be going electronically directly into your checking account. Many employers will also let you send money to one or more other financial accounts. If not, then you can set up an automatic transfer of savings from your checking account to a financial account dedicated to each of your savings goals. You will likely always be saving towards more than one goal so have an account for each. For example, you WILL be saving towards retirement from the very first paycheck you receive! You may be skeptical about that one, but wait until we discuss retirement in detail later. You will have your emergency fund account. Have another account for whatever other short-term goal is the priority such as home down payment, vacation, or new car.

Save Early

The earlier you start savings towards your goals, the longer your savings will have time to compound and grow. Compounding your savings means your interest or dividends will soon earn more interest or dividends, thus enabling your savings to grow even faster. This is why even a small amount of early savings grows faster than a larger amount of savings started later. See a more detailed explanation in *Part Five > The Magic of Compound Savings*.

Autopay at Least a Minimum Amount Towards Savings Goals

With all those savings goals and all those bills piling up, everyone will have lean times at some time. You should still strive to pay at least something towards each savings goal *even if it is a small amount at first*. $25-$50 towards a savings goal is better than $0. Furthermore, I suggest certain savings goals such as retirement and emergency funds are vital even while striving to pay off credit cards. Sometimes it will be hard, but you will have some peace of mind knowing you are making progress towards your savings goals even if struggling towards other goals.

Simplify your finances by putting both your regular bills and savings on autopay. Set them up to automatically pay the bills and route your savings to your savings accounts.

Bank Your Raises and Other Windfalls

Once you have a routine of saving towards your goals by paying yourself first with automatic transfers to separate accounts, look for opportunities to increase your savings. Once credit cards are paid, save at least part of windfalls such as tax returns, bonuses, inheritances, and lottery jackpots ☺. It is okay to splurge with some of the windfall, but remember to pay yourself first with part of it, too.

Do the same with raises. At least half of every raise should go towards your various savings goals, yes, especially retirement. Save at least half the raise BEFORE you get used to spending it and you won't even miss it.

Look for Ways to Increase Your Savings

The more you can save by spending less, the more you can save towards your goals. Look thru my savings tips next and my spending wisely tips in Part Four and make many of them a habit.

Invest Your Savings Based upon Your Time-Horizon

Where you put your savings depends upon how soon you need it. So savings you won't need for a long while (five or more years) should be mostly in stocks and stock funds. These savings will grow the most and you don't care much during the inevitable period when they go down, because they historically come back up within five or less years. In contrast, savings you may need in the near term, such as vacation and emergency funds, should be somewhere safe. When we get to "Part Three – Investing", we will discuss "risk versus rewards" and see that low risks yield low returns while high returns require taking on more risk.

Saving tips

You may think I'm hopelessly naive about how hard it is to actually save. So let's turn to a few specific examples that could save you hundreds of dollars per year that you can then use to pay credit cards and fund your savings goals. I will cover this topic more thoroughly in "Chapter 22 - *Spending Wisely*" with specific tips on saving money by spending wisely, but for now let's give just a few examples to show that it could be easier than most people think.

- **Insurance** - Use high deductibles for your home and auto insurance. Raising your deductible from $250 to $1000 could lower your premiums by 15-25%. Most companies give you a further discount if you get your auto and home insurance from the same company. Every few years, comparison shop to see if you are still getting the best deal.
- **Taxes** – It's nice to get a refund at tax time and some people use this as an enforced savings account. Nevertheless, this means that you are paying too much each paycheck in taxes. Use a web tax calculator (http://www.kiplinger.com/tools/withholding/) and last year's tax return to calculate how much tax you should be paying and then adjust your tax withholdings thru your payroll office. For example, it you got a tax refund of $2400, you could "save" $200 each month. Use this to stop *paying* interest on credit cards and start *earning* interest on investments.
- **Energy bills** – The biggest part of your energy bill comes from running your heating and air conditioning. Save at least ten percent by turning your thermostat up or down 2-4 degrees and putting on a sweater and extra blanket. If someone is wearing short sleeves during the winter, then you can see you are paying too much for energy bills. Shop around for your electricity supplier. Many states deregulated electricity suppliers and now you can shop around and get your electricity from a variety of different companies and prices. Your electricity supplier can now be separate from your local electric company that will still read your meter, get your electricity from your desired supplier, and bill you. This

could save you 10% - 40% per kilowatt-hour. Check the website of your power company or state to see the companies you may choose from and their prices. Do even better and make everyone more comfortable by installing a programmable thermostat that automatically sets the temperature up or down on set times of the day. For example, in the winter up to 67 when you wake up, down to 60 when everyone leaves for work and school, back to 67 when people come home and down to 60 at bedtime. It works like magic and saves you money for better uses.

- **Credit cards** – If you carry a credit card balance and can't pay it off right away, ensure it's on a low rate card. Example: Shifting a $10,000 balance from a card charging 17% interest to one charging 12% will save you 5% or $500 of interest per year. Taking advantage of a 0% balance transfer offer for 8-15 months could save even more.

These are just a few examples to illustrate that IT IS POSSIBLE to save money and better use that savings to live within your means, pay off credit cards, and save towards your goals.

Belt-tightening, Cutting Budget Fat, or the "Latte Factor"

Another source of savings is the one you have been dreading that I would get to -- belt-tightening. The term "Latte Factor" comes from financial author David Bach in his book *"Finish Rich"* which refers to the many little things we spend money on regularly that add up to significant money over time. Whatever you call it, we all have it, and we should be looking for and reducing it: cigarettes, lattes, fast food, muffins, pedicures, dining out, pizzas, movies, sodas, candy bars, beer, bottled water, happy hours, fast lane tolls, etc.

Most of these seem small, but see how they add up. Examples: lunch five days a week, $8 x 5 x 50 = $2000 per year. Lattes and a muffin four days a week, $7 x 4 x 50 = $1400. Happy hour twice a month, $20 x 2 x 12 = $480. Converting this "latte" spending into paying off debts or savings goals is worth even more when you remember the power of compound interest over time. For example, reducing each of these three indulgences by half for ONE year and compounding at 7% over the next twenty years would quadruple your money: ($1000 + $700 + 240 = $1940 compounded @ 7% for 20 yrs. = $7835. (See Part Five, Chapter 1 *"The Magic of Compound Interest"*.) One more example - I'm not going to yell at you for smoking cigarettes because they will kill you thirty years from now or because your clothes and car smell like a bus station bathroom.

(This is a financial book after all.) However, consider this: smoking four packs a week at $7.00 per pack will waste $1500 per year, equaling $21,000 every ten years if invested at 7% return - plus all those extra medical bills later.

Find your budget fat or "latte factor" by tracking on a notebook or smartphone for two weeks all the little indulgences that you could reduce. Add them up see how much you could save in a year and shift to your debts or savings goals. Then go to a web compound calculator to see how that could grow to a huge amount by compounding over 20-30 years. Moreover, notice how many of these indulgences aren't really healthy?

Finding fat in our spending habits may mean breaking habits like Friday night pizzas, Sunday brunches, mid-morning muffins, Saturday movies, etc. However, belt-tightening does not have to mean doing without. Doing without something completely may not be sustainable over the long-term as we relapse. We are going to splurge, but do it wisely, less frequently, and less expensively. See what you can cut in half or substitute for something less expensive (and healthier). Examples to trade: bag lunch for buying lunch several days a week, package of granola bars from home for daily muffin or candy bar, water filter for bottled water, $5.00 carryout or grocery store pizza for delivered pizza, cooked meal for eating out, cable movie for movie theater or DVD, free concert for date night, tea bags for lattes and sodas, etc. Reduce eating out or carryout from weekly to monthly and use a coupon. Pull home-cooked leftovers out of the freezer instead of frozen dinners. Limit impulse items from the grocery store to 1-2 items per visit.

Involve the kids in belt-tightening decisions so they can understand what's happening, contribute to the decisions, and learn life's financial lessons early. Family financial situations should not be an embarrassment or mystery. It's easier to understand that money is limited and should be prioritized, rather than that "no" is the answer to their every spending request.

Saving psychology

Saving is easier when you know how to make it easier and where to look for the fat, but there is still the problem of willpower - or sometimes *won't* power. Even with our good intentions, how do our impulses trip us up? Instant gratification and wanting something now can trip us up, even when part of the brain is trying to tell us that this purchase is going to cost our credit card 18% more in interest. Here are some tips for helping to get our emotional side of the brain on board with the program our rational side of the brain is trying to yell at us.

- Know the difference between "needs" and "wants". If it is merely a "want", think about how much do you really want it or how many times will you actually use it.
- Drastically limit impulse spending by how often you do it and how expensive is the item. Especially for expensive items and items not on sale, think about it overnight; you will be surprised how little you want it the next day. At least comparison shop for a sale.
- Pay cash instead of using a debit or credit card. Studies show that it's easier to limit spending when we actually see real cash leaving our hand.
- Have specific goals for your financial future, such as paying off credit cards, saving for a house, going on a cruise, etc., and think about how impulse and "habit" spending is impeding those goals.
- Compare a purchase to a higher priority goal and think whether it is worth delaying that goal.
- Reward yourself when you reach a savings goal. For example, every time you pay off a nasty credit card balance, go for ice cream or a movie.
- Pay a penalty when you fail to reach a savings goal. For example, make a donation to the political party or cause you oppose.

More information

- http://savedplus.com/home - This smartphone app provides a new twist on automating your savings. It automatically transfers to your savings account a percentage of any spending you do from your checking account. Just link your checking and savings accounts, set up your saving goals and percentages, and watch your savings grow.
- http://www.mvelopes.com/ - There are many websites and apps for budgeting and I'm going to highlight many of them throughout the book. This one is good for the "envelope" method of curbing spending by putting money you need in different envelopes to keep it separate from other money and not spending more when the envelopes are empty.

Summary

- There are many things to save for, so you should set and prioritize your goals. Discussing priorities is even more important if you are part of a couple.
- Prioritize key savings goals, then any optional savings goals:
  1. opening a retirement account from your first full-time pay check
  2. paying off credit cards as quickly as possible
  3. creating an emergency fund of at least 2-4 months
  4. saving for college when a child is born, and then
  5. optional goals such as a car, home, vacation, etc.
- It's usually easier to save more than earn more when we consider that saving $10.00 is equivalent to earning around $12.50 when you add about a quarter more for income and Social Security taxes.
- "Pay yourself first" by setting aside money for your savings goals first BEFORE you have a chance to spend it.
- The easiest way to ensure you pay yourself first is to move your savings into a separate account automatically before you ever get a chance to see it in your checking account.
- Autopay at least a minimum amount towards your savings goals. $25 is better than $0.
- Bank at least half of your raises and other windfalls by increasing your savings and debt paying before you have a chance to spend them.
- Look for ways to increase your savings. The more you can save by spending less, the more you can save towards your goals.
- Reducing the fat in our budgets and spending habits doesn't mean going without completely, but could add up to significant savings that will make it easier to live within our means, pay off debt, and save towards our goals.
- Saving is easier when you know how to make it easier and where to look for the fat, but you also need to know tips for handling problems of will power.
- Know the difference between "needs" and "wants".
- Drastically limit impulse spending by how often you do it, how many items you get at once, and how expensive is the item.

Chapter Seven

Develop a Money Management Plan (Budget)

- Why budget
- How to budget
- Follow thru on your budget

Why budget?

We have discussed living within your means and how to save towards your goals, but now we need a plan on how to actually accomplish these steps and know whether we are being successful. We could call this a money management plan, but most people call it a budget. You might be tempted to skip this chapter, but know that there are various ways to do a budget and I'm going to show you an easy way, thus increasing the chances that most people will actually do it. Everyone should do a simple money management analysis at certain key times such as getting a new job, buying a house, getting married, having children, getting divorced, planning for retirement, setting a new savings goal, or whenever your financial situation changes. You must know how your expenses and real spending compare to your income. Most people would further benefit from regularly or periodically following-thru with the additional steps I will outline to develop a plan and review how well it is working.

Many people shy away from budgets as too much work or from too little knowledge or wonder why go to all that trouble? Because a money management plan or budget gives you the hard data you need to live within your means, identify areas for potential savings, match what you should do with what you currently do, make hard choices about how to meet priorities, find areas to economize, determine how much you should be able to save in key areas, identify "wants" and "needs", and figure out whether you can afford that next big expense. Would you start a new trip without a map or GPS? Well a budget gives us a similar tool to help ensure our financial journey will go well, too.

How to budget?

Here are the easiest steps to develop a money management plan and use the data to help you follow sound financial principles and reach a more secure financial future.
1. Determine how much money you have coming in and going out (called cash flow).
2. Specify a goal to help control your cash flow (pay off debt, save for a new car, retire early, etc.)
3. Create a spending plan to balance your money going in and out (Yes, this is the budget part, but it is vital.)
4. Periodically review your spending plan and adjust where necessary. (Life happens and sometimes your budget needs to adapt to it.)

Determine Your Cash Flow

Budget tools

First, determine your current "cash flow", the "before" picture of where your money is currently going. Identify and list where your money is going each month. Choose the method that is easiest for you: spreadsheet, paper, or online. I like using a spreadsheet so it can do the math for me and is simple to change. A spreadsheet is just an easy to use grid of boxes so you can line up, change, and calculate categories and numbers. Your PC probably came with a spreadsheet (Microsoft Works or Excel) or there are several free ones on the web including Google Docs (https://www.google.com/intl/en_US/drive/start/apps.html). You can start a simple one from scratch or select a free, ready-made template. Go to this book's website to download a simple version that does that math for you. See more choices here: http://www.budgetsaresexy.com/. Another choice is to use a financial website that offers budget applications along with other money management tools. One of the most popular is www.mint.com. Smartphone users may value the growing list of money management apps such as "Mint", "Quicken Money Management", CoinKeeper, or "Pageonce". Of course, sometimes nothing beats just a blank sheet of paper, sharp pencil, and trusty calculator.

Income

Once you have picked your tool, let's get started. First, list and total your monthly, net income. If it varies by month, then average it (total for a year and divide by 12 months). This is the amount of money that you're saving and spending must be less than to live within your means. Some people tell you to list your gross income and then make you list all your deductions, but we are doing this the easy way with your net pay after all deductions, since that is what you really care about. If your income is from commissions or other variable sources, then use your worst, recent year's income. Learning to live on that frees up anything above it to devote to paying debts, increasing emergency funds, and savings goals.

Expenses

Now list and total your monthly expenses.

1. Start with the easy, fixed ones: housing, car, insurance, telephone, internet, cable, student loans, etc. Include savings like college funds that are not already deducted from your paychecks, for example, your retirement 401(k)s.
2. Get a monthly average for the ones that change each month, such as utilities, gasoline, groceries, etc.
3. Turn annual and quarterly expenses into monthly averages, such as insurance, vacations, and subscriptions.
4. End with the ones that are harder to pin down, such as eating out, clothes, tunes, gadgets, entertainment, etc. Include credit card interest, but not purchases that should be totaled under appropriate categories.

Most amounts can come from your checking and credit cards statements, but you may need to dig out bills or hunt them down on the web. Especially, categorize credit and debit card statements, because they likely will reveal the most secrets about just where your money is rushing every month. Don't worry about exact numbers; rounding and estimating are fine. Do NOT have a category called "ATM withdrawals"; estimate where all that cash is going or better yet, jot down your cash spending for a week or two. Then enter it in your appropriate budget category. A growing number of smartphone apps make it easy to enter and track your daily expenses as you make them, such as "Toshl".

Here are categories you may consider.

Expense	Initial amount	Goal amount	Month 1 actual	Month 2 actual
Mortgage or rent				
Homeowners association fee				
Yard care				
Electricity				
Gas				
Water / trash				
Insurance				
Car payment				
Car maintenance				
Gasoline				
Internet				
TV / movie subscriptions / rentals				
Landline and cell phone				
Student loan				
Kids college fund				
Kids allowances				
Kids Daycare				
Kids entertainment				
Kids schools expenses, outings, and lunch.				
Gifts				

Groceries				
Health care				
Subscriptions				
Memberships				
Charities				
Entertainment				
Dining out				
Lunches				
Coffee, sodas, muffins, snacks				
Clothes				
Electronics				
Hobbies				
Vacations				
Income	=			
Expense Totals	-			
Credit card/Debt payoff	-			
Savings goals	-			
Left-over or over-spent	=			

There is practically no end to the list of expenses, but when you have entered yours, add them all up and don't faint. If you have income left over, this is the amount you can save, increase debt pay offs, and spend. If your expenses exceed your income, then you have work to do so your debt level and financial security don't worsen.

1. Set a goal

After seeing whether you have money left over or are overspending, think about your financial goals and discuss with your partner. Set a goal of why you would like to im-prove your cash flow. For example, live within your means, buy a car, save for a down payment for a house, get ready for the baby, pay off the credit card, go to Hawaii, be-come a millionaire by age 55, etc. There is always something to pay off or save for. Focusing on your next goal helps you stay on track and develop good financial habits, security, and peace of mind.

2. *Create a balanced budget*

Many people think a budget may be hard to start, harder to do, and hardest to keep. People may think budgets keep us from doing something we want to do, like spend, but they may also be the best tool to enable us to do something we want to do, such as one of our goals. It did take a little work to get to this stage, but now comes the payoff.

Review your cash flow spreadsheet or paper list and be surprised about just where and how fast your money is going. Don't let it get you down, but use it as the best tool to ensure your financial future.

1. See how much you have left over each month or are overspending. If you are overspending or not saving enough, now you have data to see how big the problem is.

2. Calculate how much you have left over to save towards your goals. We have repeatedly discussed "saving" even when you have multiple demands on your money. Now you can use this cash flow analysis to determine how much you can save and where you can free up more money to better save or pay debts.

3. Review which categories you can reduce to live within your means and boost savings and debt pay offs.

See which spending categories could be most easily reduced. For example, think whether eating out so often is more important than whatever your stated goal is. Zero in on both the big items, such as insurance and the little items, such as your "latte spending" on many little indulgences. Spending less doesn't necessarily mean depriving yourself; it could also mean spending more wisely. See the chapter on "*Spending Wisely*" for ideas to make this task easier. If your overspending and debt keeps getting bigger, then see the chapters on "*Credit Cards and Debts*".

Now take the same spending categories in your cash flow list and assign new amounts to some of them. In the sample budget above, complete column three "Goals". Total and revise the spending and savings amounts until the amount of good cash flow enables you to meet your goals. Of course, there are plenty of circumstances where this is easier said than done, so read on for more tips on how to better accomplish this along life's journey.

4. *Review and revise your budget*

At the minimum, you should repeat this cash flow and adjustment analysis whenever your income, expenses, or goals change. However, you can get even more benefits, when you periodically review your budget to see how well you are doing and revise it where needed. Decide how often is "periodically": monthly, quarterly, annually. In the sample budget above, use the "Monthly" columns to review periodically how well you are keeping your own balanced budget. Keep it simple, so you are more likely to follow it. Focus on your goals and successes more than your failures. Reward your successes. Even when we don't follow our budget religiously, just creating one usually is an eye-opener as to just where our money goes, and in which areas can we most easily economize.

This is an absolutely vital step towards living within your means, reducing your debts, increasing your wealth, and meeting your goals. You must know what your income, essential expenses, and savings goals are in order to know how much is left over for "wants", debt relief, wealth building, and your goals.

Follow through on your plan with the right mindset and tools

Managing your money is part psychology, part knowledge, and part tools. A money management plan / budget is a tool that helps manage both your cash flow and your mental impulses to spend beyond your means. Also consider other tools that help manage both your money and your mindset. Consider budgeting spreadsheets, websites, and smartphone apps on a long-term basis. Use a prepaid card rather than a credit card to force your discretionary spending to stay within the amount that you load on your prepaid card each month. Or set aside a set amount of cash each month for your discretionary spending and stop your spending when your monthly stash of cash is gone. Use email or text alerts from your bank, prepaid card, credit cards, and other financial accounts to remind you of your spending, balances, and bills. Use direct deposit, automatic bill paying, and automatic savings to ensure you cover your priorities and simplify your financial life. Using the right tools and mental mindset should help ensure that living within your means and saving towards your goals become a habit more than a straitjacket.

More information

You have many budgeting applications, spreadsheets, and websites to choose from, so there is no excuse not to find the one right for you. Here are more.

- http://gnucash.org/ - I usually highlight easy to use websites for the general reader, but here is one for people who want all the bells and whistles. GnuCash allows you to track bank accounts, stocks, income, and expenses. "As quick and intuitive to use as a checkbook register, it is based on professional accounting principles to ensure balanced books and accurate reports," according to their website.
- https://www.learnvest.com/ - This budgeting website is good for people who want help with the financial basics.
- http://www.yodlee.com/consumers/ - This budgeting website and smartphone app is good for knowledgeable users who want to customize their money management application with dozens of add-on widgets.

Summary

- A budget is a money management plan for_accomplishing your financial goals and knowing whether you are being successful.
- A money management analysis or budget gives you the hard data you need to live within your means, identify areas for savings, match what you should do with what you currently do, make hard choices about how to meet priorities, find areas to economize, determine how much you should be able to save in key areas, identify "wants" and "needs", and figure out whether you can afford that next big expense.
- Use the tool best for you: spreadsheet, paper, website, or smartphone app.
- List your monthly income, expenses, and savings goals.
- After seeing whether you have money left over or are overspending, set a goal of why you would like to improve your cash flow such as better living within your means, reaching a savings goal, or reducing debt.
- Revise the spending and savings amounts until the amount of good cash flow enables you to meet your goals.

- Everyone should redo a simple money management analysis / budget whenever your finances change such as getting a new job, buying a house, getting married, having children, getting divorced, planning for retirement, setting a new savings goal, or your debt is increasing.
- Analyzing your budget is an absolutely vital step towards living within your means, reducing your debts, increasing your wealth, and meeting your goals. You must know what your income, essential expenses, and savings goals are in order to know how much is left over for "wants", debt relief, wealth building, and your goals.

Chapter Eight

Where to Save

- How to choose a bank
- Where to save

How to choose a bank

We have discussed your savings goals and money management tools to help achieve them. Now that you are on the road to saving all that money for all those different things, where do you save it? Let's start with checking account at a bank. What we need most is a checking account to receive our income and pay our bills. So don't get distracted with things like interest that is going to be negligible, rewards programs, one-time offers, or big brand names. Banking is one business that is still very competitive, so it pays to comparison shop. Switching banks can be a big hassle, but many banks now provide kits to make this easier. If yours doesn't, then just use a kit from another bank by doing an internet search for, "checking account switch kits". Use the internet and compare these:

- Fees and what you have to do to avoid them

- Convenience of branches and ATMs
- Online banking features and costs
- Mobile banking features

Fees and what to do to avoid them

If you want to know what banks are really, really good at; it's coming up with more types of fees than you can imagine. So determine which fees are most important to you and compare them. Start with monthly fees, overdraft fees, and ATM fees. You should be able to find free checking that may waive the monthly fee if you keep a certain minimum balance, enroll in direct deposit of your paycheck, or have other accounts at the bank. ALWAYS enroll in direct deposit of all of your monthly checks to get reduced fees, quicker access to your funds, less hassle, and no lost checks.

Banks will probably be quick to sign you up for overdraft protection for when you don't have funds to cover a check, debit card purchase, or ATM withdrawal. Yes, you definitely need this to avoid check bouncing fees, but ensure you do it the right way. Avoid the courtesy overdraft protection that charges you a fee whenever you go over-limit. Do you really want to pay a $25 overdraft fee for writing that $10 check? And those fees can skyrocket quickly. Instead, link your checking account to either a savings account or bank credit card so any over-limit activity is paid from one of those sources. A linked credit card will charge you very high interest, but much less than overdraft fees. Ensure you pay this balance in full and don't use that card for anything else, so it's always free to cover overdrafts and emergencies. Better to avoid overdrafts at all, so review your balance every week, before major bills, or before big purchases. A mobile app is perfect for this. Setup text or email alerts for a variety of situations such as low balance alerts.

Convenience of branches and ATMs

Even though it is becoming rarer, many banks will have free checking, so the next issue is which branches and ATMs are convenient to home and work? Ensure you check out the fees for using ATMs, both their's (better be free) and others' (some will reimburse you for a few withdrawals per month from another bank's ATM). Remember that there is a double whammy for using another bank's ATM; both your bank and the other bank will charge you a fee. At least you have control of ATM fees. Plan your cash withdrawals ahead so you don't have to use other bank's ATMs.

Online banking features and costs

It's easier than ever to pay your bills and manage your money with online banking and is well worth your effort to learn how to do it. Instead of writing and mailing checks, you can go to the bank's website, setup payees, schedule recurring bills automatically, and send other checks to anybody whenever you need to. Moreover, it's easy to track your payments in the past and even your balance in the future as you can see the coming, scheduled payments and deposits - so there is much less excuse for going overlimit.

Mobile banking features

One of the newest ways to bank is mobile banking with your smartphone. With instant access to view your bank balance and ATM locations, there is even less excuse to go over limit or pay avoidable fees. One cool feature I like is taking a photo of your paper check to deposit it without having to go to the bank. Now I'm waiting for the mobile feature that allows me to withdraw money without having to go to the ATM, but it would probably have a fee.

We are even starting to see financial services aimed specifically for mobile devices. The first services include these two that require mobile devices and include checking accounts, debit cards, and online bill paying:

- https://www.simple.com/
- https://www.gobank.com/

Where to save

- Where to save your money
- Internet Banks
- Credit Unions
- Savings Accounts
- Money Market Accounts and Funds
- Prepaid debit cards.

Remember that banks have several kinds of checking accounts with different features and fees. So not only do you need to compare several banks, but also types of banks and different accounts within banks. Try to find the brochure or webpage that compares each of the bank's accounts side-by-side for easy comparison. That bank on the way to work may be convenient, but at least compare a few choices starting with these web bank comparison sites:

- https://www.checkingfinder.com/
- http://www.depositaccounts.com/checking/reward-checking-accounts.html
- http://www.findabetterbank.com/
- http://icba.org/

Sometimes your local banks will be more competitive than the big, national banks, so don't overlook them. Moreover, local banks and credit unions often have higher customer satisfaction ratings than the big banks.

Where to save your money

Don't mix your checking account funds with your savings funds, even to maintain a required minimum balance. It's just too easy or tempting to dip into your savings when they are not clearly separated. Furthermore, you may wish to have a separate savings account for each of your savings goals, such as emergency funds separate from your savings fund for vacation, wedding, auto, or house down payment. You may even want a separate account for your big annual expenses, such as insurance, property taxes, or membership dues so you are not scrambling when they come due. It's simple to add up your annual expenses, divide by 12, and automatically send that amount to a separate savings account just for annual expenses. None of these options pays substantial interest, usually less than the rate of inflation, but with your savings, security is the primary goal.

Your college and retirement savings are altogether different, so see the sections on *"Saving for College"* and *"Saving for Retirement"*. We will cover options for your long-term savings in the section on *"Investing"* where we will learn that to get higher returns, we will have to take greater risks that may not be appropriate for many of your short-term savings goals.

You have a variety of options for where to put savings depending upon convenience, interest rate, and time until you may need your funds. You may wish to put different types of savings in different places. Consider the following options in addition to your regular bank.

Many banks are only online with few or no branches or ATMs. I suggest that their unique features make them uncertain choices for checking accounts, but serious contenders for savings accounts. Because they have lower infrastructure costs, they pay higher interest rates, may have lower fees, and frequently have attractive introductory offers. On the other hand, they may not have the personal touch or be as convenient if you have to mail deposits and can't use live tellers. Review their fees for debit cards and transfer fees and whether they reimburse you for several ATM withdrawals per month. Many people use regular banks for their checking and transfer money to internet banks for better savings rates.

Even some of the big banks have separate internet bank accounts. Find plenty of current reviews by searching for "internet only banks". Also, check out these:

- http://research.fdic.gov/bankfind/ - Ensure your online bank is FDIC insured here.
- https://www.simple.com/ - You have many choices in online banks, but this one is a bit different in a variety of ways including claiming to be more customer and fee friendly. The feature that caught my attention is the capability for users to better categorize bills, spending, and saving goals into the proverbial envelopes or buckets. Then you get a picture of how you are doing this month in each envelope or towards which savings goal.

Credit Unions

Credit Unions are non-profit financial institutions that are limited to members of particular organizations. Their advantages include paying higher interest rates for savings, charging fewer or lower fees for accounts, having lower credit card rates, and charging lower rates for loans. Their disadvantages might include fewer ATMs, branches, and features. So as usual, compare their rates, fees, locations, and features. I have used a credit union for many years for saving accounts, loans, mortgages, and a credit card without going even once to a branch or ATM. Credit unions have different membership requirements, some letting in direct or more distant family members. My membership is thru my wife's sister. Several credit unions let you join after making a one-time donation to a particular charity including:

- Pentagon Federal Credit Union

- Alliant Credit Union
- Connexus Credit Union
- Lake Michigan Credit Union

Find a credit union you may be eligible for here:
- http://www.creditunion.coop/ - website of the Credit Union National Association with information and search method for credit unions you may be eligible to join.
- http://www.asmarterchoice.org/ - Search for credit unions.

Savings Accounts

Savings accounts are the most convenient and flexible supplement to checking accounts, but pay the lowest interest. You can find them at banks, internet banks, and credit unions. Consider having a savings account at your regular bank linked to your checking account to cover overdraft protection. Moreover, banks will sometimes reduce your fees by having both a savings and checking account or a combined minimum balance level. This account could be savings for your annual expenses or vacation fund to which you want to transfer funds easily back and forth. Keep your longer-term savings funds (like emergency funds or down payments) at a place that pays higher interest.

Don't be complacent about accounts as banks are not shy about suddenly imposing new fees. It can be daunting to change your checking account with its many automatic deposits and bill paying, but not so with savings accounts. If your bank treats you badly over your savings account, first call them, tell them you are comparing rates for an account elsewhere, and ask them what they can do for you to stay. If they don't satisfy you, then do your comparison, move your savings, and gleefully (but politely) close the offending account. I once had a savings account with a giant bank that suddenly imposed a *$20* per month fee! I quickly closed the account and waited patiently for the customer service rep to ask me why. I eagerly replied that they had invented the "reverse savings account" in which they paid me $1.47 interest per month and then took $20.00 for the privilege of using my money!

Money Market Accounts and Funds

These are like savings accounts, but may pay slightly higher interest in return for high minimum balances. It's still easy to withdraw your money – as long as you keep that high minimum balance. You'll have to decide whether tying up so many funds is worth whatever higher interest they may be paying at the time. Like savings accounts, interest rates go up or down based upon inflation and other economic factors.

Money Market *Accounts* are offered by banks and are federally insured. Money Market *Funds* are offered by mutual funds and may pay slightly higher rates. They are not insured, but are considered very safe, as none have yet lost money, since they are backed up by the mutual funds themselves.

Prepaid debit cards

A surprisingly large number of people do not have any kind of bank account and deal with check cashing stores, money orders, and cash. I recommend that these consumers consider prepaid debit cards that offer online accounts, bill paying, direct deposit of paychecks, text alerts, and access to ATMs in addition to debit cards. Compare low-fee cards and its fees against the variety of fees you pay for check cashing and money orders.

Summary

- Choose a bank and savings account by comparing fees and what you have to do to avoid them, convenience of branches and ATMs, online banking features and costs, and mobile banking features.
- Determine which fees are most important to you and compare them. Start with monthly fees, overdraft fees, and ATM fees.
- Overdraft protection is good to have, but ensure you choose the method with the lowest fees, often by linking to a savings accounts or credit card.
- You have control over when you pay ATM fees, so just *don't* by planning ahead.
- Mobile banking on your smartphone is really nice, but online banking, bill paying, auto-paying of bills and savings, and future balance forecasting are practically essential.
- Even when most savings interest rates are negligible, it is nice to aim for higher rates for longer term savings, which you can often find at credit unions, internet banks, certificates of deposit, and money market accounts and funds. For *short-term* savings goals, security is more important than the rate of return.
- Use separate savings accounts for separate savings goals such as emergency funds, annual expenses, savings goals, investment cash, etc.

Chapter Nine

Saving for College

- 529 plans
- Prepaid tuition plans
- Coverdell ESAs
- Roth IRAs
- Savings bonds
- Financial aid

We have discussed many types of savings goals, how to save, and where to put your savings. Now let's turn to two savings goals that are quite different, saving for college and retirement. These savings goals take a lot of money and many years or decades to accomplish. Therefore, you save in different ways, use different savings tools, and have different tax rules.

No doubt you have heard that college is hugely expensive; you may have even experienced it yourself recently. Whether the parents or the student pays, college will be one of the biggest expenses in life. According to the College Board, the 2016-2017 average cost to attend an in-state public university was $20,090 and $45,370 for a private college. Of course, it will be more – much more – when your child is ready since college costs are rising twice as fast as inflation while states are cutting back their funding. If you can bear a good fright, get a good grip on your chair and go to http://www.finaid.org/calculators/scripts/costprojector.cgi to see the projected cost when your child is ready.

You may still be paying off your own student loans and your spouse's student loans and then along comes that first bundle of joy and now you need to start saving for his or hers college, too? And then the next child comes and…. Well take a deep breath and don't panic, because you don't necessarily have to save for all of it, but you certainly can save for some of it, hopefully for at least one quarter to one half. Along with all your other savings goals, try to set up a college savings account with at least something, even if you only start with $50 per pay period or month. It's vital to start as early as possible so your savings have a longer chance to compound and grow. Don't delay; start as soon as you get that new Social Security number. If you start immediately, contribute $100 per month, and compound 7% per year, you will have more than $42,000 when college begins. Waiting five years until kindergarten to begin and you will only have $25,000 when college starts. So contribute at least a token amount early, even if the reality may be that day care expenses could be just as expensive as in-state tuition and is your first priority. Just remember that when day care expenses end, really ramp up your college savings.

Since education is not only good for your own child, but also all of society, the U.S. government is here to help you in the form of tax breaks. That is where the special savings tools for college come in. There are many to choose from.

- 529 plans
- Prepaid tuition plans
- Coverdell ESAs
- Roth IRAs
- Savings Bonds

529 plans

529 plans (named for the section of the IRS code) enable you to save for college expenses with special tax breaks. You do not get a Federal income tax break when contributing to your 529 account, but you do not have to pay taxes on the earnings. Many states do give you a break from state taxes on the amount you contribute to your

account. Each state has their own plan with their own rules which you will need to review, but you aren't limited to your own state's plan. If your state does offer a tax break for its own plan, it's almost always worthwhile to stick with it, but if not, you can choose any state's plan to get lower fees or better investing options. An account with any state plan can be used for any eligible college in the country for qualifying college expenses including tuition, room and board, fees, and books.

Unlike the Coverdell Education Savings Accounts (ESAs), there is no income limitation on eligibility to contribute to a 529 plan and most states allow very high contribution amounts.

Some states offer plans directly for free or thru financial advisors for a fee of around 5% every time you make a deposit. Why would you pay around 5% of your college savings when you can do it yourself for FREE! Avoid the fees and go directly to the website of the state plan. On the website, you can get information, sign up, pick your investment options, and setup automatic contributions from your checking account. Remember to always put your savings goals on autopilot. It's easy to get started and you can set it and forget it if you choose. The plan will send you account statements periodically to monitor your progress.

Once you set up an account, you choose how you want your contributions invested. Different states have different options, but with most you can make it as simple as choosing a target-date mutual fund that automatically invests in a mix of stocks and bonds and grows more conservative to safeguard your funds as the college years near. Alternatively, most states enable you to mix your own selections among a variety of mutual funds with stocks, bonds, and indexes. You can generally change only once or twice per year.

Remember that these are investments and there WILL be periods when they will shrink. However, over time stocks are still the best investment to grow the most and beat inflation. You can pick conservative investment funds that are less likely to shrink or more aggressive investment funds that are more likely to grow. We all are fearful of the first risk of investing which is that our money can shrink, but we also need to remember the second risk which is that the *buying power* of our money will shrink thru inflation even if the absolute value grows. This is especially true for college costs that are growing at twice the rate of inflation, on average 7%, so our investments need to grow at the same rate just to stay even. It's usually only stocks that will grow over time at an average of 7%+ per year. But don't let any of this investing stuff deter you. You can usually make it easy on yourself by selecting a "target date" fund that matches the year your

child will enter college and leave the investing stuff to the experts. See the chapters on *"Investing"* for more information
.

Summary of Benefits
- Grows with federal tax-free earnings.
- Most states offer state tax breaks.
- Is a great way for grandparents to contribute. Grandparents can fund an account with up to $13,000 per year per grandparent without worrying about the federal gift tax.
- Does not count heavily against you when applying for college aid. The Federal financial aid formula only assesses 529 balances at the parent rate of 5.6% instead of the child's rate of 20%.

If your child doesn't go to college, you can transfer to another beneficiary or withdraw the funds and pay income tax and a 10% penalty on the earnings, and possibly state tax penalties if you got state breaks on your account.

Compare state 529 plans and get more info here:
- http://sites.savingforcollege.com/kiplinger/plan_details.php
- http://www.savingforcollege.com/
- http://529.morningstar.com/state-map.action

Prepaid tuition plans

Many states offer a second type of college savings plan called "prepaid plans" in which you can prepay future college tuition at today's prices. Note that this only covers tuition and certain fees, but not room and board. State plans differ on additional fees due and in-state residency requirements. Most allow you to withdraw your money if the child goes to a private or another state college.

There is also an independent 529 prepaid plan for 270+ participating private colleges. This plan has no sign-up fees, grows free from Federal taxes, and is free from tax in some states. Get more information at its website:

https://www.privatecollege529.com/OFI529/

Prepaid plans have a lower participation rate than regular 529 plans, but here is an idea to consider. Once your child has been accepted into a college, prepay then for their senior year tuition at today's price.

Coverdell Educations Savings Accounts (ESAs)

Coverdell's are like Roth IRAs (Individual Retirement Accounts) but for education instead of retirement. You pay taxes before you contribute up to $2000 per year per child, but you can withdraw both your contributions and earnings tax free if used for qualifying education expenses. What qualifies for education expenses is broader than 529 plans; you can use them for things such as tutors and computers as well as pay for pre-college, private K-12 schools, and religious schools. Unlike 529 plans, there are income restrictions for parents; in 2017, modified gross adjusted incomes up to $220,000 for married couples to contribute the full $2000 and phased out to zero. When applying for financial aid, Coverdell's are assessed like 529s at the parent's lower rate of 5.6% rather than the child's higher 20% rate.

As with retirement IRAs, you can set one up at banks, mutual funds, and brokerages. As always compare fees and commissions. Like IRAs, Coverdell's can hold a wide variety of investments including stocks, bonds, and mutual funds, and things like Certificates of Deposit.

Roth IRAs

IRAs (Individual Retirement Accounts) are used to save for retirement, and early withdrawals are normally subject to a 10% penalty. (See the chapter on *"Saving for Retirement"*.) However, early withdrawals for qualified education expenses are one of the exceptions and you do not have to pay the 10% penalty. There are plenty of details, which you should review in the IRS Publication 970 here: http://www.irs.gov/publications/p970/ch09.html. This applies to both traditional IRAs and Roth IRAs. However, using Roth IRAs for educational expenses has other tax advantages. Since you already paid taxes on the contributions you put in your Roth IRA, you don't have to pay taxes on them when you withdraw them for any reason at any time. However, if you withdraw earnings before age 59 ½, you will have to pay income tax on the earnings.

The advantage of using a Roth IRA to save and pay for college is that it gives you flexibility. If your child gets a scholarship or doesn't go to college, you still have the savings for retirement. The disadvantages are that you miss tax breaks offered by 529 plans, there are income and contributions limits for IRAs, and you have to pay taxes on Roth IRA earnings if under age 59 ½ or held less than five years. Moreover, using Roth IRAs for education is counted as income (unlike 529 plans) when it comes to applying for college financial aid. The entire amount of IRA withdrawals must be included as income when applying for financial aid. Finally, if you should decide to tap your IRA to pay for your child's college expenses instead of your retirement, remember that no one offers loans to cover retirement expenses while there are many ways to save, pay, and borrow for college.

Savings bonds

When you use Series EE or I US Savings Bonds for education expenses, you don't have to pay federal income tax on the earnings. Get more information on the US Treasury website:

http://www.treasurydirect.gov/indiv/products/prod_ibonds_glance.htm

Summary

	529 Plan	Coverdell's	IRA	Roth IRA
Limit on earnings to participate	No	Yes	Yes	Yes
Maximum contribution amount per year per child	No, but there may be for income tax breaks	$2000	$5000	$5000
Tax breaks when paid in	Not for Federal, but yes for many states	No	Yes	No

Taxed when with-drawn on amount you paid in	No	No	Yes	No
Taxed on earnings withdrawals	No	No	Yes	Yes
Penalized 10% on early withdrawals for education	No	No	No	No
Penalized 10% of earnings if not used for education	Yes	Yes	No	No
For financial aid, assessed at the low parent rate or higher child rate	Parent	Parent	Child's income in the year following withdrawal	Child's income in the year following withdrawal

How education savings options affect financial aid

I have touched upon how these options affect your chances of getting financial aid, but let's end with a review. The Federal financial aid formula is most interested in current income far more than savings, and with children's assets more than parent's. Therefore, when reviewing aid requests, the formula only expects parents to contribute 5.6% of their savings assets in calculating the student's Expected Family Contribution (EFC), but 20% of students' savings. Therefore, 529 accounts, prepaid plans, and Coverdell ESAs are all considered parent assets at 5.6% rather than children's assets at 20%. Additionally, when you use funds from these options, it does not count as income in calculating next year's aid. Savings in the child's name such as "Uniform Gifts to Minors Act" funds are thus considered more than parent's assets. None of the parent's retirement accounts is considered, but if you withdraw funds from a retirement account, such as an IRA or 401(k), then those withdrawals are counted as income in calculating next year's aid. Private colleges may use a slightly different formula. So it does matter *where* you save your college savings when it comes to applying for college financial aid.

There are many things to consider when saving for college, but don't let that deter you. Saving early is vital. You can mix your college savings among any of these options for flexibility, but double check the details as they do change and there is more fine print that I have glossed over. You can get all the excruciating details about IRS tax breaks while saving and paying for education in their Publication 970: http://www.irs.gov/publications/p970/index.html

More information:

- http://www.finaid.org/
- http://www.savingforcollege.com
- http://www.collegesavings.org

Summary

- Since college will be one of the most expensive things in life, you don't necessarily have to save for all of it, but you certainly can save for some of it, hopefully for at least one quarter to one half.
- Along with all your other savings goals, try to set up a college savings account with at least something, even if you only start with $50 per pay period or month. Put these savings on autopilot.
- It's vital to start as early as possible so your savings have a longer chance to compound and grow.
- The most widely used college savings plan is the 529 college savings account provided in every state with federal tax-free earnings, usually state tax-free contributions, no limits on parents income, no limits on per child contributions, and a small 5.6% hit for college financial aid consideration.
- Do NOT make 529 contributions thru financial advisors and pay up to 5% in fees. Go to the plan's website and do everything you need for free.
- Coverdell ESAs have more contributions restrictions and limits, but can be used for a wider variety of educational expenses including K-12 private schools.
- When we are dealing with all these fine points of tax breaks, you know it's going to get complicated, so double check IRS Publication 570 for the details.

Chapter Ten

Saving for Retirement

- Start early
- Know your options, goals, and plans
- Defined contribution plans - 401(k)s
- Individual Retirement Accounts (IRAs)
- To Roth or not?
- How to invest your retirement savings
- Summary timeline
- Retirement web calculators

You may be tempted to skip this chapter until the "right" time comes, especially for younger workers. However, it may well be one of the most important chapters in the book, because it affects not only your retirement future, but also your savings future. At least read the first two sections now.

Retirement planning is not an exact science because you don't know the answers to some of the key questions such as how long will you live in retirement, how much will your investments earn, and how much will your income need to be. Nevertheless, it is certain that how well you live financially in retirement depends upon actions you take throughout your life (just as it is in other areas such as health and relationships). Despite the uncertainty, you do control key aspects of retirement planning such as how much you save, how early you start saving, how you invest, when you retire, the retirement lifestyle you aim for, and the major expenses you will carry into retirement, possibly including mortgages, car payments, and other debts. See the later chapter on *"Spending in Retirement"* for details about how to structure your retirement income after retiring, but read on here for details about how to save for that big event. Reduce the chances that your "retirement self" won't want to take a time machine back to smack around your "younger self" for gross mismanagement of your retirement planning.

Start early

Do you want a retirement where you barely get by - or live comfortably? Well, you control much of your financial fate and the decisions you make now will determine this.

The two key actions you should strive for right now are:

- Start early, even with a small amount.
- Increase your percentage every time you get a pay increase until you are contributing 12% - 15% of your pay, including any matching amount your employer may contribute to your 401(k) or 403(b) type account.

Always keep this in mind: the longer you wait to save for retirement, the more you will have to contribute from each paycheck later on. It is common to think that it will be easier to save in the future because you will have a bigger salary, but it is just as common that you will also have bigger debts, more responsibilities, and additional expenses. Moreover, you may encounter potholes along life's journey when it is necessary to scale back retirement savings, making an early start even more critical to your future. When you do hit those potholes and have to reduce savings, DO NOT be tempted to raid your retirement savings. Leave savings to work their compounding magic rather than dig your retirement savings hole even deeper. Procrastination in saving for retirement lessens the magic of compound interest, makes saving more difficult, reduces your retirement lifestyle and choices, and could increase the number of years you have to work.

Even a small savings amount early in life has a bigger impact than a larger amount later in life because it has longer to grow thru the magic of compound interest. See the later chart in, "Plan how to get there" for an example of how starting early reduces the monthly amount you have to save. Start your retirement saving with your very first, full time paycheck – even if it is a small amount and even if you are still paying off credit cards and starting an emergency fund. From day one, consider this as an expense equal to paying off student loans and higher than dining out and shopping.

Know your options, goals, and plans

- Know what your retirement income options are.
- Determine your retirement savings goal.
- Plan how to get there.

Know what your retirement income options are.

Your retirement savings may come from a combination of these sources:

- Social Security benefits
- Defined benefits plan – pension provided by an employer
- Defined contributions plan – 401(k) type plans offered thru an employer, but you contribute from your pay check
- Individual Retirement Accounts – IRAs established thru a financial institution in which you contribute savings and see investments grow with tax breaks
- Other savings – all other savings you have invested

Social Security Benefits

Contrary to popular belief, Social Security benefits will still be around when you are ready to retire. Social Security is a political sacred cow that few politicians would allow to expire. However, benefits will be less generous in the future, as a growing elderly population takes a bigger share of the Federal budget. The longer you have until retirement, the greater the likelihood of changes. Nearly everyone will receive Social Security benefits when they retire, but I hope I am not the first to tell you, that it will be very difficult to live on Social Security benefits alone. The average Social Security retirement benefit in 2016 was $1341 per month. So you had better plan on supplementing your Social Security benefits with *several* of the following sources. Get an estimate of your potential benefit: www.ssa.gov. You should go to the SSA website and review your estimate and earnings annually, for example on your birthday. You should review your earnings to ensure they are accurate since that is a primary factor in determining the amount of your benefits.

Defined benefits plan – pension provided by an employer

Defined benefits plans are pensions provided by an employer, or at least they used to be, for pensions are rapidly disappearing. In 2010, less than one-third of workers had access to pensions, and the number is continuing to shrink. You are most likely to have pensions if you work for the public sector, military, large companies, or companies with labor unions. You might consider one of these if you are thinking about switching careers.

Saving for Retirement

Since you won't be able to retire comfortably on Social Security benefits alone, how well you live in retirement depends upon how much you save during your working years. Fortunately, as with saving for college, the U.S. government is here to help you save for retirement. There are several kinds of savings plans designed with different kinds of tax breaks specifically for retirement savings.

Determine your retirement savings goal.

You are more likely to be successful when you set specific goals rather than wander aimlessly. Most advice suggests that you aim for retirement income to match 70%-80% of your final salary to have a comfortable retirement. However, your particular situation will depend upon such factors as whether you will have a spouse to share expenses and income, how early you retire, when your mortgage is paid off, how much traveling you want to do, how expensive your hobbies are, whether you move to a less expensive area, and whether you will still be taking care of children or elderly parents. Social Security will probably provide around 30% of your final salary if you retire at your normal retirement age, around 20% if you retire early at age 62, and around 36% if you work until age 70. Get a personalized estimate of your SSA benefits at the SSA site: http://www.ssa.gov/estimator/

If you expect to get a traditional pension from one of your employers, subtract that from the 80% of replacement income you need. After SSA and pensions, the rest of your retirement income must come from your own retirement savings. This is why your lifetime savings habits will determine how well you live financially in retirement. That is a lot of money, but how much might it be for you?

Let's go thru several common examples of how you can estimate your retirement savings goal. A simple rule of thumb advises savings equal to 25 times the amount you hope to withdraw your first year of retirement. This is the flipside of the common advice that in your first year of retirement, you can safely withdraw 4% of your savings (plus inflation in future years) in order that your savings will likely last your lifetime. (For more discussion and variants of this advice, see Chapter 23 *"Spending in Retirement".*)

Method 1 – 25 times your estimated retirement needs:

$90,000 – Amount of projected final gross salary.

$70,000 – Amount of projected final salary after deducting the 22% you have been saving for retirement. (7% SSA + 15% personal savings – adjust as needed)

$56,000 – (70000 * 0.80) 80% of final salary = first year income in retirement

$17,000 – (56000 * 0.30 rounded) 30% of retirement income can typically come from SSA and pensions. Adjust this percentage down if you plan to take early SSA benefits and up by the amount of any pensions you expect to receive from an employer. Even better would be to get the estimated amount of your actual SSA and pensions and enter those amounts here.

$39,000 – (56000 – 17000) amount of income that needs to come from your own retirement savings after subtracting SSA and pensions.

$975,000 – (39000 * 25) 25 times amount of first year retirement income from savings – amount you should save before retirement to keep your same standard of living.

Method 2 – 25 times your estimated retirement needs:

This method is more precise and easier to do the closer you get to retirement. Estimate your monthly expenses in retirement. Throw in a few hundred extra for unforeseen and missed expenses.

Hypothetical example:

$5000 – Monthly expenses needed in retirement.

$2600 – Minus amount of SSA and pensions including spouse's.

$2400 – Equals monthly amount that needs to be withdrawn from savings.

$28,800 – Annual amount from savings (2400*12 months)

$720,000 – total amount of savings you need before retiring (28800 * 25)

Method 3 - A less precise method for estimating your retirement savings goal:

Different experts suggest a range of retirement savings goals ranging from 8-15 times your final salary.

$90,000 – final salary.

X   10 – average amount experts advise us to save for retirement

$900,000 – Amount you should save for retirement.

Perhaps the most useful numbers are forecasts of how much your retirement savings accounts will enable you to withdraw each month in retirement. Seeing how much or little income your savings are getting you is more meaningful than some of these other hypothetical and humongous numbers. Studies show this is a great way to spur retirement savings and more 401(k) plans are doing it. See the retirement calculators at the end of this section for aids in calculating this yourself, especially for your IRA and other savings.

You will probably get a wide variance between the methods. Additionally, your situation depends upon such factors as how early you retire, whether a spouse will be sharing in the expenses and income, whether you can expect a pension, and how high your expenses will be in retirement. Of course, the earlier you retire, the more you will have to save to make up for lower SSA and a longer period to withdraw your savings.

These simple methods give you a rough estimate on how much you should aim to save. Don't faint and do read on. It is not as hopeless as it sounds. So much of retirement planning depends upon a wide array of future situations and, early on, is just guessing. Thus, the numbers aren't meant to be precise, but rather to show you how challenging the task in front of you is, and convince you to get serious doing it while you still have time to save and compound. Research studies do show that people who estimate their retirement numbers do save more for retirement.

See the end of this section for retirement calculators on the web so you can start your own more detailed planning. Remember to adjust the generic calculators for your particular situation and goals.

Plan how to get there.

Now that you know about your options and can calculate a rough idea of your retirement savings goal, how do you get there? Whatever amount of retirement savings you calculate that you will need, it will seem like a huge amount of savings, but that depends upon when you start saving. Go to a "savings goal calculator" like the one on bankrate.com to see how much you should save to meet a savings goal: http://www.bankrate.com/calculators/savings/saving-goals-calculator.aspx

Monthly amount to save assuming a savings goal of $975,000 from our previous example

Years to retire-ment	40	30	20	10
Monthly savings amount @ 7% annual return	$371	$799	$1871	$5633
Monthly savings amount @ 9% annual return	$208	$532	$1459	$5038

Don't let the amounts frighten you, but note two things:

1. How important it is to start saving early and get compounded returns over a longer period. (You might be getting tired of reading this, but I'm not tired of explaining it.) See how waiting ten years, more than DOUBLES the monthly amount you must save for the *rest* of your working career.
2. Higher returns compound more quickly and make your savings effort easier, so choose an investment mix made up mostly of stocks, which is the only regular investment that has consistently earned those higher returns over an extended period.

Of course, in reality, you won't be saving the same amount throughout your lifetime. The amount should grow as your income grows, so common advice is to save around 15% (including employer matching contributions) of whatever your income is. Saving 15% of your income throughout your lifetime is the simplest and best way to ensure your retirement will be comfortable and comparable to the standard of living you had before retirement. (Some advisors do suggest as little as 10-12%, but that likely would mean you having more pension income, working longer, ensuring all debts are paid off, and /or accepting a lower standard of living.)

You may not be able to reach that 15% level immediately, but at least start with 5-6% and then increase it by 1 - 2% each time you get a salary increase until you reach the

15%, including any employer matches. Timing your *savings* increases with your *salary* increases means you won't even miss the extra savings money from your pay check very much, but it will mean all the difference in your retirement. *ALWAYS contribute enough to get any free money matched by your employer. (See below under 401(k)s.)*

One of the most important financial principles of this book is to start retirement saving early, make it automatic, and increase it with your raises until you reach the 15% level.

Yes, I will repeat this often.

Of course, there will be times along life's financial journey when meeting that 15% retirement savings target will be tough, maybe even very tough, especially for young families. Whether a spouse stays home with the children or you have day care expenses, you may need to delay or scale back your 15% target. This is another reason why it is extra important to start saving early before extra demands on your pay check arrive.

Start work / start saving

With your first paycheck, you should be contributing at least 5-6% of it to retirement and increasing it by 1-2% each year. You should be comparing your expenses and savings goals against your income to determine how much you have left over to spend. That includes paying off credit cards as quickly as possible – always more than the minimum. When the credit cards are paid off, switch that money to increase your emergency fund from a minimum amount to at least 4-6 months of living expenses. After you have a full emergency fund, don't increase your life style, but switch part of that money to your next savings goal, for example, a home down payment or vacation. However, this is also a perfect time to increase your retirement savings with part of that money before you use it to increase your life style. Taking advantage of these early opportunities to increase you retirement savings means you will be better able to scale back when child expenses arrive or your financial journey hits potholes. Here is a good place to remind you that saving for college must be in *addition to*, not *instead of* retirement – although it may be another excuse why it is temporarily hard to meet the full 15% target. Remember that you and your child can get loans to pay for college, but no one is going to lend you money to pay your retirement.

Mid-life Saving

By their mid-forties, most people are over halfway to retirement. This is a good time to review your financial situation. Hopefully, you are entering your peak earnings years which should also mean your peak savings years, especially when the kids are out of school, ramp up your retirement savings. Review your retirement savings situation to see where you are and where you should be. These web tools help you get detailed estimates of how much you can spend in retirement and should be saving now based upon your projected SSA and pension benefits along with your retirement savings.

1. https://www3.troweprice.com/ric/ricweb/public/ric.do?van=ric
2. http://www.calcxml.com/do/ret02?skn=74
3. http://cgi.money.cnn.com/tools/saveyoung/index.html
4. http://personal.fidelity.com/planning/retirement/quick_check.shtml
5. http://www.kiplinger.com/tools/retirement-savings-calculator.html

These tools may be a real eye-opener as to just how well you are saving for your retirement. Now is the time to ensure you are meeting the 15% retirement savings level – or more if the calculators above confirm you have been lagging the last twenty years.

Fifties – start dreaming, increase savings

Upon reaching your early fifties, it's okay to start dreaming about your retirement – certainly for planning for it. Are you ready for retirement if you lose your job? Will your major expenses be paid off before retirement? When will your spouse be ready for retirement? What will you do for health insurance until you are eligible for Medicare at age 65? When will you start Social Security? Move beyond thinking about it to action:

- Use web retirement calculators to review where you stand in relation to where you want to be at retirement.
- Save the maximum you can. These are probably your prime earnings years with most major expenses behind you. For most people, this is the period when they save the most money.
- Start making "catch-up" contributions to your 401(k) and IRA accounts at age 50. In 2017, IRS rules allow age 50 and over workers to make an extra $6500 to 401(k)s and $1000 to IRAs.

- If you still have 401(k) type accounts with previous employees, consider consolidating all of them into one IRA account. This will enable you to better manage, track, diversify, and account for them.
- If you need help, consider discussing your financial situation, goals, and investments with a professional. Many companies that offer 401(k) accounts also provide Human Resources staff to discuss your options. You can also get information from advisors at mutual fund companies like T. Rowe Price, Fidelity, or Vanguard. To get detailed advice for your specific situation, see a financial planner who will meet with you at an hourly rate. Get referrals from friends or these websites:
  - http://www.fpanet.org/
  - http://garrettplanningnetwork.com/

Fidelity Investments offers a simple guide to see how well you are doing along this savings path. They suggest that at age 35, you should have saved 1 times your salary, age 45 – 3 times, and age 55 – 5 times. Other experts suggest different amounts, but the point is to increase your savings if needed while you still have earnings years ahead and time to compound. If you didn't start saving early, never got around to saving the 15% target, or hit too many potholes along life's journey; the amount you should save may seem daunting compared to what you have thus far, but don't despair. See the concluding retirement section on *"Catching Up"*.

Defined contribution plans - 401(k) and 403(b) type accounts

1. Contributing to 401(k) type accounts
2. Withdrawing from 401(k) type accounts.
3. Roth 401(k) type accounts.

Contributing to 401(k) type accounts

By now, you know you are responsible for your own retirement and need to save big bucks to get ready for it, but how exactly do you go about it? In the U.S., there are several financial plans designed specifically for saving for retirement and getting tax breaks for doing it. The best is a "defined contribution" plan, which is the fancy term for retirement savings plans offered thru employers in which employees make the contributions deducted from their salaries. These are known as 401(k) plans for the section of the tax code, but there are other terms for certain professions including 403(b)s for colleges, non-profits, teachers, and hospitals; 457s for state and local government workers; and the Thrift Savings Plan (TSP) for the military and Federal workers. I will use the shorthand 401(k), but most rules are the same for the other types as well.

They are attractive because they are easy to use, you don't have to pay taxes on the amount you contribute nor on earnings until you withdraw the money, there are no eligibility restrictions as with IRAs, and most employers will match a portion of your contributions. In 2017, you can contribute up to $18,000 per year, which rises periodically with inflation. Once you reach age 50 or over, you can also contribute an additional $6500 in "catch-up contributions". This is a great way to beef up your retirement savings during your final peak earnings years.

Company Match

One of the most important things you should know about your 401(k) plan is how much is the "company match"? Most companies that offer 401(k) type plans will match a portion of your 401(k) savings, frequently 25-100% for each dollar you contribute up to 5-6%. This is as close to FREE money as most of us will ever get, so you should ALWAYS contribute enough to your 401(k) to get your full company-matching amount. THIS IS ONE OF THE MOST IMPORTANT RULES FROM THIS ENTIRE BOOK! Do not throw your FREE money away. Always contribute enough to your 401(k) to get your full company-matching amount - always! If you let your free money go, you'll never get that back.

401(k) Investment Options

Companies' 401(k) type funds vary widely in quality, choices, fees, and performance. If your fund choices consistently fail to match the markets' performance (as most actively managed mutual funds fail to do), consider switching to an "index" fund. Index funds are designed to closely match the performance of a particular group of stocks, bonds, or other investments and have very low management fees.

Avoid this common pitfall. Some companies match employees' 401(k) savings by contributing company stock. After a while, a significant portion of your 401(k) account might be made up of your company stock, which creates an imbalance of investments.

Diversification of savings among a large group of investments is the best way to ensure a crash in one portion doesn't damage your whole portfolio. This includes your company stock, so if it gets to be a large portion of your fund, sell some of it and move the funds to another asset that you have less of.

403(b) Accounts

403(b) accounts are for colleges, non-profits, school systems, and hospitals. They are similar to 401(k) accounts, but be aware of a few differences if you are covered under a 403(b) plan. They are much more likely to provide fixed and variable annuities as well as mutual funds. Annuities pay a fixed or variable income to retirees *for life* Good so far; however, the potential problem to be aware of is that these annuities and their 403(b) accounts may have high fees that keep your retirement savings from growing as much as lower fee alternatives. Choosing low fee investments is one of the most important investing principles we will discuss in the section on investments. Be leery of any investment that has fees of more than 2%, as this reduces your savings and compounding by that amount each and every year. Annuities have many attractions we will discuss further in the section on "*Spending in Retirement*", but if your annuity investment fees are more than 2% per year, consider investing in low cost ETFs and mutual funds during your employment and then buying an annuity when you are getting ready for retirement.

A second issue with certain 403(b) plans is that they sometimes may be small funds with a small number of employees with poor investment options or high fees. However, a special provision allows these participants to switch their retirement contribution to any financial institution that is willing to establish a 403(b)-7 account, such as big mutual funds companies. Your payroll office may not be familiar with this provision, but you can probably get your new investment company to assist you to make the switch.

Get more information about 403(b) plans here:

- http://www.403bwise.com/ - Get a wide variety of 403(b) information.
- http://www.403bcompare.com/ - This website is operated by the California State Teachers' Retirement System, but is a good place to research 403(b) providers and their fees.

Withdrawing from a 401(k)

After a while, you should have a nice pot of money in your account and there are times when it looks mighty tempting to raid it for other things. Here are the withdrawal considerations. There are rules for early withdrawals before age 59 1/2, regular with-drawals during retirement, and mandatory withdrawals the April after age 70 ½. In all cases, you owe income tax since you did not pay it when you put in your savings.

If you withdraw 401(k) savings before age 59 ½, you owe a 10% penalty. There are no exceptions to owing the income tax, but there are some exceptions to the early with-drawal penalty including permanent disability, large medical expenses, death, and the end of employment after age 55. Some plans may let you withdraw for certain "hardship expenses" such as home repairs after a disaster or impending foreclosure, but you still have to pay the taxes and 10% early withdrawal penalty. A usually better option is get-ting a loan from your 401(k) up to half your contributions balance or $50,000 for any reason. You don't have to pay taxes or a penalty as long as you repay it within five years, or 60 days after leaving your job.

When you leave a job, you can leave your 401(k) savings with your old employer (if you have at least $5000), transfer your funds to your new employer's plan to consolidate your funds (if they have one), or rollover to your own IRA if you want greater investing flexibility or lower fees. If your old employer has good investment choices with low fees (more likely from big companies) you might wish to leave your funds; conversely, take your funds with you if it's your new employer with the nice choices and low fees. If nei-ther employer has especially good choices and low fees, then rolling-over to an IRA probably offers better options, but pay *close* attention to the transfer/rollover rules. Try to avoid having retirement accounts scattered among many former employers. It's easier to review your savings strategy and progress when most of your savings are in one or two places.

There are several ways to review your 401(k) plans so you can decide what to do. Hopefully, yours has a website, but you can ask your human resources department for information. Generally, annual fees over $50 per year are considered high. See how your company's 401(k) plan compares to others here: http://www.brightscope.com/ratings/. You can review the performance of the mu-tual funds within your 401(k) at websites such as www.morningstar.com.

You can also withdraw the money and use it for other things, but don't do it. You will be forfeiting a huge chunk of your money as you will have to pay the income taxes you have avoided thus far, plus a 10% early withdrawal penalty. Not only have you lost 25-49% of your money, but you have undone your good savings efforts up to this point. Re-sist the temptation to spend these retirement funds. Not only do you lose a big portion of your money, but you are losing the compounding that savings would have earned and digging yourself a savings hole that will be very difficult to fill-in later. Moreover, it is hard to make up those lost savings since the amount you can contribute to a 401(k) each year is limited.

When thinking about leaving a job, ensure you are "vested" with enough time on the job to qualify to keep your employer contributions. Leave too soon and you might forfeit those employer matches – your free money.

Roth 401(k) accounts

Roth 401(k) accounts are different than traditional 401(k) accounts in that you pay taxes on your contributions now, while getting to withdraw both your contributions and earnings tax free after age 59 ½ and being open for at least five years. So paying taxes on your *contributions* now means you can withdraw them anytime tax and penalty free, plus your *earnings* will be completely tax exempt after age 59 1/2. Remember that traditional 401(k) accounts only *defer* taxes until later, so you will have to pay taxes on both your contributions *and earnings*. See the discussion at the end of this chapter for the pro and cons of which account is best for whom.

Individual Retirement Accounts (IRAs)

Only around half of US workers have access to 401(k) type accounts and far fewer than that still have pensions. The remaining workers are still responsible for funding their own retirement and the method for doing so is the Individual Retirement Account (IRA) including the Roth IRA. Yes, people with 401(k)s can also use IRAs if they meet the eligibility requirements. If you are self-employed or moonlighting, there are special retirement accounts you can check out including SEP IRAs, Simple IRAs, and the older, more complicated Keogh plans.

The tax-deferred amount you can contribute to an IRA is much less than a 401(k). In 2017 this was $5500 and an additional $1000 for over age 50 catch-ups, or up to the amount of your income if less. However, whether you can get the full amount tax deferred depends upon whether you are covered by a retirement plan at work and the amount of your income. For more IRS details, see their Publication 590: https://www.irs.gov/pub/irs-pdf/p590a.pdf

You can contribute savings to your IRA that are above those IRS limits, but you don't get the tax-deferred advantages on the amount that exceeds the limits. I recommend you do NOT mix your tax deferred and taxable savings in your IRA. Save yourself a big headache because it's going to be extra complicated when you withdraw your IRA contributions and have to keep track of how much of each year's withdrawals are taxable or not. You can put extra savings over the IRA limit in a separate investment account that doesn't get tax benefits, but can be used for anything any time.

Note that you can contribute to your IRA up to the tax filing deadline, April 15 after the earnings year. Each married spouse can contribute to an IRA even when one spouse is not working. So if one spouse stays at home or has little income, the working spouse can fund a separate IRA account for the stay at home spouse.

You can open an IRA at most banks, credit unions, brokerages, and mutual fund companies. IRAs provide more flexibility in investments than 401(k)s including real estate and US coins, but if you stray from publicly traded stocks, bonds, and investment funds; carefully review the rules. IRAs generally have lower expenses and fees than 401(k)s, especially 401(k)s from smaller companies. When you leave a job, you can generally leave your 401(k) there or move it to your new employer, but also consider rolling-it over to an IRA if your 401(k) plans have poor choices or high fees. *Review and carefully follow* the rules any time you roll over a retirement account from one place to another to avoid triggering the early withdrawal penalties. For example, there is a short window to make that transfer.

When can you withdraw from an IRA?

You must begin withdrawing from an IRA the April after age 70 ½, and there is a 10% penalty for withdrawing before age 59 ½, but there are a few exceptions. There is no penalty for:

- spending it on qualified education expenses (see the chapter on *"Saving for College"*,
- buying a first home with up to $10,000 of contributions ($20,000 for couples),
- purchasing health insurance if you are disabled or unemployed.

You cannot borrow from your IRA as you can from your 401(k).

Roth IRAs

Roth IRAs are different than traditional IRAs and similar to Roth 401(k)s in that you do pay taxes when you contribute to a Roth IRA, but you get to withdraw your contributions tax and penalty free anytime, and earnings are tax free after age 59 ½. Roth IRAs and 401(k)s are particularly good choices for young workers since it is better to pay the taxes now when you are at a lower tax rate than later when you likely will be paying a higher tax rate.

The income and contribution limits to a traditional and Roth IRA are the same. You can contribute to both, but the combined total still cannot exceed the IRS limit, which in 2017 is $5500.

While the amount of your income may determine how much of your contributions to a traditional IRA is *tax deductible*, for Roth IRAs, it determines how much you can contribute at all (since none of it is tax deductible). The amounts can change annually, so check the IRS website for updates, but this illustrates the limitations on income.

To Roth or not?

When Roth 401(k) accounts and IRAs were introduced, savers got more flexibility, but also the never-ending debate of which one should I choose? Defer taxes until later with a traditional account, or pay taxes on contributions now and withdraw contributions tax and penalty free anytime and earnings tax free at retirement?

Traditional advice has held that it is better to postpone taxes until later because you get more money now to compound and grow. Most financial articles include statistics to show how much more you will have in retirement when you defer taxes. However, they rarely mention that much of that extra money will have to go to pay your taxes that you have deferred. Additionally, one has to wonder how many people really invest that extra tax refund or just spend it?

Equally common is the advice to pay your taxes when your tax rate will be lowest. It is usually assumed that your income and tax rates will be lower in retirement, but this may not always be true. In retirement, you probably won't have as many tax deductions from mortgage interest, children, and retirement savings. If you are working when in retirement, your earnings could be at least as great. Even more likely is that the salaries of young workers are less than it will be in retirement, so they should especially consider Roth 401(k)s and/or Roth IRAs.

Older workers may also find Roth's attractive, especially as a way to pass tax free savings to their heirs. That is because unlike traditional IRAs, Roth IRAs do not have the requirement for mandatory withdrawals after age 70 ½. Roth 401(k)s do have the mandatory withdrawal at age 70 ½ requirement, but you can avoid this if at retirement, you convert your Roth 401(k) into a Roth IRA. Workers of any age and situation may also prefer paying their taxes with Roth accounts now while they are still in their peak earning years and thus not have to worry about paying taxes in their leaner retirement years.

Roth accounts give you more flexibility for withdrawals in the future because you can always withdraw your contributions tax and penalty free for any reason (although you would still pay taxes on your earnings if withdrawn early). Therefore, people sometimes consider Roth's like an emergency fund that is sometimes raided for other big expenses, such as a down payment for a home, college expenses, or emergencies. Remember that traditional 401(k)s and IRAs *defer* taxes so you will still have to pay taxes on both your contributions and *earnings*, while Roth *earnings* are completely tax exempt as long as you wait until age 59 ½.

Finally, since the future is so difficult to predict, many people want the flexibility of having both traditional and Roth 401(k) accounts and IRAs. Having both in retirement gives you options for withdrawing which kind of savings in what kinds of situations to minimize your taxes.

Converting to a Roth IRA or 401(k)

You can also convert a traditional IRA, or a 401(k) when you leave a job or retire, into a Roth IRA. Some employers will let you convert traditional 401(k) savings into the newer Roth 401(k) funds, if they offer them. There are several issues to consider when deciding. The income limits for *new* contributions don't apply when converting to a Roth. You will have to pay income tax on the amount you convert since you did not pay tax when you contributed originally. To avoid converting so much in one year that it pushes you into a higher tax bracket, you may wish to convert partial amounts in multiple years. The closer you get to retirement, the less beneficial it is to convert since you have less time to make up the amount paid in taxes. It is also less beneficial if your expected tax rate in retirement will be significantly less than what it is when you are making the conversion since you generally want to pay the taxes when your rate will be lowest.

The rules and math for deciding whether to convert can be complicated so you may wish to use one of the many calculators on the web to help you decide.

How to invest your retirement savings

401(k) type plans may offer a variety of investment options including stock mutual funds, bond funds, index funds, target date funds, and perhaps alternatives such as stable value funds, real estate funds, and income funds. Some plans offer a big buffet of options, others just a small menu. With IRAs, you have even more choices as you can invest in just about anything (the more exotic your investment, the more you should review the rules). It can be bewildering, so how do you choose? As we will see in more detail in the section on *"Investing"*, investing can be as simple or complex as you choose and the complex options aren't necessarily more profitable than the simple options.

For now, here is what you need to know about investing for retirement. Investments go both up and down over time. The more risk you take with those ups and downs, the higher your return *on average over time*. Historically, over time, stocks *average* greater returns than bonds, which *average* greater returns than cash investments like money market funds and CDs. When there is a long time before you will need to use your investments, you should invest most of your savings in the riskier, but higher yielding investments like stocks. Only stocks can give you the growth you need to reach the amount you need for retirement. As you approach the time when you need the money, like retirement, shift a portion to less risky investment types like bonds and cash.

One of the biggest mistakes young workers make is to invest a large portion of their retirement savings in conservative, low yielding funds. This will make it much harder to see your savings grow big enough to provide you the income you need in retirement. The two bear markets during the first decade of the new century caused too many people to abandon stocks in terror, thus dooming themselves to "safe" investments that don't even keep pace with inflation. Well here is a new risk you should think about before abandoning stocks – living to 100, but dying broke. Young workers should invest most of their retirement savings in stock funds that can grow more quickly and provide much more money – even with the inevitable, big market drops. Let's see a simple example.

- Investments of $30,000 in bonds yielding 3% at the end of 30 years = $73,705.
- Investments of $30,000 in stocks growing at 7% at the end of 30 years = $243,495.

Which would you rather have? Actually, the answer is some of both. The best way to ride thru the periods of up and down markets is to have a mix of safer and riskier investments, but change the mix as you get closer to retirement. What does this mean? Here is a common guideline and several examples. Subtract your age from 110 and that percentage of your retirement savings should be invested in stocks. Divide the rest among bonds and possibly a small amount to alternative investment types such as safer money market or riskier real estate funds. Examples:

- Age 25: 110 – 25 = 85% in stocks and 15% bonds and alternatives.
- Age 40: 110 – 40 = 70% in stocks and 30% bonds and alternatives.
- Age 55: 110 – 55 = 55% in stocks and 45% bonds and alternatives.

You can avoid the hassle and risk of choosing individual stocks and bonds, by sticking with mutual funds or "Exchange Traded Funds" (ETFs). ETFs are baskets of stocks and/or bonds that track certain indexes to meet specific investment types or goals. If your 401(k) account offers ETFs, choose them over mutual funds as they have lower expenses, leaving more money for you which compounds over time. ETFs are a good choice for you IRAs as well. Another good investment type with rock bottom expenses are "index funds" which aim to track a particular investment index or group of stocks/bonds such as the DJIA or S&P 500. Since they are only tracking a specific group of investments, they don't rack up big trading expenses or taxable earnings from constant trading.

Find the ETFs, index funds, or mutual funds that your plan offers and divide your savings among them with your desired mix. For further diversification of risks and growth potential, divide your stock portion among funds specializing in large, small, and international companies. Diversification of your investments into multiple types spreads out your risks and evens out some of the inevitable market ups and downs. You don't get the full upside of markets, but you should avoid *some* of the downside. This contributes to peace of mind and hopefully lessens the chance that you will panic and withdraw all your stock investments at the bottom of a downturn (selling low) and miss most of the upturn (buying high). Don't go overboard with your diversification mix as it may complicate your investments more than safeguard them.

Review your allocation mix once per year and reallocate the category that has grown too large because their prices have gone up and move savings to the category that has shrunk because their prices have gone down or risen slowly. This annual reallocation not only keeps your desired allocation percentages, but also ensures that you sell the category that is doing well with a high price and buy the category that is doing worse with a low price. Yes, you read that correctly, sell what is doing well and buy what is not. This is a good way that anybody can follow the strategy of "buy low, sell high" and avoid the panic strategy of "buying high and selling low". You sell winners and lock in profits before they fall, and buy beaten down investments when the price is low before they recover and rise.

Still sounds too complicated? Relax, remember that I said it could be as simple as you want. "Target date funds" make investing as simple as it can be. Target date funds come with dates that you can match to your expected retirement date and they automatically adjust the mix for you as the years go by. For example, if you plan to retire in 2044, choose the "2045 Target Date Fund" offered by your plan and contribute all your retirement savings to it. Simple, quick, and you don't have to think about it again if you don't want to.

Enjoy seeing your savings grow when the economy is good and do yourself a favor when the economic news and markets are bad – don't look at your 401(k) and IRA statements. Don't stress too much over the inevitable ups and downs of the stock markets. It has always and will always go both up and down, down and up, sometimes even way down. Over your investing lifetime, you are likely to see at least two *very* down (bear) markets, but remember they have always recovered. Rather than despair over your plunging retirement balances, view bear markets as a fantastic buying opportunity – getting stocks on sale and being able to buy extra shares cheaply for the same savings amount. Then rejoice when the up (bull) market returns and all those extra shares you bought at a cheap price now soar. Thus, having a bear market early in your retirement savings career can be a major buying opportunity yielding big boosts later in your retirement savings journey. This is another reason why young and mid-career workers should have most of their retirement savings in stocks rather than conservative investments like bonds and money market funds – even in bear markets – especially in bear markets.

A bear market near or early in your retirement can seriously impact your retirement fund, which is why you are shifting from risky stocks to less risky bonds and cash as you get closer to retirement. See the section on *"Spending in Retirement"* for more detailed information about this phase.

Catching Up

By now you know that how well you live in retirement depends upon actions you take (or don't) while working, that you are responsible for saving most of your retirement income, that you have several tax-advantaged accounts to help you save, that you should be increasing your retirement savings, and (as always) the best way to save is to put your savings on autopilot. You may think that this is a daunting task, but regardless of your age or circumstances, there are things you can do to be better prepared. First, estimate where you currently stand with your particular circumstances using the procedures we described previously or the retirement website calculators listed at the end of this section. Use a simple web calculator to see how much you need to start saving at any point in your career. The CNNMoney "What you need to save calculator" asks for your age, income, and amount currently saved to provide you an estimate of how much you should save each year to meet 80% of your income in retirement. Remember to adjust any generic calculator for your specific circumstances.

http://cgi.money.cnn.com/tools/saveyoung/index.html

If you are young, save for retirement even with all the other competing demands for your money. If you are in mid-career, increase your retirement savings with each pay increase until you are saving 15% including company 401(k) matches, and start doing some planning and estimating for your circumstances. If you are over fifty and behind, you need to take immediate steps to prepare. The inescapable truth is that you must save more and work longer if your retirement savings are low. Scale back your lifestyle now to find savings because it will be even worse in retirement. See the sections on budgeting, saving, and spending wisely. Plan to be out of most debts before retirement. Save the maximum you can including maxing out your 401(k) and IRA contributions, beginning over age 50 catch-up contributions, and then saving in regular taxable investment accounts.

If your savings still fall short, the single best way to better ensure a financially comfortable retirement is to work longer. This is true even for a few extra years, but is especially true if you can work until your SSA "normal retirement age", which is age 67 for anyone born 1960 and later. This yields several benefits:

- You receive a higher SSA benefit.

- You have a chance to contribute more to your retirement savings.
- You delay withdrawing from your savings and have fewer years to make those savings last.
- You might have longer access to employer provided health benefits while you wait to get Medicare at age 65.

Fortunately, if your savings still fall short, there are other things you can do. When we get to the chapter on *"Part Four, Chapter 7 - Retirement"*, we will discuss retirement income options in more detail. For now, just note that you will have options then including scaling back your lifestyle, working longer, delay applying for Social Security, working part-time, applying for a reverse mortgage, and moving to a lower cost area.

Summary Timeline

Saving for retirement is one of the longest tasks you should be doing, so let's summarize this topic with a timeline.

Day One on the Job – Start contributing at least 6% of your salary to a retirement account: 401(k) if your employer offers one, Roth IRA if not. Aim to increase this 1% with each pay increase until you reach 15%, including company matches. Young workers should have most of their investments in stock funds and consider bear markets a great buying opportunity.

Age 35: If family financial pressures are heavy, don't fret about scaling back retirement savings somewhat – especially to pay off credit card debt. Remember that you can borrow from your 401(k) for a down payment for a home.

Age 45: You may be halfway to retirement. It really is time to get those retirement savings up to 15% so you can enjoy the benefits of long-term compound savings. Review how you are doing with some of the retirement calculators on the web.

Age 50: You should be approaching your peak earning years and this is when many people do most of their saving. Take advantage of that with the "catch-up" rules allowing you to contribute an extra $6000 to a 401(k) and $1000 to an IRA in 2017.

Age 55: The early withdrawal penalty disappears for 401(k)s (but not IRAs) if you leave your job and need the money.

Age 59 ½: Early 10% withdrawal penalty ends for retirement accounts.

Age 60: When you are a few years away from retirement, calculate the amount of your one or two years of retirement expenses and shift this amount of your retirement investments to safe cash investments or short term bonds so if the market drops, you will have more time before having to tap your decreased stocks for retirement income.

Age 62: Earliest date eligible for Social Security benefits, but know that your benefits will be reduced by at least 25% from your "normal" retirement age.

Age 65-67: Normal retirement age for Social Security depending upon your birth year. Eligible for Medicare at 65 - know that if your delay it, you will pay a penalty. With Medicare, you still must pay premiums, co-pays, and deductibles.

Age 70: Receive maximum amount from Social Security. Apply for it even if you are still working.

Age 70 ½: You must start taking minimum withdrawals from most types of retirement accounts by the following April, (but not for Roth IRAs).

See these retirement planning tools:

- http://analyzenow.com/ - Independent site with a wide variety of computer tools, resources, and retirement tips.
- http://cgi.money.cnn.com/tools/ - Many financial tools and information from this media website.
- https://www.fidelity.com/retirement/calculators/retirement-calculators - Advice, tools, and calculators.

Summary

- Despite the uncertainty of your distant retirement finances, you do control key aspects of retirement planning, including how much you save, how early you start saving, how you invest, when you retire, the retirement lifestyle you aim for, and the major expenses you will carry into retirement such as mortgages, car payments, and other debts.
- Start your retirement saving with your very first, full time paycheck – even if it is a small amount and even if you are still paying off credit cards and starting an emergency fund.

- It is common to think that it will be easier to save in the future because you will have a bigger salary, but it is just as common that you will also have bigger debts, more responsibilities, and additional expenses. Expenses tend to expand with your salary.

- Since you won't be able to retire comfortably on just Social Security benefits; how well you live in retirement depends upon how much you save during your working years.

- One of the most important financial principles of this book is to start retirement saving early, make it automatic, and increase it until you reach the 15% level timed with your raises.

- Remember that you and your child can get loans to pay for college, but no one is going to lend you money to pay your retirement.

- There are several types of tax advantaged retirement accounts. If your employer offers a 401(k) type account – use it. Otherwise, start an IRA. Start with Roth accounts and later mix in traditional tax deferred accounts to get a flexible mix of accounts. Put extra savings into regular taxable investment accounts.

- Always contribute enough to your 401(k) to get your full company-matching amount - always! If you let your free money go, you'll never get that back.

- Investing can be as simple as picking a "target date fund" or as complex as you want. However, remember to follow the investing principles in the section on *Investing* whether for your retirement savings or taxable investment accounts.

- Your retirement savings success is better ensured when you start early, gradually increase your savings rate to 15%, and invest mostly in stocks.

- Remember that how well you live in retirement depends upon actions you take (or don't) while working.

Part Three

Introduction to Part Three - Investing

When you spend less money than you earn, you get much more than just financial peace of mind; you get extra money for debt payments or savings. At the beginning, you probably have many goals to save for, but after a while if things go well, you may have extra savings or a sudden windfall for wealth building and financial security. The sooner your debts are paid off, the faster you can save and compound, but even while paying off your debts, you should be saving towards your retirement and the kids' college. Before long you should see growing savings and notice that just sticking it in a savings account or CD pays very little. You cannot build wealth by keeping your long-term savings in a savings account or money market fund; you probably won't even keep up with inflation. So what should you do with your long-term savings? You should invest it in appropriate types of investments that meets your goals and time horizon. That may be easier to say than do, but the guiding principle of this section is that investing can be as simple or as challenging as you want it, and the more complex isn't necessarily the most profitable.

In "*Section Two – Saving*", I covered how to do it and where to put it for specific goals: emergency fund, auto or mortgage down payment, college, or retirement, etc. Usually, the place to put savings for these specific goals is someplace safe, easy to get to, or tax-advantaged, such as savings accounts, CDs, money market funds, college 529 accounts, 401(k)s, and IRAs. Now in this "*Section Three – Investing*", let's move on to putting savings into a wider variety of longer term and more complex investments with the goal of getting a much better return on our savings. Chapters will cover risk versus reward, types of investments, and strategies for investing.

Chapter Eleven

Risks versus Rewards

- Risks versus rewards
- Balancing risks and rewards

Risks versus rewards

The most basic principle of investing is the tradeoff between risk and reward. The greater the investment risk, the bigger the potential reward should be; the safer the investment, the lower the expected reward. Be skeptical of any promise for high reward with little risk. Too many people are scammed because they ignore this most basic investing principle. Conversely, don't expect to grow your investments very much without taking on some degree of calculated risk.

Risks

All savings and investing have some degree and type of risk from losses, inflation, or liquidity based upon uncertainty of what will happen in the future; the greater the uncertainty, the greater the risk.

Losses

The major risk in investing is that we will lose money. We all know about the risk that the value of our investment will go down and we will sell at a loss. The business, industry, market, or even the entire economy could do badly. The business or organization that issued stocks or bonds could do badly and stop paying interest or dividends. They could default on their bond debt or go bankrupt and our stocks or bonds could be worthless. The business climate or economy could turn bad sending most investments down.

Inflation

An often overlooked risk is that inflation will grow faster than our savings and therefore, the buying power of our savings will be less, meaning our future savings will buy less than today. If your savings do not compound or grow faster than the rate of inflation, then your savings will lose value or buying power as time goes on. Many people fail to realize that even if you do not lose money from your savings directly, you may still lose value from inflation. So keeping your savings in safe savings accounts or a mattress will protect you from losses, but not from inflation eroding your buying power. If your savings account pays you 1% interest, but inflation is 3%, then your savings will lose 2% of buying power that year. If this 2% losing trend continued for 25 years, your savings will lose 50% of its buying power during that time period when you thought your money was safe.

Liquidity

There is also the "liquidity" risk; how easily can you turn your investment back into cash when you need it without losing money. For example, it is easier to convert a savings account into cash than real estate into cash. Stocks can be sold for cash, but will the price be lower or higher at the time you need your cash?

All investments have some risk from losses, inflation, or liquidity, but different types of investments have different types and degrees of risk. Stocks have greater risk of losing value in the short term, but the least risk of not beating inflation over the long term. Different types of bonds are better at preserving your capital, but falling behind inflation. Savings accounts, certificates of deposit, and money market accounts are very "liquid" when you need your money and safeguard savings well, but your money will be eroded by inflation. Even doing nothing with your savings or putting your money under the mattress risks being eroded by inflation (not to mention someone throwing away or stealing your mattress).

Rewards

Your incentive or reward for taking on this risk by investing your savings is the expectation of getting a "return" on your money. You give your savings to someone to use (person, bank, business, or government) and hope they will return your money plus more. Your "return" will be in interest (savings account, CD, money market account, or bond), dividends (from stocks), or growth (or loss) in the value of your investment (stocks, bonds, collectibles, and real estate). The greater your risk and the longer your investment's future uncertainty, the more you want to be rewarded for investing and risking your savings.

Conversely, the lower the risk, the less someone is willing to entice you with compensation so the less your return will be. This is why savings accounts pay so little interest; because there is little uncertainty and risk of loss or liquidity (but you will still lose money from inflation). Over an ***extended*** time period, stocks have historically provided the greatest total return (dividends plus growth). Their historical return of 7-10% usually beats inflation handily, but this is for the *average* stock over an *extended* time period. In the short term, a particular stock has much more uncertainty and, consequently, the greatest risk of loss and liquidity which should yield a greater *potential* return.

Now it should be clear that you should be skeptical of any
promise of high returns with little risk.

Balancing risks and rewards

When you develop your investing goals, you will want to balance liquidity (how easily you can get your money back), safety (preserving money from loses and inflation), and total return (how much you are rewarded for what degree of risk). Later, we will add other investing factors such as tax-efficiency and fees, but for now let's finish risk versus reward. It's common advice that each person must decide for them self how comfortable they are with risk and uncertainty; are they going to stay awake at night worrying or panic at the next down market? However, this advice leads too often to too many people being risk-averse at the wrong times and settling for tiny returns needlessly that don't even match inflation. For example, many people who experience a deep "bear" (down) market develop a deep aversion to risk and are reluctant to invest in stocks. But this is precisely the best time to be buying stocks – when they are cheap and before you miss most of the inevitable rebound. Talk of avoiding risk also usually means avoiding *potential* loses, but forgets about the *certain* risk of inflation.

A better guideline is to concentrate on liquidity - when will you need to convert your savings investment back to cash. Stock prices will go both down and up and might take several years to recover from a deep hole. So don't invest any money in risky stocks that you will need within the next few years. Invest that money in safer investments, for example when you are within a few years from paying for your student's college or your retirement. Conversely, don't save your college or retirement money in safe, but low yielding money market funds when college or retirement are many years away. You will likely be missing out on many years of big returns, and your savings will lose buying power from the erosion of inflation. Once again, let me be explicit about this common mistake that too many young savers make – when you are in your twenties, thirties, and forties, MOST of your retirement savings should be in stocks as the main investment that historically has grown fast enough to get you to the retirement savings goals you need. So I don't repeat too much, refer back to the chapter on *"Saving for Retirement"* for more details.

Thankfully, there are things investors can do to reduce risk. For example, we will discuss "asset allocation" and "diversification" where you invest in several types of investments to spread and reduce your risk. However, before we get into investing strategy, let's first have a detailed review of our investment choices and their risks and rewards. We will start with a survey of our investment choices including bonds, stocks, many types of investment funds, and alternative investments. When we get into investment principles and strategies, I'll discuss how you can make investing as easy or challenging as you want. Whether you want all the details or just the bottom line, knowing the fundamentals will help make your lifetime of investing more successful. Most importantly, it will better help you reach your savings goals.

Summary

- The most basic principle of investing is the tradeoff between risk and reward. The greater the investment risk, the bigger the potential reward; the safer the investment, the lower the expected reward. Be skeptical of any promise for high reward with little risk.

- All savings and investing have some degree and type of risk from losses, inflation, or liquidity based upon uncertainty of what will happen in the future; the greater the uncertainty, the greater the risk.

- If your savings do not compound or grow faster than the rate of inflation, then your savings will lose value and buying power as time goes on. Many people fail to realize that even if you do not lose money from your savings directly, you may still lose value from inflation.

- You cannot build wealth by keeping your long-term savings in a bank account, certificate of deposit, or money market fund; you probably won't even keep up with inflation.

- The greater your risk and the longer your investment's future uncertainty, the more you want to be rewarded for investing and risking your savings, so the greater your expected return. Conversely, the lower the risk, the less someone is willing to entice you with rewards, so your return will be less.

- When you develop your investing goals, you will want to balance liquidity (how easily you can get your money back), safety (preserving money from loses and inflation), and total return (how much are you rewarded for what degree of risk).

- Rather than focus on the risk of losing money, concentrate on liquidity -- when will you need to convert your savings investment back to cash. Thus, keep short-term investments in safer, low return investments and long-term investments in riskier, higher-return investments.

- The guiding principle of this investment section is that investing can be as simple or as challenging as you want it and the more complex isn't necessarily the most profitable.

Chapter Twelve

Bonds

- What are bonds?
- Why bonds?
- What risks do bonds have?
- How to buy bonds?
- What are the investment strategies for bonds?
- Where to get more information?

The best way to reduce your overall investment risks is to spread your savings among several different types of investments with different risks, rewards, and characteristics. So let's review our main choices, starting with bonds.

What are bonds?

Bonds are loans used by businesses and governments to borrow money, whereas stocks are how ownership of a company is divided up. Bondholders lend money to the business or government and get the promise of their money back at a specified time, plus interest. Since many organizations need to borrow money, there are many kinds of bonds such as corporate, municipal, government agencies, U.S. government, foreign government, and mortgage and asset backed securities.

Bonds have many differences from stocks which is one reason investing in some of both is a good way to minimize the risk that either one will do major damage to your savings. Buying bonds is more complicated than buying stocks. Here are the things to consider.

- Duration – time to maturity
- Yield – interest rate divided by price
- Quality – borrower's creditworthiness
- Price – amount paid for the bond

Duration – The maturity date is the future date that the borrower will repay the principal (amount borrowed). Bonds' duration generally vary from one to thirty years and are grouped in these categories:

1. Short-term: up to 5 years
2. Medium-term: 5 - 12 years
3. Long-term: more than 12 years

Yields – Bonds pay interest (called the coupon amount) in three ways:

1. Fixed rate of interest paid periodically. For example, 4% annually of the bond's principal paid twice per year; or bond's original face value of $1000 x yield of 4% = $40 / 2 semi-annual payments = "coupon payment" of $20 paid twice per year until maturity regardless of the price fluctuations.
2. Floating interest rate that is reset periodically based upon an index such as U.S. Treasury bills.
3. Fixed rate of interest paid only at maturity. These are called "zero-coupon bonds" as you don't get any payments until maturity when the bonds are paid in full face value plus the compounded interest. You buy these bonds at a discount, for example paying $75 and getting $100 at maturity.

Fixed interest rates/coupon amounts do not fluctuate, but prices do which causes the effective yield to fluctuate. Thus, yield at a particular time is the original coupon amount divided by the purchase price that may be higher or lower than the face value of the bond at maturity. Continuing our example above, buying a 4% bond for a discount of $9875 would give you a yield of 4.05% (0.04 / 9875 = 4.05). You would still receive the same coupon amount each year of $40, but you only had to pay $9875 to get it instead of

$1000 resulting in your higher yield of 4.05% compared to the 4% yield of the investor who originally bought the bond for $1000.

Quality – The better the credit of the bond issuer, the less risk it will fail to pay back the bond and interest, and therefore the lower the interest rate it would need to pay on its bonds. Ratings agencies issue grades to bonds so you can have a good idea of a bond's safety. AAA, AA, A, and BBB are considered investment grade that is safe. Any rating lower such as BB, B and down to D are considered potentially risky or speculative, and thus the bond issuer would have to pay a higher interest rate to get investors to buy them.

Prices: When you buy a newly issued bond, you will pay its face value and if you keep it to maturity, you should get that full value back. However, bond prices on the secondary market after issue fluctuate based upon many factors we will discuss below.

Why bonds?

- Preserve savings – borrowers guarantee to repay all of your capital at maturity.
- Predictable income – most bonds pay interest semi-annually at a rate that does not change.
- Low volatility – bonds have fewer price ups and downs than stocks and the swing amounts are less.
- Diversification – spread your risk among different types of investments.

Most bonds are considered low risk investments because most pay back your principal at a specified maturity date, plus pay you a set amount of interest periodically until then. While certain stocks may pay dividends equal or greater than bonds and have wonderful records of increasing dividends, the company does not guarantee stock dividends, which can be reduced at any time as we saw during the Great Recession of 2008-2010. There is less uncertainty (risk) with bonds over stocks because you know what you can expect: a specified rate of interest until maturity when you will get all of your money back. This is why they are called "fixed income" investments and have less volatility than stocks.

What risks do bonds have?

Like all investments, bonds do have some risks. Always remember that the lower the risk, the lower the return. Bond features that can affect the risk/reward ratio and value of bonds include price, market interest rates, *maturity*, redemption features, market conditions, *default* history, credit ratings, and tax status.

Price

Bond prices fluctuate between the date the bond is issued and the maturity date based upon interest rates, credit-worthiness of the issuer, supply and demand, and general economic conditions. The price you pay may be above (selling at a premium) or below (selling at a discount) the face value (par) and is quoted as a percentage of "par". For example a quoted price of 98.75 means you would pay $9875 for a $1000 bond (in bond lingo – buying the bond at a discount below par).

Interest rates

Both market interest rates and interest rates of individual bonds affect the bond's price and yield. When market interest rates rise, this causes the price to fall for bonds with lower interest rates, since they are now less attractive than new bonds with higher rates. This is the main way an investor can lose money with bonds. Therefore, bond prices are very sensitive to market interest rate changes and bond prices move *opposite* of market interest rates.

Maturity

Shorter terms bonds usually pay lower interest rates because their shorter duration has less uncertainty and makes them safer. Longer-term bonds usually pay higher interest rates for their greater uncertainty and price fluctuations of the longer holding period. For the same reasons, longer-term bonds may have greater price fluctuations when market interest rates fluctuate.

Redemption features

Some bonds have features that enable them to be cashed in before the maturity date and these features affect the bond's interest rate. Some bonds may have provisions that enable the issuer (call provision) or investor (put provisions) to cash in the bonds before the maturity date based upon whether market interest rates have risen or fallen. "Call provisions usually offer higher interest rates to compensate the investor for losing his bond early and having to reinvest at a lower interest rate, while conversely, "put" provisions usually offer lower interest rates. Some bonds (convertible bonds) can be converted to stocks and thus have lower interest rates for the right to combine the fixed income of bonds with the potential for growth of stocks.

Market conditions

Bond prices are sensitive to general market conditions, but usually differently than stocks. Bondholders like moderate market conditions that ensure government and corporate borrowers can repay the bonds. However, remembering the strong link between bond prices and interest rates, bondholders react to how the general economic climate and news might affect interest rates more than how they might affect such things as business profits. Thus, news of a very strong economic trend might actually send bond prices *down* from fears that a robust economy will lead to higher inflation and interest rates. Conversely, weak economic news might send bond prices higher from expectations that this means interest rates will go lower and send bond prices higher. This helps explain why bonds and stocks frequently move in different directions and why investing in some of both will result in less risk and volatility in your overall portfolio.

Credit quality

One of the biggest factors that affect the interest rate of a bond is the credit-worthiness of the bond issuer. The greater the risk that a business, government, or agency will default (not pay) on its loan principal or interest, the higher the return or interest rate. This is why bonds of the U.S. government pay the lowest interest rates while start-up companies and shaky foreign governments pay the highest. These speculative bonds rated "BB" or lower by credit rating agencies are sometimes called "junk bonds" and other times "high yielding corporate bonds". Buying them is one of the common ways to increase an investor's fixed income, but always remember that high returns always mean higher risk, so limit the amount of junk bonds you buy to a small percentage of your holdings. Bond ratings can change over time as the credit worthiness of the borrower changes, so periodically review your bond holdings.

Tax Status

Some government bonds are exempt from income tax, but these usually have lower interest rates.

Summary of key points

We can see that many factors help determine the price and interest rates of bonds, but let's summarize with the most important points. All of these factors help provide a wide range of bond yields, but the most important factors in getting higher yields come from lower quality bonds (more risk the company will default) or longer maturity dates (more uncertainty about the future). Remember: higher rewards, higher risks. Bonds are great ways to get fixed income that is higher than offered at banks and less volatile than stocks. However, you can lose money if you sell bonds before the maturity date because bond prices fall when interest rates rise. Conversely, bond prices rise when market interest rates fall, so bond prices move inversely (opposite) to market interest rates. This price fluctuation is greater for bonds with longer maturities because of the increased uncertainty about the more distant future.

How to buy bonds

- Individual bonds
- Bond funds

Individual Bonds

Not only are bonds more difficult to understand than stocks, but also harder to buy. This makes bonds less "liquid" than stocks, (harder to buy and sell). Stocks are sold on several stock exchanges with most stocks selling tens or hundreds of thousands of shares a day so you are always likely to find a buyer or seller when you need one. Bonds are sold "over the counter" by decentralized independent dealers, brokers, and bankers, while particular bonds may be sold infrequently. The bond market is dominated by large institutional investors such as pension funds, insurance companies, and financial institutions who get the best prices. To buy bonds directly, contact your broker, financial advisor, or independent dealers who are increasingly available on the internet. Many websites and brokerages will enable you to find bond information and prices online for commonly traded bonds, but bond prices for infrequently traded bonds may be difficult to find from all those independent dealers with no central exchange. You should shop around to see what prices are being offered by bond dealers because they may vary widely due to many supply and demand factors. Additionally, you do pay fees and commissions to your broker and the dealer. Brokers' websites usually have bond-screening tools that help you find bonds you are interested in while reviewing prices, yield, quality rating, maturity, and coupon payment frequency. Note that individual investors may not get as good of prices for individual bonds as institutions get for huge bond purchases:

- http://www.investinginbonds.com/ - bond lookup tools, calculators, and articles.
- http://finance.yahoo.com/bonds - bond screener, news, and education.

The best way to avoid losing any savings from bonds is to hold individual bonds to maturity, but there may be times when you would consider selling them. For example, the price has gone up significantly so take some profit, or the quality rating of a bond has dropped significantly to junk level. All bonds have to be sold on the secondary market. Start with your broker or financial advisor for help.

The most popular bonds in the world are U.S. government bonds, both because there are trillions of dollars of them and growing, and because they are considered the safest investment you can have. Of course that safety also means they have among the lowest yields of any bonds – remember low risk, low return. The U.S. government has many types of bonds including the small denomination savings bonds popular as gifts as well as the standard Treasure bills, notes, and bonds based upon length of maturity. TIPS (Treasury Inflation Protected Securities) even have a yield that rises or falls with inflation, but at maturity will pay the higher of the original or adjusted value. Another nice feature of buying U.S. government bonds is that anyone can buy them directly without paying any fees to middlemen, so they are unquestionably the easiest bonds to buy directly. This is best if you plan to hold them to maturity as selling them early on the secondary market means going thru a broker with fees. You can no longer buy paper bonds, but get the details and create an account for buying, holding, and tracking your electronic government bonds at the Department of Treasury website, Treasury Direct:

http://www.treasurydirect.gov/indiv/indiv.htm

Bond Funds

If buying bonds seems complicated, it's because it is, which is why most regular investors buy bond mutual funds or exchange traded funds (ETFs) instead. Mutual funds and ETFs have professional managers who can navigate most of that bond stuff for you and select an expert mix of bonds better than you can, especially in areas like high-yield junk bonds and foreign bonds. You can find a fund to match just about any category and maturity length you are interested in, so spread your bond money among more than one bond type, company, industry, or government borrower. Moreover, most bond funds pay interest monthly rather than semi-annually as most bonds do.

When you analyze bond funds, you will basically see total returns and current yield. Total returns will include both the interest paid and any rise or decline in the bond fund's price. Yield shows how much you can expect to receive in interest. When comparing bond funds you are interested in, review returns from different time periods such as 1 yr., 3 yr., and 5 yr. and as always, compare the expense ratios to look for low expenses. Bond Index ETFs are similar to mutual funds, but follow a bond index rather than have active managers, resulting in lower fund management fees and probably less taxable, capital gains from buying and selling bonds.

Many resources will help you navigate the bond fund choices including:
- *Money* magazine offers bond fund recommendations.
- Morningstar.com provides free and premium bond fund screens and ratings.
- AAII.com among others offers premium mutual fund screens including bonds.

So bond funds are easy and convenient, but of course that means they have a cost. In addition to the expenses you pay the fund managers, which result in a lower return, you lose some of the best features of bonds, the predictability that you will get all of your money back at a specific time, plus a set interest rate. Bond funds include a variety of bonds that spread the risk, but also lead to price fluctuations and lack of a maturity date and predictable return. So individual bonds are still worth considering, especially if you plan to hold them to maturity, want to time them to mature at a certain time such as the kids college or your retirement, or desire to try out the really easy Treasury Direct online bond program. Another way to get the predictability of individual bonds without the work is to have an investment advisor or brokerage firm manage your bond portfolio – for a fee of course, perhaps around 0.5%.

What are the investment strategies for bonds?

- Risk / Reward Ratio
  - o Losses
  - o Liquidity

- o Inflation
- o reward
- Strategies
  - o Diversification
  - o Laddering
  - o Predictable income
  - o Tax free income
  - o Different economic climates
  - o Bonds versus stocks

Risk / Reward Ratio

Let's review the risk / reward ratio for investing in bonds based upon the investment risk factors we reviewed in the last chapter.

Losses

Bond investors have three worries about losing money.

- Borrower will default and not pay back your money or coupon payments. To minimize this risk, review the bonds' credit rating, AAA (low chance of default) down to D (risky).
- You may have to sell your bond or fund for less than you bought it for. Absent a default, if you hold your bond until maturity, you will get your full par (face value) back. This is not true for bond funds which have no maturity date.
- Your bond may be called (paid) early which forces you to reinvest your money in an investment that may have a lower yield than your old bond. To avoid this, buy bonds that do not have a "callable" feature, but this may also mean getting a lower yield.

It may be hard to predict interest rates rise and fall, but we have been thru several recessions and recoveries recently with more certainly to come, so do heed this. Beware of bond funds when interest rates are rising, since this will cause their prices to fall. During a recession, the Federal Reserve likely will help lower interest rates to stimulate the economy and this will cause bond prices to rise, which is a great time to be in bond funds. As the economy improves and inflation starts to rise, the Federal Reserve likely will push interest rates to rise which will cause bond fund prices to fall. This is the time to be out of bond funds. Except – everyone say it together now – bonds held to maturity will get the full par value back regardless of interim price fluctuations.

Liquidity

Remember liquidity is how easily you can cash in your investment to get your money back. Bond funds are easy to cash in, but how much you will get back depends upon the current price. Individual bonds held to maturity will automatically return your full par value, but selling individual bonds on the secondary market may not be so easy, especially with infrequently traded bonds. Not only are you at the mercy of interest rates and supply and demand, but also finding a broker or dealer interested in your particular bond at an attractive rate for you. Your broker or financial advisor can probably do this for you for a fee.

Inflation

Especially during periods of economic bad times and volatility, it is so tempting to just put all of our money in very safe investments, such as CDs and government bonds. It gives us peace of mind without realizing the hidden danger chipping away at our safe investments and that danger is inflation. If our money is not growing at least as fast as inflation, then the buying power of our money is diminishing even if the absolute value isn't. So if our super safe government bonds are only yielding 1% while inflation is growing at 2%, then we are really losing 1% per year of buying power. Of course, this is better than losing 5-10% from declining investments. Just remember that the safest bonds with the smallest yields may not keep up with inflation, so it may be beneficial to choose bonds with a yield that can at least keep up with inflation or diversify your bond investments in several types.

Rewards

The risks of most bonds don't really seem all that bad, especially when coupled with the ready means to manage them. So it's not surprising that most bonds are considered relatively safe investments and therefore their rewards are relatively small as well. In fact, yields on some super safe government bonds may not be much higher than money market funds or CDs that have only minimal risks from price losses, early redemption, defaults, or liquidity. Nonetheless, the benefits of bonds include predictable income, preservation of capital when held to maturity, and diversification; while providing a wide range of types, maturities, and yields to accomplish this.

Bond strategies

Diversification
The main reasons for buying bonds is to preserve your savings from loses, diversify your investments, and earn fixed income. Bonds are considered a relatively safe investment, but like any investment, it's still better to diversify your holdings among different bond types, maturities, and industries. I've discussed many generalities about bonds, but there are still a lot of differences between types and when one type is sinking, another may be rising. For example, bad news about munis, junk bonds, or foreign bonds may send investors fleeing into super safe U.S. Treasuries. Diversification is another instance that is easier to do with funds than individual bonds unless you have a large sum to invest in bonds.

Laddering
Buying short-term bonds provide less price volatility during interest rate moves, but low yields; while buying long-term bonds give higher yields, but more price volatility. One way to reduce bond risk and smooth out yields is to use a "ladder" strategy of buying short, intermediate, and long-term bonds with different maturities so they mature at regular intervals. When a bond matures, reinvest it for a date one year after the end of your ladder and repeat, thus always extending your bond ladder by another year. For example, you could buy a series of bonds so they mature each year for the next fifteen years giving you a mix of short, intermediate, and long-term bonds. Each year a bond will mature and you can reinvest it for another bond that matures at the end of the next one, five, or fifteen years. You should structure your bond ladder to meet your circumstances and goals. Another possible scenario is while waiting for interest rates to rise, you could buy a ladder of short and intermediate term bonds set to mature when you hope rates will be higher. You can ladder indefinitely, adjust for changing circumstances, or time them to mature at a specific date when you will need the cash.

A ladder gives you flexibility as bonds mature each year giving you access to cash without having to sell bonds. This enables you to buy longer-term bonds with higher yields. As long as you hold the bonds to maturity, you won't worry about rising or falling interest rates and prices. When bonds mature in a period of rising rates and falling prices, you will still get your full par value and can buy new bonds at a higher interest rate. During periods of falling rates and rising prices, you could take capital gains and you would still be buying new, long-term bonds with the best yields.

Predictable Income

A steady, predictable source of fixed income is particularly prized by retirees. Bond funds pay monthly, while bonds typically pay twice per year. To earn a regular income from bond interest payments, buy a series of bonds that pay you income each month. For example, six bonds that pay twice per year in different months to receive 12 regularly spaced checks or even 12 bonds for 24 checks timed throughout the year. If you are well diversified, then consider devoting a small portion to risky, high yield bonds for greater income, but don't get carried away.

Tax Free Income

Some investors prefer bonds to get tax-free income. U.S. government bonds are free from state and local taxes; nice in high tax states, but not so much in states with no income tax. Municipal bonds (munis) are offered by local governments to finance expensive infrastructure such as sewers and roads. They are exempt from Federal, state, and local taxes if paying taxes in the same locality. So why wouldn't everybody want tax free bonds? Well tax free bonds have lower yields than most taxable bonds so you need to compare your tax free bond yield plus your tax savings versus the yield from taxable bonds. Generally, munis are less attractive to people in lower tax brackets and most attractive to people in high tax brackets. Your considerations on buying tax-free bonds may include your tax bracket, alternative minimum tax eligibility, yields versus taxable bonds, effect on Social Security benefits, and whether they will be held in 401(k) or IRA type retirement accounts that are already tax-advantaged. Some of the tax rules can get pretty arcane on certain bonds, so check the rules carefully. Web calculators like these can help do the math to compare taxable and tax-free bonds to see which would be better for your situation and tax bracket:

- http://www.tipsinc.com/ficalc/calc.tips

Different economic climates

Even when rising interest rates are negatively affecting bonds, you should not abandon them altogether since diversification of your savings from stocks and cash is still a vital part of your overall investing strategy. But there are steps you can take to soften the sting. Many bond experts recommend investment grade bonds rated A or AA with maturities from 5 to 10 years for the best mix of preserving capital in safe bonds while getting adequate yields and low price volatility. However, in particular economic climates, other mixes may be better. For example, when rising interest rates are expected, choose short-term bonds bonds, which won't fall as much as longer term, or TIPS (Treasury Inflation Protected Securities) which will see yields rise with inflation and prices hold steadier from increased demand. You can find a bond fund's average maturity length by entering it in Morningstar.com's quote box. Additionally, when U.S. interest rates are rising, you may be able to get some relief by investing part of your bond allocation in foreign bonds in countries where interest rates are not rising.

Bonds versus Stocks

Here are some key differences between stocks and bonds:

- Income from stocks and bonds are taxed differently. Interest from bonds is taxed at the higher, ordinary income rate, the same as wages, while dividends from stocks are taxed at a preferential lower rate, the same as capital gains. (This lower, preferential tax rate for stock investors over wage earners is a main reason many wealthy people tend to pay a lower "rate" in taxes than their secretaries.)
- Both stock and bond prices go up and down. In fact, bonds have had more losing years since WWII than stocks. However, the volatility (wild swings up and down) of bonds is much less than stocks. The low volatility of bonds gives peace of mind (low risk, low return). The high volatility of stocks provides more potential for growth and loss (high risk, high return).
- You can make or lose money by selling either stocks or bonds, but if you hold a bond to maturity, you will not lose your original investment.
- If a company goes bankrupt, bond holders have precedence to get paid before stockholders.

- Only bonds pay a predictable income. A borrower can only skip a bond coupon payment by defaulting, but a company can skip or lower a stock dividend payment for any reason.

More information

- http://online.wsj.com/public/page/news-fixed-income-bonds.html - Offers comprehensive information relating to the bond market.
- http://www.investinginbonds.com/marketataglance.asp?catid=31 - Lookup information about specific bonds with bond news and information.
- http://finance.yahoo.com/bonds - Lookup information about specific bonds along with educational articles and calculators.

Summary

- Bondholders lend money to a business or government and get the promise of their full money back at a specified time, plus predictable interest.
- Bonds have many differences from stocks which is one reason investing in some of both is a good way to minimize the risk that either one will do major damage to your savings.
- There is less uncertainty (risk) with bonds over stocks because you generally know what you can expect: a specified rate of interest until maturity when you will get all of your money back. This is why they are called "fixed income" investments and have less volatility than stocks.
- The low volatility of bonds gives peace of mind (low risk, low return). The high volatility of stocks provides more potential for growth and loss (high risk, high return).
- Bonds are great ways to get fixed income that is higher than offered at banks and less volatile than stocks. However, you can lose money if you sell bonds before the maturity date because bond prices fall when interest rates rise.
- Bond prices are very sensitive to market interest rate changes and bond prices move *opposite* of market interest rates. This price fluctuation is greater for bonds with longer maturities because of the increased uncertainty about the more distant

future. When you expect rising interest rates, concentrate on short-maturity bonds.

- Bond funds are easier to buy than most bonds and you can find a fund to match just about any category and maturity length you are interested in. Bond funds include a variety of bonds that spread the risk, but also lead to fees, price fluctuations, and lack of a maturity date and predictable return.
- Diversify *among* bond types just as you use bonds to diversify among your total investments.
- The benefits of bonds and bond funds include low volatility, predictable income, preservation of capital when held to maturity, and diversification; while providing a wide range of types, maturities, and yields to accomplish this.
- Bond risks may include low yields that may not exceed inflation, volatility when interest rates move, issuer default, and liquidity issues when buying or selling on the secondary bond market.

Chapter Thirteen

Stocks

- Why stocks?
- What risks do stocks have?
- How to buy stocks?
- What are the investment strategies for stocks?
- Where to get more information?

We know that all investments have both risks and rewards. We have seen how bonds are generally considered low risk, low reward, so now let's turn to an investment that is considered high risk, high reward - stocks.

Why stocks?

Stocks are ownership shares in a company. Companies use stock to raise capital for the company and to compensate employees in lieu of cash. Unlike bonds which are loans to the company, stock never have to be repaid, but sometimes is bought back by the company as a means to use a portion of its cash to raise the stock price and benefit stockholders. When you buy stock, you own shares in the company. As owners of the company, "common" stockholders have the right to vote for the board of directors and on certain company decisions and have the expectation of sharing in the profits of the company.

There are two kinds of stock: *common* and *preferred*. Maybe you guessed that the most common type of stock is the *common* kind, while *preferred* stock has certain preference over common stock; specifically, preferred stockholders have first claim on a company's dividends and assets if the company runs into trouble. For example, if a company goes bankrupt, bond holders get first priority to be paid followed by *preferred* stockholders, and lastly, *common* stockholders. Common stocks generally have lower yields that are variable and higher growth potential with more price volatility. Preferred stocks are similar to bonds in that they usually have fixed yields that are higher than common stock, but they have lower growth potential and can be "called" or bought back by the company at a stated price. Some dividends of preferred stock called "nonqualified dividends" are taxed at your higher "ordinary" tax rate rather than the lower capital gains rate. "Qualified dividends" of preferred stocks are taxed at the lower capital gains rate, so pay attention to which kind you have if you buy preferred stock, as well as whether your preferred stock is "callable" and at what price.

http://quantumonline.com/ - Good website for information about preferred stocks.

You can make money from stocks two ways: from the stock's dividends (if they have any) and by selling your stock at a higher price than you paid for it - growth. Most stocks have high liquidity, meaning they are very easy to buy and sell, much easier than bonds, real estate, and most alternative investments. But the real reason to buy stocks is because historically they have the highest return of any other standard type of investment. From 1928 thru 2012, stocks have returned around 10% per year, including dividends. So if your investment goal is long term, the high *average* return of stocks is one of the best ways to get there. As we saw when discussing "saving for retirement", investing a substantial percentage of your retirement savings in stocks is the only way to accrue the huge amounts needed for a comfortable retirement.

What are the risks of stocks?

Of course, these high returns also mean high risks. Stocks have three risks you should consider. The main risk from stocks is that you could lose money by selling for less than you bought it for. You could even lose all of your money if the company goes bankrupt because most of its assets may go to pay its debts, and bond holders get paid before stockholders. The second risk is that stock prices are very volatile, (frequent and large swings up and down). A third risk is that stock prices or the stock market in general could be down for a long time, even years. It took around seven years for stock prices to recover from the Great Depression of the 1930's and five and one half to recover from the Great Recession in our lifetime.

Many unpredictable things can cause this volatility. Stock prices are theoretically influenced mainly by profits or the expectations of future profits, but in reality can also be influenced by a wide variety of factors including general market conditions, industry conditions, news headlines around the world, and beating or failing to beat analysts' financial expectations.

How to buy stocks

- Individual stocks
- Stock funds
- Stock brokers
- Picking Stocks

Individual stocks

Stocks have many kinds of data beside price to help you buy, sell, and review individual stocks. Key ones include the following:

Price – The price is all-important, so there are many ways to look at it.
- Open / close – the first and last price the stock sold for that day.
- High / low / last – the price range the stock has traded for that day.
- Bid price – the current price someone is willing to pay to buy the stock.
- Asking price – the current price someone is willing to sell their stock for.

Dividend – the last amount in dollars and cents the company paid to stockholders for each share they owned.

Yield – The dividend amount divided by the stock price shows the return or percentage of your stock investment you hope to be paid compared to the amount it takes you to buy the share.

Ex-dividend date – Since stocks are bought and sold frequently, this is the date used to determine who gets the next dividend.

P/E ratios – One of the most widely used measures of a stock is its "price earnings ratio" (P/E) so let's discuss it in more depth. The P/E ratio is a quick guide as to whether a stock is cheap or expensive and how enthusiastic investors are for it. Specifically, the P/E shows how much investors are willing to pay for future earnings of the company. The P/E is calculated by dividing the current stock price by the "earnings per share" (EPS) of the last four quarters or estimated for the next four quarters. Example:

Stock price per Share	or	$100	=	P/E of 20.20
Earnings per Share (EPS)		$4.95		

In this example, investors are currently willing to pay $20.20 per each dollar of earnings from the company, so the higher the P/E, the more investors are willing to pay and the more they think the company will grow their earnings. Conversely, the lower the P/E, the less investors are willing to pay because they are skeptical of the growth potential of the company.

Reviewing the P/E ratio of a stock can help investors:

- See what the market currently thinks of a company's growth potential (the higher the P/E, the more the expected potential).
- Run stock screens to find companies with desired P/E ranges (for example, for inexpensive, *value* oriented stocks with P/Es under a certain level or *growth* oriented stocks above a certain level).
- Be wary of expensive stocks that may not be able to justify lofty expectations. For example, is a stock with a P/E double or triple the market or industry average, in bubble territory and ready for a crash? This lesson was learned too late by too many in the dot.com/tech bubble crash in the late 1990s. Don't relearn this lesson again the hard way just because time has gone by.

You have to be careful about comparing P/Es among stocks directly because companies in different industries have different growth potential. For example, tech companies are normally assumed to have more growth potential than utility companies. It's better to compare a company's P/E to the market average, its industry average, the company's historical average, or a company in the same industry.

Usually the best middle range for P/Es is 10-25. The historical average P/E for the S&P 500 is around 15 depending upon how you calculate it and what time period you use. P/Es are widely used by *"growth"* or *"value"* oriented investors to find stocks that match their investing style. For example, value investors look for companies with low P/Es to find beaten down companies that are inexpensive, and hopefully, ready for a re-bound. Growth oriented investors look for companies with higher than average P/Es to find fast-growing companies likely to continue growing faster than rivals and rising in stock price (hopefully).

Stock funds

Since it can be challenging and risky to analyze, select, and hold individual stocks, many investors choose to invest instead in professionally managed stock funds to spread their risk among many stocks. We will review each of these in coming chapters including the benefits and risks:

Mutual Funds – A professionally managed investment company that pools investors' money to buy an assortment of stocks, bonds, money market instruments, real estate, and other securities generally based upon a particular investment style. The price of a share is changed only at the end of each business day.

Exchange Traded Funds (ETF) – An investment fund that is traded on stock markets like stocks, but usually with the goal of tracking a particular index for stocks, bonds, industries, or commodities. The price can fluctuate throughout the trading day.

Index Funds – A type of mutual fund or ETF that pools investors' money to buy stocks with the goal of matching the performance of a specific market index such as the Dow Jones Industrial Average, Standard and Poors 500, S&P *SmallCap index, or many others.*

Stock brokers

You buy stocks thru a stock brokerage firm and there are three types, each with different strengths: full service, discount, and mutual fund companies. Full service brokers like the big names of Wall Street are more expensive, but offer more personalized advice. Discount brokers are inexpensive and best for do-it-yourself investors. Many of the biggest mutual fund companies offer brokerage services and may be best if most of your investing is with that company's mutual funds.

Here are things to consider when choosing a brokerage firm.

- How much advice do you want? If you want to talk to a broker and get investing advice, then a full service broker may be worth the extra cost. If you plan to make your own investing decision, then a discount broker will save you significant costs while offering a wide array of investing resources.
- What will you mainly want to invest in? Each enables you to buy and sell stocks, but brokers differ in the resources they offer in other areas such as mutual funds, EFTs, bonds, and alternative investments. Especially, review the costs and breadth of offerings for mutual funds and EFTs.
- What are the costs? Fees can vary widely, even among discount brokers. In addition to stock trading fees, review fees for inactivity, buying bonds and funds, moving money around, and other services you may need. Remember that fees can reduce your investment returns, so they should contribute to your investing success.
- What kind of services do you want? Brokerage firms offer an increasing array of services and resources such as research reports, stock screeners, online tools, education resources, check cashing, streaming stock quotes, investment ideas, social media, portfolio management tools, mobile apps, and customer service. Check them out, but sometimes, it's the website or trading interface that really matters because that is what you actually deal with most often.
- Do you want an office you can visit? Many discount brokers do not have offices you can visit. Everything is done online.

To get started, I recommend reviewing any of the regular brokerage reviews provided by many magazines and websites such as *Barrons* and *AAII*. Many brokers offer incentives to join and it's easy to try them out until you find the one that suits you. You may want to commit only a small amount of cash while you try it out. It's also easy to change brokers if you decide to.

Picking stocks

We will look at investing styles and strategies soon, but now let's consider exactly how do you buy stocks. There are basically two methods for picking individual stocks, fundamental or technical analysis.

Fundamental Analysis

Fundamentals analysis tries to find good stocks by finding good companies and reviews the companies' business fundamentals to determine which company is going to earn growing profits. It tries to determine the true value of a stock relative to its profits or assets. Professionals and experts have many ways to try and value a company, determine its profitability and growth potential, and estimate when a stock is a good deal. Different investors may review such data as price earnings ratio, price book ratio, price to sales ratio, price to cash flow ratio, debt to equity ratio, book value, return on equity, return on assets, revenue, past earnings, future earnings, and many more most of us know little about. It should work even better when analysts can estimate the company's *future* profits and data, but as we have frequently discussed – the future is hard to predict consistently. There is no end to books, articles, and websites that will explain all this to you, but the reality is that most of us have little knowledge or time to find and calculate most of this, while the pros and experts aren't much better at predicting the future than the rest of us.

Technical Analysis

A second method pays little attention to a company's fundamentals, but isn't necessarily any better or easier for most people to understand and use. Technical analysis reviews past patterns in stock prices, volume, momentum, and investor behavior to try to predict future stock price movements. It can't predict the future, but aims to combine past and current data with investor psychology to predict how investors *likely* will act in similar situations as they have in the past. Technical analysts review charts of stock price movements and volume over time to spot trends, momentum, and patterns that in the past have led to predictable price movements up or down. They use trend lines that in the past tended to act as "support" where stocks bounced off a price level *floor* several times and then rose, or "resistance" where prices bounced off a price level *ceiling*, tried to punch thru, and then fell or breakout above it. The support and resistance trend lines show where either demand or supply is likely to be dominant over the other. For example, technical analysts might buy a stock that was rising but still far below a previous "resistance" level or sell a stock that had repeatedly failed to break above a resistance level and was falling.

Technical analysis adds in price patterns with shapes and names like "head and shoulders", flags, and "triple bottoms" to predict what frequently happens to prices when they breaks out of these common patterns. Technical analysis also uses plenty of data, calculations, and statistics that combine price and volume data to discern signals about which way prices are most likely headed. Here are some good technical analysis websites that provide more information and free charts to use:

- www.StockCharts.com
- www.FreeStockCharts.com
- http://bigcharts.marketwatch.com/

Fundamental analysis is especially used by long-term investors and technical analysis by shorter-term traders. Academic experts especially consider technical analysis unsupported at best and superstition at worst. Nonetheless, it seems probable that many if not most serious stop pickers use some of both. Fundamental investors screen good companies with their favored fundamentals, and then sneak a peek at the stock charts to determine the best time to buy. Technical analysts may screen good companies from their charts, but confirm final selections based upon company data. A stock with both good fundamentals and technical charts could be a winning combination.

Despite all these analysis methods, some experts suggest that monkeys have almost as good of a chance at beating the market indexes as any other method, so what is a small investor to do? I'll devote most of the rest of *"Part Three* – Investing" to reviewing this question, including a super simple method for people who don't care about any of this.

For those of you that are still interested in picking stocks for the thrill of beating the market indexes and can deal with the agony of defeat, follow me, but before you get your hopes up, let me say that this book is not about picking stocks. There are whole sections of libraries, bookstores, and websites filled with many fine books, old and new, on that topic. Nonetheless, I do want to give you enough information to point you in the right direction.

I suggest that for investors who don't want to master a library of investing books, but still want to invest in stocks, the place to seek help is obvious – from people who do fancy themselves to be experts, have read most of those books, and have already experienced those ups and downs. No, that doesn't include the brother-in-law nor office water-cooler guys, but there are plenty of reasonable options. Remember, we would rather do most of our learning from other people's mistakes than our own.

- **Investment newsletters** – There is no shortage of these for every investing style and experience level. Some are expensive and some not. The advantage is that you can get advice emailed to you that is as timely and specific as you choose for whatever investing style you prefer.
- **Investing Websites -** Many news, investing, and personal finance websites will provide specific tips about stocks as well as general information, news, stock screens, and portfolio managers. Here are just a few among many fine websites that are mostly free although many offer premium upgrades:
  - http://finance.yahoo.com/
  - http://www.marketwatch.com/
  - http://money.cnn.com/
  - http://www.morningstar.com/
- **Stock screeners** – Here are websites that enable you to search for stocks that meet certain criteria you select. Some even provide preset screens for selected investing styles:
  - http://finviz.com/
  - http://www.cnbc.com/id/15839076
  - http://www.zacks.com/screening/
  - http://caps.fool.com/Screener.aspx
  - http://www.morningstar.com/Cover/Tools.html
  - http://screener.finance.yahoo.com/newscreener.html
- **Stock picking services** – Many investing services will provide you all kinds of tools, stock screens, advice, commentators, and information. Many of these can be quite expensive and can rope you in at seminars and trade shows. My advice for free is to wait a few days before signing up, research any you are interested in, and take advantage of any free trial period.
- **Full service stock brokers and financial advisors** – If you are going to pay for advice, perhaps you want a real person to talk to, help you review your situation and options, and even manage your portfolio for you. Always take the time to understand what they are proposing to you and how they are being compensated for that advice. Some make more fees the more often you trade or invest in certain products.
- **Magazines and newspapers** – There are many good magazines and newspapers that provide investment information and offer specific stock suggestions. For $20

- $50 per year, you get a wide variety of information delivered to you by mail or tablet that you can read and analyze at your leisure. *Barrons, Forbes, Fortune,* the *Wall Street Journal,* and *Business Week Magazine* cover the market from the business perspective. *Kiplingers* and *Money* magazines cover investing from the personal finance perspective. The latter two are my favorites because they offer investing suggestions and personal finance information for the small investor.

- **Insider buying** – Who would know more about their company than its executives, officers, and board members? When insiders buy their own company's stock, it's bound to be because they think it is a good deal and will make money. As a friend, who built his own website to find insider buying, frequently said, "There are many reasons why an insider might sell their company stock, but there's only one reason why they would buy it." You can find out when insiders are legally buying their own stock because they are required to make the information public on the Securities and Exchange Commission (SEC) website. There are many websites that make it much easier to find that information and some even provide email alerts:

  o http://insidertrading.org/
  o http://www.gurufocus.com/InsiderBuy.php
  o http://www.insidercow.com/

Remember that if stock pickers were usually right, they would be gadzillionaires instead of paid stock pickers. So, it is always worthwhile to understand why you are investing in a stock and do some research. It may even be useful to get a second opinion (although there is an investment style called "contrarian" that holds that doing the opposite of the "herd" is more profitable). Here are several websites that offer free ratings on individual stocks. Enter a stock symbol and get the rating, along with the usual important data:

- http://www.morningstar.com/Cover/Stocks.html - star rating
- http://www.fool.com/ - CAPS rating
- http://biz.yahoo.com/r/ - Analysts' mean rating
- http://www.zacks.com/stocks/zacks-rank - Zack's rank
- http://pwstreet.com/app/ - Soon there is bound to be many mobile apps for smartphones and tablets. This is one of the first.

Investment strategies for stocks

- Risk / Reward Ratio
    - Losses
    - Liquidity
    - Inflation
    - reward
- Strategies and principles
    - Growth
    - Value
    - Dividends
    - Diversification
    - Different economic climates
    - Stocks versus bonds

Risk / reward ratio

Let's review the risk / reward ratio for investing in stocks based upon the investment risk factors we reviewed previously.

Losses

There is always a risk you can lose some of your money if you sell your stock at a lower price than you paid for it. You could even lose all of your money if the company goes bankrupt. Although this is rare, it does happen even to big, established companies like Enron, Worldcom, Six Flags, and Lehman Brothers. "Buy low, sell high" sounds obvious, but that doesn't mean it's easy. In fact, everyone is going to have stocks that decline in price since stocks are very volatile with frequent ups and downs. How do you deal with it? For active traders this may mean limiting your losses early while they are small. For long-term investors, it may mean riding out the time period it takes to recover and collect your dividends in the meantime. You don't actually have a loss until you sell and when you do sell at a loss, the government gives you a tax break.

Liquidity

Remember, liquidity is how easily you can cash in your investment to get your money back. Most stocks have medium liquidity risk because they are among the easiest investments to sell. It generally only takes minutes to contact your broker and sell your stock by phone, mobile app, or website, although with a small commission. On the other hand, when you need to sell stock may not be the best time to do so because of a price decline and it may take years to regain the price you paid for it. Therefore, it's common advice to NOT invest in stocks with money that you may need within the next few years. This is why it is common to start shifting part of your college and retirement savings to a safer investment when you are a few years away from needing it.

Inflation

If your savings do not grow as fast as the inflation rate, then you are actually losing money – or at least buying power. Despite the recent bear markets, stocks are one of the best investments to grow faster than inflation – *on average, over time*, especially if you are getting dividends.

Rewards

High risk – high return. Stock investors take higher risks because they want higher returns than you can usually get in most other investments. Actually, as we have seen, stocks have high risk of losses from price volatility, medium liquidity, and low inflation risk. Investors take these risks in hopes of sharing in a company's profits and making more money than they could in safer investments. Stock investors can be rewarded two ways, selling their stocks for a profit or receiving dividends. All investors hope to see the price of their stock increase, even soar, but dividends are the more dependable way to profit. Many, but not all, companies pay dividends, which is the straightforward way that companies share their profits with the company's owners, their stockholders. There is growing pressure on more companies to pay or increase dividends, but company directors may prefer to keep profits to expand the company, buy other companies, increase research and development, move into new markets, develop new products, buy back their stock, dodge taxes, or save for a rainy day. Any combination of these may – or may not – make the company more profitable and increase the stock price.

Stock strategies

The way to make money in stocks seems so simple, buy low, sell high. Even more attractive is humorist Will Rogers' advice, "buy some good stock and hold it till it goes up, then sell it. If it don't go up, don't buy it." So why do too many of us too often do the opposite and buy high and sell low? We will get to the big picture strategies of diversification and "buy and hold" in a coming chapter, but let's discuss some basic stock investing strategies and tactics here which try to improve your chances of making money with winning investments.

Growth

The "growth" investment style is perhaps the most popular, especially in strong bull markets. Investors strive to find companies with strong potential for rising profits and stock prices. Rising stock prices depend on *expectations* of more rising stock price and profits so prices can be volatile based as much on managing expectations as results. A second risk is that it is too easy to overpay for growth stocks based upon very high P/E ratios and difficulty in exceeding ever rising expectations. Stock screens will let you screen for potential high growth companies and many mutual funds offer growth investing styles.

Value

A "value" oriented strategy tries to find companies that are a really good deal, have very low P/E ratios, and are undervalued; but with undiscovered potential. Generally, these companies have suffered big declines from bad news, are out of favor with investors, may be in suffering industries, are promising but undiscovered small-cap companies, or have low expectations of growth or profits. Some of these companies deserve investor skepticism; some may be due to overreaction. The challenge is to know the difference, but it may take a long time for the market to agree with you and be willing to pay a higher price.

When you can find good companies that are really cheap, investors can see big profits so this is a very popular investing style. Moreover, value stocks may be less volatile since they are already beaten down and may have very nice dividend yields due to the new lower stock price. Again, stock screeners and mutual funds help investors use the value approach.

Dividends

Concentrating your investments on stocks that pay dividends provides many benefits. Historically, dividends account for 40% of the stock market's total return and as a group, dividend paying stocks easily outperform non-dividend paying stocks. Of course, the most obvious benefit is that you receive income even if you don't sell the stock. A regular stream of dividends makes it easier to hold stocks for the long term even when they have declined in value. Additionally, steady dividends tend to stabilize or even help increase stock prices because it makes them more attractive and comparable to fixed income investments like bonds and CDs. Moreover, your stock dividends may increase over time whereas bond and CD interest rates are fixed.

There are special considerations to review when looking for good dividend paying stocks. You want to maximize the chance of finding companies that can continue to pay those nice dividends. The highest yielding stocks may not be the best investment. Increasing yields can result from either falling stock prices or rising dividends. High yields may be the result of declining stock prices of companies with declining business fortunes or investors' favor. Be wary of companies that may be about to cut their dividends. Look at the "dividend payout rate" found on many web or brokerage stock pages and avoid those with pay out rates above 50% as unsustainable. Remember to diversify. Many high dividend paying stocks may be clustered in particular industries such as financial companies, utilities, REITs, or telephone companies. Avoid having too many stocks in the same industry and avoid the fate of even many professionals whose overexposed portfolios crashed along with the stocks of high-dividend paying financial companies in the 2008 financial meltdown.

A good long-term dividend strategy is to buy and hold stocks with a good history of raising their dividend rates over many years. Therefore, regardless of the ups and downs of the stock prices, you will still be getting a rising payment from rising dividend rates. The most famous list of companies that match these criteria is the "Standard and Poors Dividend Aristocrats" which lists companies that have increased their dividends for at least 25 years. You can find this list and others here:

- http://www.standardandpoors.com/
- http://dripinvesting.org/Tools/Tools.asp

Here are three websites with a wide variety of free and premium information, tools, dividend screens, and recommended portfolios for dividend paying stocks:

- http://dividenddetective.com/

- http://www.dividend.com/
- http://www.dividendinvestor.com/

When looking for high yield stocks, remember that "preferred" stocks have higher yields than a company's "common" stock and may be an easy way to lock in high yield investments with relatively low price volatility. Additionally, many foreign stocks pay higher dividends than U.S. stocks and are a good source of diversification.

Diversification

Diversification is the strategy of reducing your risk by spreading your savings among different investments so that if one type of investment is doing poorly, it won't devastate your entire savings. We will discuss diversification with "asset allocation" soon, but here I want to emphasize the importance of diversifying your stock portfolio by taking advantage of the many types of stocks available. Consider different types of stocks in different industries, in different parts of the world, and in different size companies. Ensure that too many of your stocks aren't in the same industry because you know most about it, like it the best, or see it on a hot streak. And don't own too much of your company stock even in your 401(k). Diversification is easier to do with funds than individual stocks unless you have a large sum to invest in stocks.

Different economic climates

Certain types of stocks tend to do better in certain types of economic environments. For example, many investors like small company stocks during early bull markets because they are more nimble and aggressive with hoped for higher growth. In bear markets, investors may like dividend paying stocks that can pay them while they wait for the next bull market, utilities that pay nice dividends and have more stable prices, or companies with products that consumers always need to buy such as consumer goods, food, and healthcare. In roaring bull markets, "growth" stocks with great potential do well. Note that different countries and regions don't always have the same market environment at the same time. For example, sometimes when the U.S. and European markets are in a slump, emerging markets may be doing fine, or vice versa.

Stocks versus Bonds

Here are some key differences between stocks and bonds which also illustrate why it's good to have some of both:

- Historically, stocks have returned nearly twice as much as bonds.
- The volatility (wild swings up and down) of bonds is much less than stocks. Both stock and bond prices go up and down. In fact, bonds have had more losing years since WWII than stocks. However, the low volatility of bonds gives peace of mind (low risk, low return). The high volatility of stocks provides more potential for growth and loss (high risk, high return).
- You can make or lose money by selling either stocks or bonds, but if you hold a bond to maturity, you will not lose your original investment.
- If a company goes bankrupt, bond holders have precedence to get paid before stockholders, and preferred stockholders before common stockholders.
- You can get regular income from both stocks and bonds, but there are differences. In early 2013, 410 of the 500 stocks in the S&P 500 paid dividends ranging from 0.06% to 11.66%, with the average being 2.51%. The average of the DJIA yield was 2.87% compared to 3.33% for investment grade corporate bonds. So the average stock dividend is generally less than the average high quality corporate bond yield because the stock investor still hopes to profit from growth. Moreover, a stock dividend is not guaranteed and can be reduced or even eliminated at any time, although they tend to increase slowly as long as the company and economy are doing well. Only bonds pay a predictable income since a bond issuer can only skip a bond coupon payment by defaulting.
- Income from stocks and bonds are taxed differently. Interest from bonds is taxed at the higher, ordinary income rate, the same as wages, while dividends from stocks are taxed at a preferential lower rate, the same as capital gains.

Guru Stock Screens

Let's wrap up this section on stock picking strategies by getting back to my original point that one of the best ways for small stock investors to pick stocks is to follow the lead of the experts. There have been many successful stock investors with many different philosophies, styles, and methods. Frequently these "gurus" concentrate on different combinations of company fundamentals and many have published their methods. This means that others can copy their philosophies by using stock screeners to copy their methods of finding stocks that match their combination of fundamentals. Several services and websites offer pre-set stock screens that enable you to find companies that match the criteria of a wide variety of stock picking gurus. Note however, that all are quick to remind us that getting potential stocks from any stock screen is only the first step that leads to further analysis before picking final selections. Additionally, any stock screen is going to be changing regularly which could lead to frequent trading and fees that eat into your returns. I previously listed websites that enable you to screen stocks for desired criteria and offer pre-set screens. Here are several web sites that offer stock screens of gurus or investment styles.

- http://www.aaii.com/ - In additional to a wealth of information, this non-profit organization offers a huge array of stock screens based upon investment gurus and investment styles for a modest annual or lifetime fee. You can see the criteria behind the screens, their investment styles, and their multi-year performance rates.
- http://validea.com/home/home.asp - For a membership fee, Validea offers a variety of guru screens based upon its interpretation of the guru's methods as well as newsletters.
- http://www.magicformulainvesting.com/ - This site is *free* and based upon Joel Greenblatt's book, *"The Little Book that Beats the Market"*. It uses a "value" investing style to find good businesses selling at bargain prices.

More information

- http://online.wsj.com/public/page/news-fixed-income-Stocks.html - Offers comprehensive information relating to the Stock market.
- http://finance.yahoo.com/Stocks - Lookup information about specific Stocks along with educational articles and calculators. Get the app for your smartphone and synchronize your watch lists between devices.
- www.aaii.com - This non-profit organization provides a wealth of resources, stock screens, education, model portfolios, annual reviews, local chapter meetings, magazines, email newsletters, and plenty more for a modest membership fee.

Summary

- The reason to buy stocks is because historically they have the highest return of any other standard type of investment. From 1928 thru 2012, stocks have returned around 10% per year, including dividends. So if your investment goal is long term, the high *average* return of stocks is one of the best ways to get there.

- These high returns also mean high risks. Stocks have three risks you should consider:
  - You could lose money by selling for less than you bought if for,
  - Stock prices are very volatile with frequent and sometimes large swings up and down, and
  - Stock prices or the stock market in general could be down for a long time, even years.

- Therefore, it's common advice to NOT invest in stocks with money that you may need within the next few years.

- Stocks have high average returns, but high volatility, low inflation risk, and medium liquidity. They are easy to buy and sell, but may have a loss at the time you need the money. Therefore to repeat again -- it's common advice to NOT invest in stocks with money that you may need within the next few years.

- Stocks are easy to buy thru brokerage firms that may offer an increasing array of services and resources such as research reports, stock screeners, online tools, education resources, check cashing, streaming stock quotes, investment ideas, social media, portfolio management tools, mobile apps, and customer service. Discount brokerages enable investors to minimize their trading expenses.

- Fundamentals analysis tries to find good stocks by finding good companies and reviews the companies' business fundamentals to determine which company is going to earn growing profits. Technical analysis reviews past patterns in stock prices, volume, momentum, and investor behavior to try and predict future stock price movements in similar situations.

- The "growth" investment style is perhaps the most popular, especially in strong bull markets. Investors strive to find companies with strong potential for rising profits and stock prices. A "value" oriented strategy tries to find companies that are a really good deal, have very low P/E ratios, and are undervalued; but with undiscovered potential.

- Investing in stocks that pay increasing dividends is one of the best stock picking strategies. Dividend paying stocks tend to grow steadily, stabilize stock prices, pay you even when the price has declined, pay you even without selling the stock, and on average pay almost as much as quality corporate bonds.

- Historically, stocks have returned nearly twice as much as bonds.

- It's not easy for small investors with day jobs to pick good stocks, but there are many resources to help including websites, magazines, newsletters, services, and stock screens.

- For many investors, especially with small investments, mutual funds, ETFs, index funds, and target date funds are a better choice than individual stocks. Consider limiting individual stocks to a small portion of your investment portfolio compared to stock funds.

Chapter Fourteen

Mutual Funds

- What are mutual funds?
- Types of mutual funds.
- Why mutual funds?
- How to choose?

What are mutual funds?

A mutual fund is a professionally managed investment company that pools investors' money to buy an assortment of stocks, bonds, money market instruments, real estate, and other securities generally based upon a particular investment style. Investors buy shares from the mutual fund company or brokers rather than exchange shares with other investors. The fund will continuously issue shares to meet demand or until managers decide to stop issuing new shares because the fund gets too big to manage well. The price for shares of a mutual fund fluctuates as the securities it holds fluctuate, but is set once per day after trading hours. The price is called the fund's net asset value (NAV). There are funds called "closed end" funds that issue a set number of shares in an initial offering similar to a company issuing stock. They have special trading considerations that you should research carefully before investing.

You can purchase some mutual funds directly from the fund company while others can be purchased thru your stockbroker, bank, financial planner, or even insurance agents. Stockbrokers' mutual fund fees, selections, and policies can vary widely so this may be one area you want to review carefully when selecting your stock broker. There are many big companies called fund families that offer a wide variety of mutual funds. Some investors like to pick the best from each company while others like the convenience of being able to exchange funds primarily within one or two fund families.

Types of mutual funds

There are basically three types of mutual funds: money market, bond (fixed income), and stock (equity); but there is an almost endless variety of combinations, sub-categories, and investment styles.

Money market funds – These funds may only invest in high quality, short-term investments from US corporations and Federal, state, or local governments. They try to keep their NAV-price at $1.00. Since the price rarely changes, your return comes solely from dividends, which are in the same low range as savings accounts, CDs, and money market accounts. Notice that "money market FUNDs" are not the same as "money market ACCOUNTS" even if a bank is offering the mutual fund. Money market accounts are federally insured like other bank accounts while money market funds are not - just as other mutual funds are not.

Bond funds – These are also called "fixed income" funds. You can find a bond fund for nearly every type of bond including treasuries, foreign, municipals, high quality corporate, high yield (junk bond) corporate, short/intermediate/long-term, convertibles, mortgage backed, and more.

Stock funds – Also called "equity" funds, you can find many types including growth, value, income, every kind of sector/industry, global, international, emerging markets, regional, country specific, index, target date, small/mid/large cap, balanced, contrarian, bear market, and more.

We will review several specialized types in more detail in the next chapter for investors who want to make investing as easy as possible: balanced, target date, and index funds, but let's continue surveying the basics everyone should know.

Why mutual funds

Risk / reward

As usual, let's review this investment's risks and rewards, but with mutual funds, it's a little trickier because there are so many types.

Money market funds - Since the risk of losing money is extremely low, I hope you can predict by now that the reward will also be very low in the form of dividends. Liquidity risk is very low since you can easily redeem your shares, almost certainly for the same price you paid for them. The risk of not keeping up with inflation is very high since the low dividend yield usually is less than the inflation rate. Therefore, money market funds are best for keeping savings that you may need soon or really want to keep safe, but it will not grow fast enough to meet long-term goals such as college and retirement savings.

Bond funds – Bond funds are riskier than money market funds since you can lose money, but that means they yield more. Bond funds have many of the same risks as individual bonds – you can lose money from interest rate changes, early redemptions, and defaults – but the risk is spread out among many different bonds and investors, which is a key advantage of mutual funds. However, a key difference is that while you can lose money from fluctuating bond fund prices, you won't lose money from individual bonds if you hold a bond to maturity (unless the company defaults on your bond). But bond funds have no maturity date, so the price is constantly fluctuating, although rarely as wildly as stocks. Bond funds are more liquid (much easier to buy and sell) than individual bonds. Whether they can keep up with inflation depends upon the type of bond and its yield.

Stock/equity funds – As you probably guessed, stock funds have basically the same risks and rewards as individual stocks – high volatility, risk of losing money, easy to buy and sell, good investment to beat inflation, and historically among the best returns, *on average over time*. They are the riskiest of the three types of mutual funds we have discussed, which means they also have the best potential for rewards, which can come from both dividends and price appreciation. Stock funds provide easier diversification than individual stocks.

Combo funds – Since different investments have different risks, it's natural to want to mix and match them. In fact, there are several types of mutual funds that strive to balance these risks including target date, life cycle, and balanced funds, which we will discuss shortly. They combine stocks, bonds, and sometimes money market funds and strive for a combination of safety, income, and modest capital gains.

Since there are a huge variety of mutual funds, there is a huge variety of risk among them. This is especially true based upon how diversified a fund is among a variety of different types of investments. A fund that invests in just one type of stock or bond such as one industry sector, world region, country, or market capitalization will be *less* diversified and *more* risky than a broad based fund that invests in many companies across multiple industries, countries, and market caps. Some mutual fund screens may include risk/volatility ratings so you can compare them with other funds in their category and among fund types.

While we are talking about risk, let me repeat that no mutual fund, not even money market funds, are federally insured against losses, but you do get tax breaks for losses as with most investments when it is time to report them as income.

Advantages

Investing in mutual funds is easier, less risky, takes less time, and costs less cash than investing in individual stocks or bonds.

Diversification

Investing in mutual funds is the easiest way to diversify your investments among a broad range of stocks and bonds. It is much less risky than owning a few individual stocks. If one of your few individual stocks crash, it will damage your portfolio much more than if one stock in a mutual fund that owns 20 or more stocks. So investing in a mutual fund gives you instant diversification that lessens the risk to your portfolio. You can further diversify your risks with the types and number of mutual funds you invest in which we will review more thoroughly soon.

Professional management

Since most of us don't have the time or expertise to consistently pick individual stocks or bonds, it's nice to turn to experts who hopefully can do better. Investing in mutual funds is one of the best and cheapest ways to get professional management for our investments.

Time savings

In addition to lacking the expertise, many of us lack the time to fully research many individual stocks as well as monitor their continued performance. Picking a diversified mutual fund is much easier with less time.

Affordability

You frequently can invest for a small amount of money, both for your initial investment and additional, future investments. Different funds set different requirements. Investors frequently buy stocks in "lots" of 100 shares that can cost thousands of dollars, and it costs even more to diversify properly among many stocks and bonds. However, many funds will let you invest in a broad based mutual fund for as little as a $1000, and some require even less.

Periodic investments

Many funds make it easy to regularly invest small amounts in existing mutual fund accounts. You can setup automatic transfers of set amounts from your paycheck or bank account each pay period or month to buy more shares. This is a great way to follow one of our basic financial principles to put your savings on autopilot. It also has the advantage of following an investing method called "dollar cost averaging" in which your regular, set amount automatically buys more shares when the price is low and fewer shares when the price is high which averages out the cost of each share.

This is a great way to save for practically any goal, not just retirement or college. Let me use this opportunity to throw in another example of the magic of compound interest. Investing just $150 automatically, every month returning 8% would give you $27,625 at the end of ten years and $88,942 after 20. For more information on the magic of compound interest, see the chapter at the end of this book.

Liquidity

Mutual funds are easy to buy and sell thru your stockbroker, financial advisor, or directly from fund companies, but you also want some confidence that the price hasn't dropped a lot since your purchase. Therefore, tailor your investment to the type of mutual fund best suited for your time horizon for needing your money back: money market funds for absolute safety in the short run, the appropriate bond funds for medium term risk and time horizon, and stock funds for long-term savings. Considering your "time horizon" for when you will need your cash is the most important investing rule I want you to learn, as it will lead you to the appropriate TYPE of investment for your specific investment goal.

Services

Many mutual fund companies offer services such as dividend re-investment plans, check writing, telephone and web switching between family funds, regular account and tax statements, and periodic deposits and withdrawals.

Disadvantages

The biggest disadvantage of using mutual funds for your investments is the range of fees and expenses they accrue to manage the fund. These costs can significantly reduce your earnings. 1.5% costs may seem small, but if a mutual fund had a 7.5% total return, then its 1.5% expense ratio would reduce your earnings by 20%. Here is an example from a SEC.gov publication:

If you invested $10,000 in a fund that produced a 10% annual return before expenses and had annual operating expenses of 1.5%, then after 20 years you would have roughly $49,725. But if the fund had expenses of only 0.5%, then you would end up with $60,858 — an 18% difference.

Buying and selling individual stocks result in relatively small fees only when you buy and sell them, while mutual funds' expenses reduce your returns as long as you hold the fund shares – regardless of whether the price goes up or down. There are a wide variety of fees when you buy and sell a fund and annual expenses eat at your returns indefinitely. Here is a list of the most common.

Some funds charge a fee, called a "load", when you buy or sell the fund. These loads are paid to the agent who sells you the fund and can range up to 8.5%. These types of funds are called "front-end" or "back-end" load funds depending upon when they charge you the load/fee. Think about how extraordinary these funds would have to perform to overcome that 5 – 8.5% load -- and then avoid them! You can always find plenty of "no-load" funds that do at least as well without handicapping yourself with a hefty up-front fee that is going to be difficult to overcome later. Paying fees reduce your returns.

Additionally, all funds, including no-load funds, have a variety of other fees and expenses needed to run the company including: purchase and redemption fees, exchange fees when exchanging funds within the same company, account fees for maintaining your account, management fees, 12b-1 fees for advertising etc, distribution fees, service fees, and "other" expenses. Funds may have several classes of shares (A, B, or C) each with a different level or combination of these fees and expenses.

How to choose

There are thousands of mutual funds based upon every imaginable investing style. Some try to balance or hedge risks, combine stocks and bonds, and even try to go opposite of the market. So how do you choose?

The most obvious way is not generally the most profitable. It is so tempting to buy the hottest funds of the month and hope they continue to zoom up. Unfortunately, by the time you spot that hot fund, its rise may already be nearing its end and you may even be buying at its peak. This is how too many investors buy *high* and sell *low*. Plenty of funds have short-term hot streaks, but the top performing funds of any quarter change rapidly and frequently. To be spotlighted may mean that they are different from other funds, take on more risk, are less diversified, or got lucky with a pick or two. **Alas, past performance is not a reliable indicator of future performance.**

Your mutual fund investing will be more profitable in the end if you choose good funds with strong *long-term* performance records, low expenses, tax efficiency, and proven managers.

Long term records

Look for funds that consistently rank near the top of their categories over *multiple* time periods. While *immediate* past performance is not a guarantee of continued future performance, it is important to review a fund's *long-term* past performance over multiple time periods. Review a fund's performance over the past 1, 3, 5, and 10 years performance to find funds that aren't necessarily hot now, but have demonstrated *consistent* performance over many years and several types of market climates. For example, review a fund's performance during the 2008 crash, 2009 bottom, and 2010-2016 bull recovery to see how a fund performed in several market environments. Compare the records of your potential pick with its peers and an appropriate index that matches your fund; for example, match a small company fund against a small company index.

Cost of investing

The more costs you pay to invest, the less you get in returns. The higher the expense ratio for a mutual fund, the less likely it can beat its competitors or even match its equivalent index. You cannot reliably predict a fund's performance, but you can easily see its costs and expense ratio that you will be paying indefinitely.

One of the most important factors in choosing a mutual fund is to compare its "expense ratio" which is the total of all its annual expenses divided by its average net assets. The lower a fund's expenses and fees, the more your investments will grow.

You can find this ratio on the fund's website or prospectus as well as numerous websites that provide mutual fund comparison information. Compare a fund's expense ratio with its peers and avoid any that are much higher than average. Average expense ratios can vary over time and by fund type, but in general, avoid stock funds with ratios above 1.5 and bond funds above 1.0. Moreover, studies have found that funds with expense ratios that are among the lowest 20% in their categories also tend to be among the best in their categories in performance.

Here is a website where you can look up and compare expenses for most mutual funds: http://www.sec.gov/investor/tools/mfcc/mfcc-int.htm

Tax – efficiency

For individual stocks and bonds as well as their mutual funds, you will have to pay taxes on your dividends (unless they are tax free government bonds) and capital gains taxes when you sell them for a profit. However, there is a key tax difference with mutual funds. Mutual funds buy and sell securities throughout the year and shareholders will have to pay taxes on those "capital gains distributions" annually even if you don't sell your shares or do buy them late in the year. Mutual funds are required to report their tax efficiency and you may want to compare this factor when selecting funds.

Managers' performance

Since professional management expertise is one of the things we are paying for when investing in mutual funds instead of our own stock picking, many experts recommend we review the records of individual manager's when buying or selling a particular mutual fund – even to consider selling a fund when a manager leaves. This may be a nice factor for other experts with time to review, but I'm not convinced this is something that individual investors can pay much attention to. How many of us really know the difference between the shooting stars and real star performers of the mutual fund world as we do in our favorite sports world? Nonetheless, some web mutual fund screeners do provide this information.

Selling your funds

Even good managers can have a poor year or two, so bailing out of a fund at the first sign of weakness is not necessarily worthwhile. Nonetheless, you may wish to consider selling a fund that consistently trails its peers, has poor performance after a manager leaves, gets too big for the managers to find enough good investments, or changes the investing style you are comfortable with. Remember that frequent trading of one fund for the latest star doesn't mean that your future return will be anywhere nearly as good as the hot performance that got your attention. Past short-term performance does not predict future performance.

Getting fund information

Bond funds can be fairly self-explanatory, but with others, it's very important that you fully understand what type of mutual fund you are getting into. Many of the largest mutual fund companies have offices in major metropolitan areas, but as usual, the best way to get information, set up an account, and manage an account is probably thru their website. Telephones also work for those who like to press 1 – 3 – 4 - 1 – 3 etc. to wait on hold to talk to a real person.

You can get the most detailed information about mutual funds from their "prospectus" which is a pamphlet that is more than just pages of dense fine-print for the lawyers. In fact, the Securities and Exchange Commission (SEC) requires them to include specific information that actually helps potential investors compare different funds. You can find information about the fund's investment goals, performance over the past ten years before and after taxes, fees, summary profile, and other information. You can obtain a prospectus from the fund and many websites, including the SEC's.

Many investing publications and websites provide suggested, mutual funds including these:

- http://www.kiplinger.com/tool/investing/T041-S000-kiplingers-25-favorite-fund/index.php
- http://www.aaii.com/model-portfolios

When choosing mutual funds, pick funds that combine low expenses with strong long-term performance.

Fund screeners, especially fee-based ones, often let you select from additional categories such as analyst ratings, risk/volatility, stewardship of shareholder interest, insider investing, tax efficiency, comparison to indexes, and more. Brokerage websites frequently provide mutual fund screeners. Here are websites with mutual fund screens:

- http://screen.morningstar.com/FundSelector.html - Includes a wide variety of data to screen for.
- http://www.kiplinger.com/tool/investing/T041-S001-mutual-fund-finder/index.php - Screen funds by type, performance, and fees.

These websites offer a wide variety of free resources about mutual funds:

- http://finance.yahoo.com/funds/ - It provides mutual fund articles, news, fund screener, prospectus', top funds, and fund family information.
- http://www.sec.gov/investor.shtml - The US government website offers publications, information, calculators, a database to review brokers and advisors, and a site to submit complaints about problems with mutual funds and other investment companies.

Summary

- There are basically three types of mutual funds: money market, bond (fixed income), and stock (equity); but there is an almost endless variety of combinations, sub-categories, and investment styles.
- Money market funds are best for keeping savings that you may need soon or really want to keep safe, but it will not grow fast enough to beat inflation or meet long-term goals such as college and retirement savings.
- Bond funds are easy to buy and sell, and pay monthly income that may beat inflation, depending upon the type of bonds. Prices fluctuate from many factors, but have much less volatility than stock funds. They are safe for mid-term savings goals (3-5 years) and provide diversification for your investments.
- Stock funds have basically the same risks and rewards as individual stocks – high volatility, risk of losing money when selling, easy to buy and sell, good growth to beat inflation, and historically among the best returns, *on average over time*. They are best for long-term savings goals, time horizons greater than five years.
- Investing in mutual funds is easier, less risky, takes less time, and costs less cash than investing in individual stocks or bonds.
- Mutual Funds provide diversification, professional management, time savings, automatic investments, little cash, good liquidity, and many services when managed thru big fund companies.
- Disadvantages may include high expenses that reduce our returns. There is no reason to buy funds with "load" charges that take a huge chunk of your savings without performance that is any better than no-load funds. Just say no to load funds even if your advisor pushes them to get his cut.
- The most common way people select funds is also the worst – choosing the hottest performers of the moment and buying high. Past performance is not a reliable indicator of future performance.
- Choose funds with good *long-term* performance over the past 1, 3, and 5 years; low expense ratios; good managers; and tax efficiency if in taxable accounts.
- Many websites provide recommendations and fund screeners so you can filter fund types, styles, long-term performance, ratings, and many other factors.

Chapter Fifteen

Special Types of Funds

- Exchange Traded Funds (ETFs)
- Index Funds
- Balanced Funds
- Target Date Funds

I hope by now that you have an understanding of the basic investments: bonds, stocks, and mutual funds. Now let's turn to several different types of funds that may be the perfect investments for most people, most of the time: inexpensive, easy, and set and forget. Investing can be as easy or as challenging as you want and challenging is not necessary more profitable. It's these types of funds that make investing especially easy.

Exchange Traded Funds (ETFs)

- What are ETFs
- Why ETFs
- Risks / Rewards
- Strategies
- More Information

What are ETFs

Exchange Traded Funds (ETFs) are funds that offer the convenience and diversification of mutual funds, but trade like stocks. You can buy and sell ETFs during the trading day at the current price rather than only at the end of the day at an unknown price as with mutual funds.

Rather than being actively managed with managers picking stocks, ETFs usually aim to match the performance of a specific benchmark index, but some track commodities, foreign currencies, and other alternative investments. There are a wide variety of ETFs that track a wide variety of indexes including broad stock indexes, small/mid/large capitalization companies, investment styles such as growth or value, global stocks, country or region specific, industry/sector such as telecommunications or healthcare, and a wide variety of bond types. Some indexes have even been created specifically for ETFs to track.

ETFs are a relatively new type of investment. The first ones were created in 1993 and the number has more or less doubled every few years. By 2017, there were over 4500. As they grow in popularity, we are seeing more and more types including more complex types such as actively managed (rather than only following an index), income (pays dividends and interest), leveraged (using borrowed money to magnify moves), inverse (tracking the opposite of an index), and life cycle (combining stocks and bonds for different stages of one's life).

With mutual funds, it is important for investors to understand the investment goals and style of the fund. With ETFs, it is also important to understand how the index works that the ETF is tracking. You can get the fund prospectus, annual reports, and performance data from the funds' websites.

Why ETFs

ETFs provide investors with a flexible, diversified pool of securities, but with much lower costs than most mutual funds. ETFs have much lower expense ratios because most are passively managed without high management expenses, 12b-1 fees, sale/redemption loads, or commissions from frequent trading. Some ETFs with rock bottom expense ratios can be nearly 1% less than equivalent mutual funds giving you nearly an extra point of return every year that is not dependent on any other factors such as market behavior or management skill. ETFs that follow traditional stock or bond indexes have the lowest expense ratios, generally under 0.2%, while ETFs that follow more exotic or complicated strategies have higher expense rations, perhaps over 0.5-0.6% - or even over 1% which is in the same realm as actively managed funds. Furthermore, Morningstar data shows that in most categories, the group of funds with the lowest expenses regularly out-performs the group of funds with the highest expenses. Here is another example where simpler is cheaper and likely better for most people for most of their investments.

Since ETFs trade just like stocks they have more flexibility than mutual funds. Investors can buy them at intra-day prices, use margin (borrowing) to buy them, employ stop and limit orders to automatically buy and sell at certain prices, and even sell them short (bet the price will go down). ETFs tend to be more tax efficient than mutual funds. Because ETFs don't trade their securities as often, they have less capital gains distributions each year than mutual funds that require taxes to be paid even when you didn't sell any shares or the NAV-price didn't rise much.

Is it any wonder that the popularity of ETFs is booming? However, I hope by now you are asking to hear the flipside before you rush in. The main disadvantage of ETFs is that you buy them through your broker and pay a commission every time you buy and sell, whereas you can often buy mutual funds directly from the fund company for free. Thus, ETFs may not be suitable for regular, small investments or withdrawals as mutual funds are perfect for. However, we are starting to see some discount brokers offering commission-free trades on select ETFs so this could be another factor to consider when choosing your discount broker.

Risks / Rewards

For the most part, ETFs have risks similar to mutual funds; the stocks, bonds, and commodities it tracks; and its investment goals. However, ETFs may have some unique issues to be aware of. Smaller, newer, or more exotic ETFs may not match their benchmark index well. Before investing, you may wish to compare funds' performance with their benchmarks. Morningstar tracks many indexes here:

- http://news.morningstar.com/index/indexReturn.html.

Older ETFs tracking a broad, established index tend to have lower expenses and work well with less risk. While the newer, smaller, more complicated, and less diversified ETFs are often more expensive and have more issues and risks. This should reinforce our basic principle that to get higher returns, you necessarily take on more risk of volatility and potential loss.

Strategies

Remember that the best way to choose funds is to select low cost funds with strong *long*-term records. A problem with investing in ETFs is that, while they usually have low costs, few have long-term records to review since ETFs have exploded in popularity and numbers very recently. Even some of the indexes that certain ETFs track have been recently created just for that ETF. Sometimes you can find historical data about what an index would have done in the past, but remember that recent, *short*-term performance is not a reliable predictor of future performance.

You can use ETFs to meet a wide variety of financial goals including "buy and hold" investing, short-term active trading, and income. They are also great for diversification and asset allocation among stocks, bonds, real estate, commodities, indexes, inverse index, income, sectors, international, and more. You can either find an ETF with a style that meets a need or first choose a category and then research the available ETFs within that category. Either way, review its expense ratio, as much of a long-term record as exists, prospectus, risk/volatility ranking from ETF websites, tracking index, and comparison with its peers and alternatives. Ensure that you understand the benchmark index it is tracking and the particular risk/reward relationship of that particular ETF and type of investments in the ETF.

More information

Frequently, the websites that are strong with mutual fund resources are also good with ETF resources, news, screeners, tools, rankings, and model portfolios including these:

- http://finance.yahoo.com/etf/
- http://www.etftrends.com/
- http://www.morningstar.com/Cover/ETFs.aspx
- http://www.xtf.com/
- http://www.nasdaq.com/investing/etfs/

Index Funds

- What are index funds?
- Comparing ETFs and index funds.

- Index fund strategies.

What are index funds?

Most investors have an itch to "beat the market", to do better than the average; but that is so hard to do. Few investors can beat the markets consistently – not even professionals. However, there are ways to consistently **match** the market – and do it with tiny expenses and broad diversification while beating the majority of professionals and making it really simple.

Use "index funds" which are mutual funds that own a pool of stocks or bonds that seek to match a specific benchmark index rather than use active managers to pick investments to try to beat the market. Index mutual funds are similar to exchange traded funds (ETFs). Usually, these have very low expenses and a wide variety to choose from. Included are traditional broad market indexes such as the S&P 500, investment styles like value and growth, small/mid/large cap companies, commodities such as gold and oil, sectors like technology and financials, internationals such as emerging market and country specific, and newer more exotic styles including leveraged and inverse indexing.

The attractions of index funds are the rock bottom expenses, simplicity, and the promise of matching their benchmarks, which more than 60% of actively managed mutual funds routinely fail to do. Study after study has confirmed what you can see for yourself when reviewing actively managed mutual funds on any web mutual fund screener: most actively managed funds in most categories fail to beat their benchmarks consistently.

Is this really that surprising considering the higher expenses of actively managed funds over index funds and ETFs, as well as the difficulty in predicting the future? A study by Dimensional Fund Advisors found another reason: that only 25% of stocks accounted for all the gains in the market index. If a manager missed having many of that top 25%, then they would have a hard time matching the market index.

Comparing ETFs and Index funds

ETFs and index mutual funds are very similar but have some differences. Index funds date from the 1970's versus 1993 for ETFs, but ETFs have exploded in popularity recently with more than 4500 compared to over 300 index mutual funds. Most of the differences relate to the differences between ETFs and mutual funds in general. You can trade ETFs throughout the trading day, but index funds, like all mutual funds, are bought and sold at the end of the day. You buy ETFs through your brokerage account with flexible buy/sell methods, but pay a trading commission, which may not be attractive if you want to invest regular, small amounts. You can buy index mutual funds straight from the fund company for no fee. Index mutual funds have a minimum investment amount, EFTs don't. Index funds have really low expense fees, but ETFs are even lower.

Index strategies

Remember that successful fund investing is based upon picking low cost funds with solid long-term records compared to their appropriate benchmark or the S&P 500. Always pay attention to the expense ratio of funds – even index funds can have widely varying expense ratios. Funds following broad based indexes should have little problem meeting their benchmarks, but as you review funds with a narrower or more exotic focus, review how well they match their benchmark over the long-term and compare to their peers.

You can use low-cost index funds to meet most investment goals by mixing and matching from a large selection. Investors can diversify with as few as three funds: total US stock, international stock, and total bond divided into whatever asset allocation percentages you prefer. This also makes annual rebalancing among them super easy. Others may wish to expand their selection to emphasize preferred styles such as value, growth, income, small cap, emerging market, tech, etc. Some people use a few basic index funds for their core holding and then allocate a small amount to beat the market in some area of interest. This "core and explore" strategy is useful whether you stick entirely with index funds and ETFs or "explore" with other investments such as actively managed mutual funds or individual stocks.

Most index fund investors like the simplicity as well as low fees and confidence of matching the market. You can allocate your investments among a few funds to meet your changing goals and age. This simplicity may also lead index investors to outperform most active traders, not only because index funds consistent beat most actively managed funds and have lower fees, but also because they are more likely to be "buy and hold" investors rather than chasing the hottest investment of the day.

Balanced Funds

Investing in index and ETF funds is one of the easiest ways to invest, but there are other, even simpler funds to use. A single "balanced fund" could be the only fund some investors need because it already combines stocks and bonds in a single fund so you don't have to worry about choosing both, diversifying your investments, and rebalancing your assets between them. Balanced funds seek a balance between growth and stability by combining riskier stocks with steadier bonds, which is what most investors should do on their own or thru a fund. An easy and safe investment strategy would be to use a balanced fund for the core of your investments and then fine tune it with additional desired investments with a small portion of your assets.

Balanced funds have several advantages. They are low cost, automatically rebalance their stock/bond mix to keep the popular 60/40 balance, and are less volatile than stock-only funds. This steady approach to investing appears to lead to better investors who are more likely to stick to a "buy and hold" strategy since their investments are less volatile. *Morningstar* data show that many investors don't actually do as well as their funds do because of frequent trades in and out of different investments; whereas investors in balanced funds generally match their fund's performance because the lower volatility and steady performance usually leads to more "buy and hold" and less panicked selling and chasing performance elsewhere.

Remember to always review the flipside of any investment. Note that because balanced funds are safer (less volatile, more diversified) than stock funds, that also means they have lower returns during the good times and less losses during the bad times. A one-size fits all investment may not be right for everyone's goals and age. A key problem with balanced funds is that they are mostly steady with a mix of 60% stocks and 40% bonds, which is not ideal for every age group or risk profile. This leads us to our last type of special funds: target date funds.

Target Date Funds

Target date funds are the simplest type of investment you can find. You can choose one fund, setup your automatic savings deposits, and forget it. They are designed for your long-term savings goals such as saving for college or retirement. You choose a fund primarily based upon its target date, so if you plan to retire around 2028, you could choose a 2025 or 2030 target date fund (retirement funds are setup to target each five year period and college funds every year).

Target date funds are made up of a basket of other mutual or ETF funds that include stocks, bonds, and sometimes commodities and cash. They are so simple to use because they are low cost, already diversified, and change its allocation to become safer and less volatile the close you get to the target date. Therefore, you do not need to worry about any of the investment strategies we will be discussing next such as diversification, asset allocation, and rebalancing.

When you are young and far from retirement, you should invest mostly in stocks that can grow your savings the best. When a bear market comes, you have plenty of time to recover from it and take advantage of it by buying more, cheap stocks. As you approach retirement, you should steadily move some of your investments from volatile stocks to safer bonds because you will have less time to recover from a down market before you need your money. Note however, that even in retirement, you will still need some stocks to last you the ten, twenty, or thirty years you will be withdrawing money in retirement. Target date funds take care of this for you in two stages, becoming more conservative as your target date approaches, but perhaps still with 50% stocks, and then more conservative with mostly bonds and cash a certain number of years after retirement.

Target date funds aim for this simplicity, but are not all alike as different companies manage these allocations differently with different percentage mixes at different stages. Even with the same target date, some companies may have 15% more in stock than other companies at any given time. At some point after the fund's target date, all the assets are shifted to produce relatively safe income so down markets won't wreck your portfolio as you are trying to withdraw money from it. However, another big difference among companies is when their target date fund reaches this final allocation. Some companies make the switch at the target date while others may go as long as 30 years after it in hopes of continuing to grow your investments in retirement. Additionally, some companies include more types of investments such as foreign bonds, real estate, or commodities for greater diversification. Since a company's target date fund is a collection of its other funds, you can expect that the performance, expense ratios, yield, and volatility will vary between the different fund companies.

Target date funds are very common in your college 529 savings accounts and retirement 401(k) type accounts and you will probably only have one company choice. If you don't choose a 401(k) fund when you start a new job, chances are you will be automatically placed in the appropriate target date fund. You can adjust the choices to your risk comfort level by picking a different target date. For example, instead of the expected target of 2030, you could choose the 2025 fund to be safer or the 2035 fund in hopes of getting more return for a longer period. If your 401(k) choices are poor with high fees, you can always contribute enough to get your company match and save more in your own IRA or even taxable accounts.

In your IRA or taxable accounts, you can choose from many different fund companies and as we saw earlier, they can vary widely. As usual, review their long- term performance and expense ratios. Expense ratios among target date funds can vary by more than a percentage point and even small difference in expense ratios can be extra important when saving for retirement and compounding over decades. Try to avoid target date funds with an expense ratio much over 1% and know that some are even under 0.2%. In addition to comparing the usual fund costs and long-term performance, with target date funds, you should also compare the asset allocation mix, goals, and timing to ensure they are consistent with your risk tolerance. Find this information in the fund prospectus or website.

Target date funds are the perfect *one* fund for "set it and forget it", but you can always set aside a small portion of your savings in some other interesting fund or investment. Even if you do "set it and forget it," as you approach retirement, you may want to review your fund's asset allocation strategy as it approaches the target date and beyond. Many people were surprised at how much most of these funds fell during the 2008 crash because they had a bigger percentage of stocks than realized.

Summary

- Investing can be as easy or as challenging as you want and challenging is not necessary more profitable. ETFs, index, balanced, and target date funds all make investing easy for anyone.
- Exchange Traded Funds (ETFs) offer the convenience and diversification of mutual funds, but trade like stocks. You can buy and sell ETFs during the trading day at the current price rather than only at the end of the day at an unknown price

as with mutual funds. Rather than being actively managed with managers picking stocks, ETFs aim to match the performance of a specific benchmark index.

- You can use ETFs to meet a wide variety of financial goals including "buy and hold" investing, short-term active trading, and income. They are also great for diversification and asset allocation among stocks, bonds, real estate, commodities, indexes, inverse index, income, sectors, international, and more.

- Use "index" mutual funds to consistently **match** the market – and do it with tiny expenses and broad diversification while beating the majority of professionals and making it really simple. They are similar to ETFs by tracking an index of stocks, bonds, or alternative investments without active management as with other mutual funds. Further diversify by investing in several types of index funds.

- EFTs and index funds have the lowest expenses of any funds, often more than a full 1% less than actively managed mutual funds. Picking low fee investments is the easiest way to increase your investing returns.

- 60% of actively managed *mutual funds* fail to consistently match the market indexes, but most ETFs and index funds do.

- Investors can diversify with as few as three funds: total US stock, international stock, and total bond divided into whatever asset allocation percentages you prefer. This also makes annual rebalancing among them super easy.

- A single "balanced fund" could be the only fund some investors need because it already combines stocks and bonds in a 60/40 asset allocation that seeks a balance between growth and stability.

- Target date funds are the simplest type of investment you can find. You can choose one fund, setup your automatic savings deposits, and forget it. They are designed for your long-term savings goals such as saving for college or retirement. They stay diversified and rebalance to become more conservative as your target date approaches.

- Any of these funds can be used as your "core" investments and then expand your diversification with a small amount of other funds or individual stocks to emphasize your preferred styles such as value, growth, income, small cap, emerging market, tech, etc.

Chapter Sixteen

Investing Strategies

- Dollar cost averaging
- Diversification
- Asset allocation
- Rebalancing
- Buy and hold vs market timing
- Surviving a bear market
- Your investment plan
- Investment do's and don'ts

We have discussed the need to always review an investment's risk versus reward characteristics and then reviewed a wide variety of investments appropriate for average investors from the basic building blocks of bonds and stocks to an array of mutual funds and ETFs, running the spectrum from challenging to simple investments. Now let's use these principles and building blocks to discuss strategies that will increase the chances that our savings will grow to meet a lifetime of financial goals.

Most investors would like to find the right investment to get high returns with little risk. You many even have seen the late night infomercials or encountered that pushy financial salesman, but unless you just started reading this book here, you should be well aware that high rewards bring high risk and low risks mean low returns. We also have seen that we need a good return to beat inflation and better meet our long term savings goals such as saving for college or retirement. We fear losing money when the market goes down, but also fear *not* making money when the market goes up.

So what is an investor to do with these competing problems? Well, thankfully there are investing strategies available that will help us lower risks while still aiming to get a good return. Note that I said *lower* risk not *eliminate* risk. We will start with basic strategies including dollar cost averaging, diversification, asset allocation, rebalancing, and buy and hold before ending with a discussion of how to use all of this to create your own financial plan to meet your personal savings goals.

Dollar cost averaging

"Dollar cost averaging" is the strategy of investing a set amount on a regular basis to average high and low prices. This is what you do when you automatically invest in your 401(k) and college 529 accounts each pay period or month, but you can also do it for any long-term savings goal. Most mutual fund companies make this particularly easy and you can avoid sales commissions. Also check with your online broker, but with stocks and ETFs, you will mostly be paying commissions.

The point of dollar cost averaging is that investing a set amount regularly, automatically means you are buying more of an investment when it has declined and is cheap, and fewer shares of an investment that has risen and is expensive. This is also a great way for small savings amounts to build up over time with less risk that you are buying all in at the top. This strategy also helps you survive market ups and downs with less emotion because you know your strategy is automatically buying more and less shares at the right times.

Diversification

As we have seen, there are many kinds of investments and different kinds do better or worse at different times and in different economic and market conditions. Different investments have different risk/reward ratios, volatility, interest rate risk, likelihood of beating inflation, liquidity risks, and income potential. So it is a good investment strategy to own a variety of investments that can increase your chances of doing well during the good times, limit the damage during the bad markets, handle different kinds of risks, and offer different kinds of rewards. This is called diversification and is one of the most important investment strategies you should practice. I have discussed risks and rewards of specific investments. Diversification is the strategy investors use to manage their risk / reward ratio across their entire portfolio.

Diversification begins with the basic building blocks of stocks, bonds, and cash, individually or thru mutual funds or ETFs. Diversifying in stocks, bonds, and cash gives you some of the benefits of each. In particular, you get the long-term growth of stocks when the market is good, and less volatility and losses when the market is bad. You can further diversify by dividing stocks and bonds into subcategories. For example, you can diversify your stocks among U.S. and foreign, large and small cap (businesses), growth and value, or among industry sectors (tech, health, consumables, utilities, etc). Bonds can be diversified among short/intermediate/long term, Treasuries and corporate, or US and foreign.

Many investors, especially young investors, have grown leery of stocks after the two bear markets around 2002 and 2008. There was much press about this being the "lost decade" for investing, but then the stock market rebounded with one of the longest ever bull markets. Numerous studies have consistently shown that stocks outperform bonds over the long-term. The long-term means every rolling 20 and 30 year period and almost every 10 year time period. So the evidence shows that, over the long term, stocks are the best way to beat inflation, grow your investments, and meet your long-term savings goals – especially for retirement. Diversification makes it easier to ride out the volatile swings of stocks by smoothing out both the up and down swings.

Some people question whether diversification is really all that important given that in 2008, nearly every type of investment plunged. However, not everything dropped equally. Bonds did not drop as much as stocks and within both, some types dropped less than others. For example, the usual "defensive" type stocks of consumer staples, health care, and utilities dropped much less than the S&P 500 average as was true in previous bear markets. Some bonds such as certain Treasuries even made money. Investors who were diversified in higher percentages of bonds did better than those with lower percentages of bonds.

So diversification is still one of the best investment strategies to lower the overall volatility of your portfolio. 2008 was an extreme event when many different parts of the United States and world economy blew up around the same time and only the third time since WWII that a bear market dropped more than 40%. Diversification still works well to protect against more normal, single cause events, such as the dot.com bubble or a hit in one industry, region, or investment style. Diversification has worked well in most other market downturns including severe ones such as 2000-02. The bottom line is that good diversification does not guarantee that you won't ever lose money, but it is the best guarantee for doing better in down markets than investors who do not diversify well.

Diversifying among a variety of asset types positions your portfolio to face the uncertainties of the future. Since we don't know which assets will do well or poorly in the future, diversification helps us be ready to take advantage of whichever one does well and be less impacted by whichever one does poorly.

Asset allocation

Diversifying your investments is one of the most important strategies for investing, but how do you do it? Asset allocation is dividing your investments among different types of investments that fluctuate independently of each other, in investment lingo, have "uncorrelated performance". It's not simply a matter of buying more than one type of investment. You allocate your assets among different types of investments that do not routinely move in the same direction at the same time. Owning a hotel stock and an airline ETF would not be diversified because they both will decline when the travel sector is hurting.

You should first choose the asset types you want to diversify with and then the percentage you want to allocate to each. The asset types with the least correlation (most of the time) are stocks, bonds, cash, and real estate so these are what most investors should use to diversify. You can further diversify within these asset allocations; for example, growth and value, large/mid/small cap, U.S. and foreign, or among industries. However, this is less important because most assets within the same type have very close correlations in performance. Most will go up and down closely together. More specifically, all plunge during bear markets, but tend to rise in different amounts during bull markets. For example, small cap and value stocks tend to do very well at the beginning of bull markets, while large cap and growth stocks do better later. So some investors vary their asset allocations somewhat during different market environments, but always remember that the future is hard to predict.

How do you choose among them for your asset allocation percentage mix? How you allocate your assets should depend upon your time horizon for needing your savings, your risk tolerance, and your investing goals.

The most important consideration when choosing your asset allocation percentages is your "time horizon" – how long will it be before you need your money? The longer it is until you need your money, the greater percentage you should invest in stocks. For example, saving for retirement, young people in their twenties, thirties, and forties should have most of their investments in stocks, perhaps 80-90%. Even with the inevitable bear market, they will have plenty of time to recover and even use the bear market to buy more stock at bargain prices. As people get older and closer to the time they will need their retirement savings, they can allocate a lesser percentage to stocks and shift to less volatile bonds. (See the chapters on *"Saving for Retirement"* and *"Spending in Retirement"* for more details.) The same is true when saving for the kids' college. As their time horizon gets within five years of college, shift your asset allocation percentages mostly to bonds from stocks to preserve your savings, because there is less time to recover from a bear market that can last five years (perhaps 30% stocks/70% bonds).

You can find plenty of suggested asset allocation models for a variety of ages and needs, but feel free to adjust them based upon your "risk tolerance". If the inevitable bear market is going to cause you to miss sleep or sell all of your stocks, then it is better to keep a lower percentage of stocks in your asset allocation target, so the stomach-churning volatility will be less and it will be easier to ride out the inevitable downturns. There is plenty of research to suggest that the classic 60/40 stock/bond asset allocation provides a return almost as good as a higher stock percentage over the long term, but with much less volatility in the short term.

Also, adjust your asset allocation based upon the priority of your investing goals, which may be to preserve your capital, grow your savings, or produce income. When preserving your capital is the priority, you will want more bonds and cash. When you want to grow your savings, a higher stock allocation is essential. When income is your priority, bonds are best with dividend paying stocks. You may be saying you want ALL three, which is why diversification is essential, but you will need to find the best asset allocation mix to meet your highest priority goals, time horizon, and risk tolerance.

Reviewing these asset allocation considerations - time horizon, risk tolerance, and financial goals - point to an alternative method of asset allocation based upon when you will need your money. I'll discuss this in more detail in the *"Spending – Retirement"* chapter, but it can also be useful in other circumstances. Divide your savings into baskets of investments based upon when you will need your money. So money you will need within the next two years, keep in super safe cash (savings accounts, money market accounts, money market funds, and Certificates of Deposit - CDs). Money you will need in 3-5 years, put in appropriate bonds that are less volatile than stocks and pay fixed income. Then invest most of the rest of your savings in diversified stocks that you will not need for more than five years, which is usually time enough to ride out most bear markets. This asset allocation method could make it much easier to sleep at night and ignore market turbulence knowing that your money is very likely to be available at the time you need it.

Rebalancing

Asset allocation is a tool to implement your diversification strategy, but after a while, your asset allocation percentage is going to get out of date as certain assets will grow faster than others at different times, and then make up a bigger percentage of your portfolio than you originally intended. Periodically rebalancing your asset allocation is how you keep your allocation mix close to your original target. Rebalancing your asset allocation on a regular basis is one of the best investment strategies to lower your portfolio risk, deal with market volatility, and impose a plan to actually make money for you. The rebalancing strategy prompts you to periodically review your asset allocation to see if its percentage has changed from the amount you originally chose because one type of asset has risen or fallen. You then sell enough of the asset that has grown and buy the asset that is less than your chosen percentage. For example, if your desired asset allocation is the classic 60% stocks and 40% bonds, and your review shows that stocks have climbed to 65%/35%; you would sell 5% of your assets in stock and buy 5% more in bonds. If you fail to rebalance, then you gradually lose the benefits of your original diversification and asset allocation target, and your portfolio becomes more volatile or less likely to match your goals and time horizon.

It's easy to see how rebalancing helps you lower volatility and risk by keeping your diversification and asset allocation target on track, but it also includes the benefit of helping you make money by buying low and selling high. Too many investors too often buy high and sell low by buying the hottest investment just before the bubble bursts and then selling it in disgust after its inevitable drop. Rebalancing forces you to do the opposite – sell your winners high and buy beaten down assets at a low price. It imposes discipline on you to do what isn't easy – sell what is doing well and buy the assets that everyone else are shunning. This strategy provides a procedure and imposes a discipline that results in buying low (out of favor assets) and selling high (winners before they inevitably "revert to the mean" and drop back down to its average). Thus, rebalancing helps you deal with market turbulence by providing you a plan, discipline, and ongoing diversification to help deal with it.

Stock turbulence during the Great Recession provides an informative example. A common asset allocation of 60% stocks / 40 bonds at the beginning of the recession in 2007 would have flipped at the bottom of the recession in 2009 to around 40% stocks / 60% bonds. At this point, it would have been emotionally challenging to rebalance your portfolio by selling your safe bonds and buying sinking stocks. But if you didn't, you would have missed much of the subsequent 200%+ bull stock market rise by skipping the opportunity to sell expensive bonds and buy cheap stocks. So following the essential rebalancing rule would have been tough emotionally at the time, but paid off big over the next few years.

You can have flexibility about how precisely and often you rebalance. To save transactions costs and taxes, you may wish to rebalance only if your allocation is more than 4-5% off target. Rebalancing once per year is common because then the assets you sell will be taxed at the "long-term capital gains" rate of 15% for assets held more than one year rather than as higher, ordinary income for "short-term capital gains". Mark your calendar to rebalance every year in January when you are thinking about new resolutions or May when the market adage, "Sell in May and go away" so often turns true.

Alternately, rather than sell your over-weight asset to buy your under-weight one, just make new contributions to your under-weight asset or future withdrawals from your over-weight asset until they are back in balance. Retirees, note that you may be able to tailor your withdrawals to your rebalancing needs. Consider taking all or most of your withdrawals from your asset type that exceeds your allocation target. For example, if your current mix is 70/30 stocks to bonds and your original asset allocation target was 60/40, then make most of your ongoing retirement withdrawals from you stock funds until the percentages again meet your target.

Rebalancing makes perfect sense in theory, but at time may be hard to actually practice because it sometimes goes against the grain of investors' emotions. During a down market, it may be hard to sell your bonds that haven't lost as much to buy stocks that may still be dropping; and during up markets, it may be hard to sell stocks that are rising nicely to buy bonds that aren't. But remember that in the long run, successful investors use a sound plan more than emotions and rebalancing provides a strategy that helps you follow the advice of the most renowned investor of our time, Warren Buffet, who offers his plan of buying when others are fearful and selling when others are greedy. This is really another strategy for buying low/selling high which is what the strategy of rebalancing encourages you to do.

Here are tools that may help with your rebalancing:

- http://www.morningstar.com/Cover/Tools.html - Morningstar.com's TOOLS page has tools to help you "Xray" your portfolio to tell you what your current asset allocation is across all your funds and to help rebalance it. A nice feature includes information about the all-important fees you are paying.
- http://www.invest-it-yourself.com/rebalancing.php – For those who like Excel spreadsheets to help with rebalancing.

Buy and hold vs. market timing

There are two types of investors, long-term investors and active traders. Active traders are in and out of trades within weeks, days, or hours. Active trading is for the pros or at least experienced and knowledgeable traders. This book is mostly aimed at average people who want simple means to meet their savings and financial goals. Most people should be long-term investors with most of their savings. If you want to join the active traders, then do it with only 5-10% of your savings and do a lot more studying and practicing. Your library is filled with FREE books to help you. For long-term investors, after you have mastered diversification and rebalancing, the main strategy you will face is whether to stick with "buy and hold" or try "market timing". This is especially true when you face one of the 3-5 bear markets you will experience over your investing lifetime.

We accept that death and taxes are certain; investors should also know that booms and busts are certain. Stocks prices can be affected by many factors including economic cycles, bull and bear markets, sector and country ups and downs, company performance, world news, and some even say randomness; so is it really surprising how volatile stock prices can be? Stock indexes have plunged 43% in a year and rocketed up 54%, individual stocks even more. Even within the same year, stock indexes have swung wildly, on average up or down 13% within the same year. So you need to be prepared for wild, even extreme swings in the short-term, but know that over time, stocks have in the past *averaged* almost 10% per year, more than any other type of investment readily available to average investors. I have noted that many times, but now it's time to note that many research studies have shown that average investors earn much less than that. Other studies show that most actively managed mutual funds fail to match the market indexes and that average investors fail to match the performance of their mutual funds. Why?

Average investors don't match the indexes' and their mutual funds' performance partly because of commissions, fees, taxes, and bid/ask spreads. However, the bigger reason is that they don't stay invested in them long enough to get the same returns. Too often, too many investors buy investments that have already risen and are near the top, and then sell when stocks or funds have declined. Just so we are all on the same page here, the goal is to buy low and sell high, but chasing hot performance and bailing out when the going gets turbulent results in the opposite.

The remedy most experts have long proposed is "buy and hold" -- buying an investment and holding it indefinitely regardless of price fluctuations. This strategy is based upon the premises that:

- The best way to match the market is to invest for the long-term.
- Despite volatility, stocks provide the best *long-term* return.
- Less trading results in lower trading costs and taxes.
- Trying to time the tops and bottoms of stock and market swings does not work for long - even for the pro's.

Buy and hold seems like a pretty easy strategy to follow, especially when everything is going up, but proves not so easy when it's going down. Then fear takes over and we want to sell, even at a loss. Some would even say that it's dumb to sit by and watch your investments sink when you could just get out, move savings to something else, and get back in later when investments are rising again. Moving in and out of investments because of price swings is an alternative strategy called "market timing". Both "buy and hold" and "market timing" have proponents so let's review them.

The main premise of "buy and hold" is that market timing just doesn't work. It has data to show that average investors underperform when trying to time the market and that even professionals cannot do it consistently. It is often pointed out that it is not surprising that market timing is so hard because you have to be right twice – first on when to sell to avoid the crash and secondly when to get back in before the best part of the next bull market. It is very common for investors to miss much of a bull market because they are still so fearful from the last bear market. They often regain their confidence and buy back in near the top of the bull market, just in time to see it crash again into the next downtown. Knowing when to get out and back in is just so difficult. For example, is a market decline the beginning of a bear, or just a temporary correction before the next rise? Data is commonly presented on charts showing that if investors miss the top twenty biggest trading days, their returns would be a small fraction of the market's and if they miss the best forty days, they would even have a negative return.

For decades, nearly all experts advocated "buy and hold" and denounced "market timing", but nonetheless, people have been doing it anyway – especially in down markets. Now, two bad bear markets in a decade have made it respectable to discuss market timing in polite company. Market timers aim to smooth out their performance by selling to avoid the worst of the declines while buying in time to get most of the upside. Market timers need reliable signals to know when to get in and out and the ability to interpret them. Signals can include both "fundamentals" such as investment class yields, ratio of advancing/declining stocks, P/E ratios, etc., or a host of "technical" indicators from reading charts.

There are many variants with one of the most intriguing having the aim to remove emotion and add rules to the timing. It is proposed to sell stocks whenever a selected market index has risen by 25% and buy stocks whenever the market declines by 10%. This contrarian approach encourages investors to buy whenever there is a dip in prices and sell whenever there has been a significant rise, but contrarian strategies are hard to follow because you are buying when everyone else is selling with falling prices and selling whenever everyone is buying in a nice rise. Note that this is not an "all or nothing" in/out strategy, but just rebalancing between stocks, bonds, cash, REITs, and/or commodities with a small portion of your investments, 10-30%. That way you won't kick yourself as hard after you sell stocks at a 25% rise and the investment continues to rise another 25% which happens often.

Marketing timing hasn't resulted in hordes of millionaires because it's hard interpreting signals, signals aren't necessarily reliable, the future is hard to predict, past performance is not always a reliable guide to future performance, you have to be right in getting out and getting back in, and you have to find an alternative investment while you wait. It's not uncommon for experts to warn about expensive, overvalued bull markets only to see the bull market continue to rise for many more months or years.

Many average investors do their own version of market timing by finally getting into a bull market after it's making headlines for reaching new highs and then bailing out with a loss when the highs proved short-lived and the declines have drained their investment.

So where do these competing strategies leave us? I like the paraphrasing in a *Money* magazine article in January 2012 of Winston Churchill's famous comment about democracies, "Buy and hold investing is the worst form of investing, except for all those other forms that have been tried." It seems to me that the historical record shows the long-term success of "buy and hold", and our biggest savings goals, college and retirement, involve long-term savings. Market timing is hard to do consistently and the record shows that most of us are bad at it with our performance records underperforming our funds and the market indexes. Even the pro's aren't consistently better. Nevertheless, there are times when prudence makes sense or fear makes action irresistible. There are times when certain investments seem very expensive, interest rates or inflation are clearly a danger to our existing investments, a bubble has burst, or economic conditions are plainly sending the market into deep bear territory. Here are actions to help us hang on with buy and hold, long-term investing.

- Rebalancing over-weight asset allocations should be one action every long-term investor takes at least annually, since rebalancing is part of a sound strategy rather than emotional fear or greed. This also encourages you to sell what is doing relatively well and buy what is cheap.

- Increase your diversification with foreign stocks and bonds and then go beyond stocks and bonds with cash, REITs, and commodities. If you must try one of the new "tactical" or "alternative" funds, keep it small until they have proven themselves. Perhaps the safest of the alternative funds are the "low volatility" ETFs that confine their holdings to only the stocks with the lowest volatility such as utilities and consumer goods.

- When you want to take an action, do it in a limited way, varying your target asset allocation by only 10-20% depending upon your time horizon, risk tolerance, and financial goals. For example, if you are fearful about an over-bought market or the decline appears to have begun, don't abandon your asset allocation in stocks, just rebalance a small portion from stocks to bonds or cash. If you must take an action, make it small, infrequent, and limited.

- Concentrate on dividend paying stocks that usually pay whether the market is up or down.

Surviving bear markets

Officially, "bear" markets are defined as a drop of more than 20%, but whenever we hear news of persistent declines, our fear sets in and emotions try to override all our investment strategies and rational behavior. It's hard to fight that irresistible urge to sell to avoid more losses, more pain. This emotional response often over-rides our rational understanding that the market will go back up sometime, that falling prices mean an opportunity to buy bargains, and that we don't actually have a loss until we sell.

Let's review the 2007-2009 bear market that coincided with what is called the great recession. It was one of three bear markets since WWII that lost more than 40% and the second in the same decade after the 2000-2002 bear. The bear market began in October 2007 and had plunged more than 55% when it reached bottom in March 2009. Some wondered whether they could ever recover, especially during one of our worst economic climates. But bear markets have always recovered; it's just a matter of how much time it takes. This time it took until March 2013. Investors who sold in late 2008/2009 suffered huge losses AND likely missed the huge gains once the bull market started. Investors who were too afraid to look at stocks again missed huge gains. Investors, who bought stocks in 2009 when others were still abandoning stocks and held them, could have run up gains of more than 100%, thus doubling their investment.

Isn't hindsight wonderful? Or perhaps "buy and hold" with our other investment strategies are wonderful, as investors who didn't panic, market time, and sell did not lose money. Investors who continued to regularly pump their savings into the market during the down period were real winners as they saw their portfolio gain from both regular savings and buying cheap investments that later soared. People who lament 2000-2009 as being the "lost decade" to investors miss the fact that *buy and hold* investors did not *lose* money and investors who continued to "dollar cost average" into stocks throughout both bull and bear markets saw their bargains picked up during the bear markets soar to huge gains in the subsequent bull markets. Investors with good diversification and regular rebalancing did better than those who didn't.

Here are some tactics to try to keep our emotions under control during turbulent markets. The less often you check your portfolio, the less danger you feel, so during those down markets, turn off the business news and just stop checking your portfolio as often. When you can't resist taking some action, just play around with a small portion of your portfolio, 10-20%. Try to save even more – this will help pump up your portfolio and do it when prices are low. Rather than dwell upon your falling portfolio, think about how these bargains are going to pay off big time when the market rises. Just because the herd is doing something like chasing rising prices and abandoning plunging stocks, doesn't mean it's correct -- especially when going over the cliff. Yes, I have mentioned this before, but the advice is pertinent here again - follow the advice of the most renowned investor of our time, Warren Buffet, who offers his plan of buying when others are fearful and selling when others are greedy. Recall that most fixed income bonds and dividend-paying stocks will keep paying you while you wait out a down market. Focus on your long-range financial goals more than the short-term market gyrations. Remember that in the long run, successful investors use a sound plan more than emotions, so ensure your dollar cost averaging, diversification, and rebalancing is current.

Your investment plan

- Develop an investment plan
- Model portfolios
- Keeping it simple

Develop an investment plan

We have reviewed investment types, strategies, rewards, and risks. Now let's put it all together and discuss how to sort thru all of this and personalize it for your own investment circumstances. Let's start by reviewing a simplified snapshot of the major investment types and how they relate to each other and the characteristics of your investment plan. This table shows how investments typically compare with each other and best meet which time horizons and savings goals. It should remind us that safe investments have low returns while high returns mean higher risks and are best for longer time horizons.

Selected Investments in February 2017

Investment Type	Sample Yield / Return	Best for Time Horizon	Best for Savings Goals
1 year Inflation rate	1.26%	n/a	Investments that do not exceed this rate will be losing purchasing power.
Savings Account	0.11	0-2 years	Preserve capital – no risk
Money Market Account	0.11	0-2 years	Preserve capital – no risk
Money Market Fund	0.31	0-2 years	Preserve capital – low risk
Certificate of Deposit 6 month 1 year 5 year	 0.35 0.59 1.22	 < 1 year 1 year 5 years	Preserve capital – no risk Preserve capital – no risk Income & Preserve capital
Treasury (3 months return) 6 month bill 2 year note 5 year note 10 year note	 0.63 1.20 1.91 2.47	 0-2 years 0-2 years 2-5 years 5-10 years	Preserve capital – Default risk only when Congress plays chicken with debt-limit deadlines.
Short-term bonds (Wall Street Journal)	2.39	Any	Preserve capital – low risk
Intermediate Bonds (WSJ)	2.86	3-5 years	Income & Preserve capital – medium risk
Long-term bonds (WSJ)	4.59	5+ years	Income & Preserve capital – medium risk from interest rate ris-

			es
High yield 100 corporate bonds index (yield)	5.42	3+ years	Income – higher uncertainty and default risk
S&P 500 Index		5+ years	Volatility risk
1 year return	22.77		Growth
3 year annualized return	12.02		Growth
10 year annualized	7.00		Growth
Average dividend paid	2.09		Growth & income
Russell 2000 Small Cap – 1 yr	36.4	5+ years	Growth
S&P United States REIT – 1 yr	8.25	5+ years	Grown & income

This snapshot is from one point in time, but illustrates how the various types of investments compare to each other, despite the fact that the rates fluctuate. Notice how many had yields less than the rate of inflation. Note that the ten year return for stocks beats nearly any other type of investment, despite the fact that this ten year period included one of the worst bear markets since WWII.

Use the internet to find your current rates:

- http://www.bankrate.com/
- http://www.bloomberg.com/
- http://www.morningstar.com/
- http://online.wsj.com/home-page

Long-term investing is more successful when based less upon emotional reactions, and more upon a sound plan and strategies. I recommend you take a few minutes to think about and write down your personal investment plan based upon your savings goals, time horizon, risk tolerance, investment needs, and level of involvement. With this in hand, you will find it much easier to select and stick with your investing strategies and asset allocation targets.

Savings goals

Write down your savings goals and your "time horizon" which is the time period you will need your money. For example:

1. Home down payment – 3 years
2. College for kids – 15 years
3. Retirement – 32 years

Risk tolerance

Risk tolerance is the ability to handle losses and deal with turbulence without panicking and selling near market lows. Think about how much could you see your portfolio plunge before bailing out? If you invested during the last bear market, use that experience as your guide. Financial advisors are supposed to get a risk tolerance profile from clients and many websites offer risk tolerance quizzes so you can get an idea where you think you stand at a given moment:

*   http://njaes.rutgers.edu/money/riskquiz/ - Rutgers University risk tolerance quiz.
*   https://personal.vanguard.com/us/FundsInvQuestionnaire - See how one of the big fund companies analyzes risk and suggests asset allocations.

People tend to think they are more open to risk when investments are doing well, and then discover they don't want to lose as much as they thought when investments are going down. So there can be a difference between our theoretical risk tolerance and our actual tolerance. If you experienced a down market, how much were you willing to lose before you sold – or did you hang on until the recovery?

There is also a difference between these *emotional* aspects of risk tolerance and our *capacity* to handle risk. A more objective way to measure risk is our capacity to handle risk based upon our financial circumstances, wealth, and time horizon. If you have a safe job and/or pension, then you can better handle potential risk than someone without. Additionally, someone with say $150,000 can probably hold out through a deeper downturn than someone with only $25,000. Most important is your time horizon, because the sooner you will need your money, the less risk you should take with your savings and the lower return you should expect. The longer it is until you need your money, the more risk you can afford to take because you will have more time to recover from any decline in your investment. A full market cycle of bear to bull is typically around five years, but bad ones can take longer, which is why large investments in stocks are most appropriate for time horizons of at least five years.

Investment needs

With your risk tolerance and savings goals in mind, prioritize your investment needs of preserving capital, growing your savings, or earning income. You probably want all three, but remember the risk / reward ratios we have discussed and how different types of investments are best for which priority.

Once your written financial plan includes your goals, time horizon, risk capacity, and investment priorities, you can determine which type of investments you want to tilt your asset allocation towards. Here are some possible examples.

Examples of Financial Plan

Goal	Time Horizon	Investment Need	Majority Asset Allocation Example
Emergency fund	Any time	Preserve capital	Savings / Money market account/fund
Home down payment	3 years	Preserve capital	CD's / money market / short-term bonds
College 1	10 years	Growth	Stocks
College 2	4 years	Preserve capital / income	Intermediate or high yield junk bonds.
College 3	2 years	Preserve capital	CD's / money market / short-term bonds
Long-term investments	5+ years	Growth	Stocks
Retirement	5+ years	Growth	Stocks / bonds
Retirement	Now	Income / Growth	Basket of stocks / bonds / cash

Level of involvement

The last element you should consider for your financial plan is what level of involvement you want to put into your investments. Consider your interest, knowledge, capability, and time. This will help you select the type of investments for your portfolio.

Easy to hard

Your investments can be as simple or challenging as your choose. If your desired level of involvement is low, choose a target date fund to match your savings goal time horizon and it will rebalance for you and get more conservative as you get closer to your goal. A balanced fund will provide you one fund with an asset allocation around 60% stocks and 40% bonds, but with no target date to get more conservative.

If you want more control of your investments, then you have two choices. Still keeping it simple is the "core and explore" approach in which you keep your target date, balanced fund, or 3 diversified index funds as the core of your portfolio and add a fund/stock/bond or two to explore a favored area, idea, or style. For example, add a bond or money market fund to make your portfolio more conservative or a REIT, stock fund, or alternative fund to tilt toward one area. Alternatively, you can move to the next step, set your asset allocation target, and select your own diversified portfolio of mutual funds, ETFs, index funds, or individual stocks and bonds.

Set your asset allocation targets

Your personal financial plan should guide your asset allocation target. Getting your asset allocation and diversification set up well is even more important than which specific investment you choose, because the percentages you choose will do more than anything else to determine your portfolio's level of growth and volatility, and consequently how well you meet your goals and ride out any market turbulence. Let's review two methods for selecting your asset allocation target, one based upon your age and the second based upon your time horizon.

Age based asset allocation

The most common guideline is based upon your age with the assumption that the longer it is until your retirement, the more risk you should take to increase the prospect of growing your savings more – and this means investing mostly in stocks. Subtract your age from 110 and that is the percentage of your retirement savings that should be invested in stocks. Divide the rest among bonds and possibly a small amount to alternative investment types such as safer money market or riskier real estate funds. Examples:

- Age 25: 110 – 25 = 85% in stocks and 15% bonds and alternatives.
- Age 40: 110 – 40 = 70% in stocks and 30% bonds and alternatives.
- Age 55: 110 – 55 = 55% in stocks and 45% bonds and alternatives.

If you want less volatility and risk during inevitable market drops, then to be more conservative, use 100 minus your age instead of 110 to shift 10% more of your allocation from stocks to bonds and alternatives. Having less of your asset allocation in stocks should mean less volatility, but also less long-term growth. On the other hand, less volatility may also help you sleep better at night and be less likely to bail out when the market has piled up losses and jump back in when the market has already run back up. Avoiding the buy high and sell low, market-timing approach may be the best way to ensure long-term growth.

These websites provide historical data to illustrate the risk/reward of a variety of asset allocation issues and portfolios.

- https://personal.vanguard.com/us/insights/saving-investing/model-portfolio-allocations - This is a great resource that illustrates data about a wide variety of asset allocations including the average, best, and worst returns, plus the number of years that saw losses. It may help give you a better idea of the asset allocation target that best fits your risk tolerance.
- https://www.fidelity.com/viewpoints/guide-to-diversification - This article shows the data that illustrates investment strategies including diversification, asset correlations, portfolios during the 2008 bear market and recovery, how the average investor's returns fail to meet index averages, how various model portfolios compare in returns and volatility, and the risk from not rebalancing your portfolio.

Time horizon based asset allocation
An alternative asset allocation method is based upon the time horizon you identified in your financial plan. For any savings goal longer than five years, divide your investments into three baskets based upon when you will need your money. This works especially well when you are ready for retirement. For example:

Basket One	0-2 years	All in CDs, money market funds, or short-term bonds or Treasuries.
Basket Two	3-5 years	Mostly short/intermediate bonds and some in higher yield bonds.
Basket Three	> 5 years	Asset allocation mostly in stocks. For example, the classic 60/40 allocation has proven to provide nice growth with only half the volatility of all stocks. Or see other model portfolios below.

As basket one is used, refill from basket three when doing well or basket two when three needs time to recover. Don't forget to rebalance basket three at least once per year.

Diversification

After your asset allocation target is set, comes the fun part of picking your investments while keeping diversification within each of your asset types in mind. This can be as simple as choosing two index funds -- a broad based global stock fund and a broad based bond fund. Or choose a broader diversification mix of US and foreign stock funds, small and large cap stock funds, high quality (low return) and high yield (lower quality) bonds, a REIT, and perhaps a money market fund so you will be ready for buy opportunities, especially during down markets. Focus on the aspect of investing you can most control – expenses. Remember that even an extra 1% in fees compounded annually can add up to big money over time. ETFs and index funds have the lowest expenses. To invest in them, choose which benchmark or investment type you want to follow; then choose the fund with the lowest expense. Don't take diversification to the extreme and hold more than ten funds which makes it too difficult to track and rebalance. When you are experienced, you may wish to set aside 5-10% of your savings to try to "beat the market".

Financial advisors and many premium websites will structure model portfolios for a variety of financial goals and ages, but you can get similar recommendations from a variety of publications, organizations, and websites. *Money* and *Kiplinger* magazines frequently provide articles with recommendations to fit a variety of circumstances which you may also find on their websites. Many of the fund companies also provide suggestions for creating portfolios for a variety of circumstances.

Websites with model portfolio recommendations:

- http://www.ipers.org/calcs/AssetAllocator.html - Lets you calculate your desirable mix based upon your age, risk tolerance, and other factors.
- http://cgi.money.cnn.com/tools/assetallocwizard/assetallocwizard.html - Let's you calculate a desirable asset allocation based upon your time horizon and risk tolerance.
- http://www.aaii.com/ - This site has a modest membership fee, but includes plenty of articles, stock and fund screeners, recommendations, and tools including model portfolios.

Income

Even when savings rates are very low, you still have plenty of options for assembling a diversified portfolio when income is your goal, whether it's for living expenses or boosting your returns whether the market goes up or down. In addition to all kinds of bonds, consider dividend paying U.S. stocks, dividend paying foreign stocks, preferred stocks, REITs, foreign bonds, high yield corporate junk bonds, "total return" bond funds, and if you are in a high tax bracket – municipal bonds. Stock sectors that typically pay nice dividends include utilities, financials, telecommunications, and REITs, but remember that going too far in one investment makes you vulnerable to a downturn in that sector. Investors willing to go even higher on the risk/reward ladder can investigate mortgage REITs, closed end funds, master limited partnerships, and business development companies – some of which had yields greater than 10% even when high yield junk bonds were paying less than 5%. However, you have to investigate these graduate level topics on your own. (I admit I have a fondness for REITs paying over 10% which I buy and hold with little care whether their price fluctuates.) With a well-diversified mix of income producing investments, you should be able to easily beat inflation, receive income, and expect long-term growth – all with less volatility.

Rebalancing

"Buy and hold", long-term investing doesn't necessarily mean static "set and forget". Don't forget to rebalance at least once per year. If you get a queasy stomach or itchy trigger finger when the market has risen 25%, seems over-bought, or is plunging; then rebalance a *small* portion of your allocations. Better to satisfy your urge for action with a small rebalance than abandoning your carefully crafted financial plan and risk buying high and selling low.

Your investment profile will change over time based upon changes in your age, wealth, family circumstances, goals, retirement plans, time horizon, risk tolerance, and job status. Fine tune your financial plan and asset allocation accordingly.

Selling

There are many reasons why traders sell stocks, but fewer for long-term investors. Long-term investors don't sell based upon emotions and price swings. They buy stocks because they want to own a good company and sell when the company is no longer a good company – which is not the same things as a stock price that has declined. Besides rebalancing, the main reason to sell is if the reason you bought the investment has changed. For example, if the company has lost its way, the fund raises its fees or changes its style, your nice dividend paying stock has slashed its dividend, or the invention of personal spaceships drive your auto stock into the ground. You may sell to correct a mistake such as chasing a hot tech stock when the P/E soared past 50 and then "reverts to the mean", that is returns to its more normal average. Investors who obsess over taxes can sell a big loser to offset gains from winners they sold.

Investment do's and don'ts

Once you have developed your personal financial plan and mastered these few investment steps and strategies, you should be well on your way to meeting your financial goals. We have seen that investing can be *simple* with index and target date funds, but not necessarily *easy* because our emotions call us to do unfortunate things at bad times. In our final investing section, let's review some further investing rules and mistakes to be even more successful. Yes, you have heard many of these before, but this is my last chance to repeat them before moving on to the next topic. "Repetition is the mother of studies," as the Romans put it.

Investing principles

- Buy low, sell high – if this is so obvious, then why do we too often do the opposite?

- Diversify within your investment types as well as among them.
- Asset allocation and rebalancing are even more important than the particular investments you select.
- Invest based upon your time horizon, investment plan, and these principles rather than emotion and price swings.
- Avoid the noise – it only makes you stray from your plan and do the wrong thing at the wrong time.
- Long-term investing is the best way to save for your goals, but if you want to short-term trade, do it with only a small portion of your savings.
- Invest for the long-term. Sell when there has been a significant change with the company or fund not with its stock price.
- Steady automatic saving even in (especially in) down markets is the surest way to your financial goals.
- Favor dividend paying stocks – they pay you whether the market goes up or down.
- Past performance is not a guarantee to future returns.
- Boom and bust cycles commonly last around five years, so plan on holding stocks for at least this long for long-term goals.
- Think like an investor more than a trader. You should be more interested in owning good companies or funds for the long-term rather than current price swings.
- Preserving your capital in a long-term investment (like CDs and savings bonds) that fails to keep pace with inflation, results in losing your money's buying power over time.
- Much of the market is beyond our control, but the one thing we certainly can control is how much we pay for our investments. Go for low fee funds as much as possible. Index funds have lower fees than actively managed funds. ETFs have lower fees than mutual funds. Even among actively managed funds, fees vary widely and there is no evidence that expensive funds beat the market any better than cheap funds. Avoid funds with "loads" – big upfront or surrender fees even from your financial advisor.
- Automate your savings. If you have a 401(k), you do this already. Do the same for your other savings goals. Automatically shift money from your checking account to your savings account for an emergency fund, 529 account for the kids' college fund, or your brokerage or fund company for your investments and IRAs.

Use your bank's bill pay or your investment's website to set savings to run automatically.

- Not even professionals can *beat* the market consistently, but there is one way to consistently *match* the market – buy low cost index funds.
- Mark your calendar. Increase your retirement savings 1% at the same time you get your annual raise. Rebalance once per year after New Year's or May Day. After your birthday, check the Social Security website to ensure your earnings are correct and remind yourself how little Social Security is going to pay you in retirement. On April 15, reset your W2 withholdings so you don't give the government such a big loan throughout the year; put the tax savings into your financial savings or payoff credit card debt.

Investing mistakes

Avoiding losses is perhaps more important than picking winners, so try to minimize these mistakes.

- Don't react to the news of the day and be whipsawed in and out, back and forth. Are you a long-term investor with a plan or the one guy who can finally beat the market? (Yes guys, I'm looking at you.) Focus on things that matter and you can control, such as fees.
- Don't follow the herd into the latest hot fad. Professionals say that by the time small investors have heard about something, the easy money is over. Then it's just a matter of transferring the wealth from the herd to the pro's.
- In your quest for greater returns, don't fall for pushy salesmen, high energy seminars, and over-the-top-yields that may turn out to be complex, loaded with fees, Ponzi schemes, or just plain risky. For the average investor, simpler is often better.
- Don't depend upon riskier investments to make up a loss or goal shortfall, ramp-up your savings instead as the surest way to wealth.
- Don't project the recent past into the indefinite future. Things do change. Both bear and bull markets end. Keep your gloom and optimism, fear and greed within bounds.
- Don't let overconfidence lead to over trading, risky bets, or abandoning your long-term plan. Yeah guys, the behavior scientists are staring at us. That win-

ning streak was probably due to a bull market or luck more than our skill. Remember that even matching the S&P index is tough -- let alone beating it.

- Don't think you are the one who can time the market well – or at least not with more than a small portion of your portfolio. The data shows that as often as not, market timing leads to *more* losses, not *less*.
- Don't pay high fees to actively managed mutual funds that perform no better than low fee passively managed ETF's or index funds (or at least only a small portion of your savings). This mistake could cost you around 1-1.5% of your savings annually, which compounds over time.

More information

I hope you now have investing strategies, rules, and knowledge to make you a successful, long-term investor. You are on your own to turn knowledge into wisdom and experience, but let's close with some tools to make tracking your growing investment portfolio easier. Your broker, fund company, and 401(k) websites likely offer a variety of tools for monitoring and managing those investments. However, you probably have accounts in multiple places; perhaps several 401(k)s, IRAs, a stock broker, 529 college account, and perhaps actual bonds, not to mention your spouse's accounts. Plenty of software programs can handle all of this for you, but these websites are more convenient, almost as powerful, and offer both free and premium versions.

- https://www.personalcapital.com/
- http://www.morningstar.com/
- https://www.wikinvest.com/account/portfolio/regx/start
- http://www.marketwatch.com/myportfolio

Part Four

Introduction to Spending

We have discussed financial principles for managing our money to live within our means, setting goals for savings and putting them on autopilot, and investing to meet our financial goals. Finally comes the fun part – spending! Let's introduce a new financial principle to increase your financial security – "Try to avoid paying full price." Follow this principle, and it will be much easier to find extra money to pay debts, increase savings for your financial goals, and further your financial security. Note that I'm not even preaching to you to live frugally – I'm saying "spend wisely". As long as you are living within your means, paying off your debts, and increasing your savings; then people will spend – just do it wisely. Then there will be more money for all those other things.

That is what Section Four is about. I will discuss how to buy expensive things that commonly require borrowing (autos, real estate, and college), deal with debt, save money when spending, and wrap up life's financial journey with spending in retirement – always keeping on the lookout for ways to spend wisely and avoid paying full price. Before beginning, remember the most important principle about spending – know how much you have available to spend and stay within that limit. You know how much you have left to spend because you periodically match your income, expenses, and savings goals. The amount you have left after subtracting your expenses and saving goals from your income is what you have left for spending on all other items, both needs and wants.

Ideally, before we paid for anything, we would save enough money to pay for it. However, a FEW things are so expensive that this is not always practical. The most common are medical expenses, automobiles, real estate, and college. The best way to deal with most (but unfortunately not all) medical expenses is to live a healthy life style and always carry health insurance - even when you are young and healthy since you can't predict accidents. As I'm writing this chapter, I'm recovering from a broken leg that happened when a car knocked me off my bicycle. So I can assure you that accidents can happen to anyone at any time, especially when you least expect it. However, I'm concentrating on discretionary borrowing and spending, specifically for an automobile, a home, and college. You could make the case that these three are close to necessities or even that they enhance your or your children's financial security. But too often we move beyond these and borrow for other discretional things that are not necessities. This is living beyond our means, which can only be continued for a limited time. Credit card debt may seem to enhance our present, but it threatens our future, so I'll examine it while we are discussing borrowing.

Chapter Seventeen

Buying a Car

- Leasing a car
- Purchasing a car
- Buying used cars
- Owning a car
- More information

Owning an automobile is one of the most expensive undertakings, and it's not only the lease or purchase price. Even if you get a great deal, you still may have endless gas, insurance, maintenance, registration, cleaning, parking, and repair bills. No wonder many people opt to use public transportation instead. Nonetheless, it's still true that most people find cars very useful or essential, regardless of how expensive they are. But, before automatically choosing to lease or buy, consider "car sharing" if you only have an occasional need for a car and want to save a lot of money. With car sharing, you typically pay a membership fee to join a company plan and then pay by the hour, day, or month when you actually use a car. There are many car-sharing companies in many major metropolitan areas and even the big car rental companies are getting into the business. To find one in your area, search "car sharing companies".

Leasing or buying a car is a major purchase, so before stepping into a dealership, you have some research to do. Thankfully, this is easier than ever with the internet. To make it easier and save you money, in this section, I will review these topics:

- Do you want to own or lease?

- Want a new car or used?
- Where can you get a loan at what rate?
- Which several autos are you interested in?
- What should you expect to pay for your selection?
- What do you need to know after driving that shiny car off the lot?

Leasing a car

Leasing a car is an alternative to buying it. At the end of the lease term, you return the car and have nothing left to show for your payments. So why do it? The advantage is lower payments than if you were buying it and you can get rid of it without having to sell it. So there are a few reasons to do it:

- You always want to drive a new car and keep getting new car leases when the previous one expires.
- You want the lowest monthly payment.
- You can't save for a down payment to buy a car.
- You need a car for a relatively short period of time such as before going overseas.

Shop around for a lease just as you would if buying. The amount of the lease depends upon the negotiated price of the car (capitalized cost), the expected depreciated value of the car at the end of the lease (residual value), the length (term) of the lease, and the interest rate you will be paying (money factor). Negotiate over these:

- price of the car just as if you were buying it – try for at least a 5% reduction and ensure it isn't much over the true market value found on many websites
- the length of the lease - typically three years because after that comprehensive warrantees may expire and you may have more maintenance costs such as tires, brakes, etc.
- any included extras such as options and warrantees
- the amount of mileage you are allowed before paying extra – typically 10,000 – 12,000 miles per year, but you can sometime pay a fee to get a higher allowance

At the end of the lease, you may have to pay extra for excess wear, damage, or extra mileage, which would lower the value of the car more than the expected depreciation value. Consider detailing the car before returning it so it looks good to avoid potential excess wear fees. You do have the option to buy the car at the end of the lease based upon the "residual value" or value of the car after depreciation. If you are considering this, try to bargain for a lower residual value when your bargaining power is strongest – shortly before the lease is up. If you want lower monthly payments, then a higher residual rate is better.

Some leases allow you to transfer it to a new owner for a fee. Find one at these websites – which also charge fees:

- http://www.leasetrader.com/
- http://www.swapalease.com/

Here is the bottom line on leasing. Leasing is just renting a car long term. Despite all those payments, you have nothing to show for it at the end of the lease. You own nothing. If you buy and keep a car past its paid-off date, you will come out ahead. Conversely, you would save money by leasing if you commonly trade in a car before it's paid off.

These websites are useful when you are considering leasing a car:

- http://www.carpaymentcalculator.net/calcs/lease-vs-buy.php – leasing calculators
- http://leasecompare.com/ - information and comparison tools
- http://www.edmunds.com – information about deals from manufacturers
- http://www.checkbook.org/auto/leasew.cfm - Pay a professional to get you the best lease and at least five bids.

Purchasing a car

Whether a new or used car, buying a car may involve researching your financing, researching your potential cars, visiting several dealers, test driving your choices, evaluating options packages, negotiating a deal, and filling out all that paperwork; but at least you shouldn't have to do it very often. In return for all that hard work and loads of cash, you get one sweet toy - that is, vital necessity.

Research

For something this expensive, and hopefully something you will have for a long time, you should do your research in advance. Only visit a dealer when you are ready to test drive. Thankfully, the internet has made shopping for a car much easier. On the web, you can research potential makes and models, reviews, safety reports, comparisons, prices, how much others are paying, trade-in value for your current car, financing, incentives, dealers, payment calculators, and car buying services. Many websites enable you to get quotes from multiple dealers. Many dealers will even let you search their inventory. The better your advance research, the more successful you will be when dealing with that sales person and getting the car you want for the best price. In addition to car type, price, and looks; consider these in your car selection and research: safety record, gas mileage, maintenance costs, and resale value. As always, the first place to start is reviewing your own budget to see how much you can afford for a down payment and monthly payments. Then start your research at these websites:

- http://www.safercar.gov/ - Review safety ratings.
- http://www.caranddriver.com/ - A good place to narrow down your choices with reviews, road tests, comparisons, and buyers guides.
- http://www.edmunds.com/ - One of the most comprehensive car buying sites for both new and used cars with information on car reviews, ratings, incentives, road tests, price quotes, dealer inventory, calculators, and used car appraisals.
- http://www.kbb.com/ - The Kelly Blue Book website is a must visit and provides price data for new cars, used cars, and trade-ins. You can also find information and tools including calculators, car comparisons, price quotes, recommendations, reviews, car buying wizards, and incentives.
- http://www.nadaguides.com/ - Among a wealth of information is a "cost to own" calculator for hundreds of cars.
- http://www.truecar.com/ - Enables you to compare prices and see the sticker price, average price, and target price for new and used autos. Their target price is sometime below the dealers invoice price because it can account for other hidden incentives the dealer gets from the auto company that you can negotiate for. *Truecar* is also one of the many "car buying services" so it can also provide you with a certificate to print and hand the dealer with the price, thus minimizing haggling.
- Smartphone apps – Of course there are a growing number of smartphone apps that are very useful when visiting dealers including apps from *Edmunds, Kelly Blue Book, Car and Driver, AAA,* and several independents.

Trade-ins

Trading in your old car at the dealer is really convenient, but you do have other options that might get you a better deal. Use *ebay.com* and *craigslist.com* to sell it yourself – you will probably get 10-15% more than from the dealer. At the very least, take your car to the giant used car chain, *Carmax* before going to the dealer. A *Carmax* quote should be good for a week and see if the dealer will beat it.

Negotiating

The keys to negotiating are to do your research, know your facts and data, comparison shop, and have multiple dealers compete against each other rather than you. The most important data in car buying is just what is the price? Actually, cars have several different prices. Get an idea of what they are for specific cars by researching the web, especially at the websites listed above. The "sticker price" is what's on the car's window and is 5-10% above the dealer cost/invoice price which is theoretically what the dealer paid for the car, except that there are many other kinds of incentives the dealer gets from the auto manufacturer. The websites above will give you an idea of what the dealer paid for the car and this should be your bargaining point as it is for the dealer. Unless you are buying one of the hottest cars, your goal is to pay less than 5% above the dealer cost/invoice price which is always less than the sticker price on the window. Try for the invoice price plus $500, especially if the car has been sitting on the dealer's lot for more than a month. Sometimes you can get near the invoice cost because the dealer is still making money from the manufacturer incentives. The window sticker may list plenty of fees, but try to avoid most of the ones not listed on the dealer invoice, which the dealer should share with you. Then there are all the add-ons such as options, packages, and warrantees. Options packages can sometimes make it difficult to compare prices among dealers.

You should head to the dealer showroom only after you have done your research and are ready for a test drive. Take your printouts and prices with you to use as the basis of your negotiations. You could even do your negotiating before going to the dealer for the test drive. After completing your research, if you find a specific car on the dealer's website that you want, you could call the dealer and ask to speak to the "internet manager". Negotiating a price over the phone may be easier and more convenient than in person. Just make it contingent on a test drive, and then go in for the test drive and paperwork.

Most Americans do not look forward to haggling, especially when you are up against someone who does it for a living, but you will do fine if you go prepared and remember a few things:

- Haggling is a time-honored custom from ancient times and still today in many places around the world.
- Success here could save you several thousand dollars.
- Before going to the dealer, get bids from at least three sources. Many websites enable you to get multiple bids emailed to you from local dealers. You may also get bids from dealers by calling or emailing them. First, search the dealer's inventory on their website and find several cars with the exact options package you want. Then you can negotiate with a dealer over the phone for a specific car. Don't be shy about going multiple rounds – give your best quote to several dealers to see if they will beat it until no one will.
- First, negotiate price without any discussion of potential financing or trade-in value, so the sales person can't give something in one area and take back in the other. Second, discuss what the dealer will give for your trade-in car, which will be less than what you could get if you sold it yourself.
- Don't reveal your "cards", they already have enough advantage as it is. Specifically, don't reveal how much you are willing to pay per month or for the car which lets them know where to start bargaining or adjusting terms to fit. Just tell them you want to discuss the price before financing.
- Ensure you shop around and do your homework before hand.
- Don't be pressured to "get this deal that is only good today". Always get quotes from multiple dealers and don't be afraid to threaten to walk away and apply some pressure of your own.
- Once you are close to a price, ask for one of these discounts paid by the manufacturer to the dealer: "loyalty" if buying the same brand as your current car or "conquest" if buying a different brand.

You can probably minimize much of this when you know exactly what model and options you want. Here is where you can have multiple dealers compete against each other for your business. Take your specifications to multiple dealers, specify what you want, inform them you are going to multiple dealers, and ask them for their best price. If you prefer a specific dealer, ask if they will beat your best offer. If the offers are still more than 5% above the invoice price, then unleash your negotiating strategies.

Financing

Ideally, you have saved up a big pile of money for at least a big down payment to reduce your monthly payments and interest. But the reality for most people is that cars are so expensive that they need to get a car loan. At least interest rates on car loans can be fairly low depending upon your credit score, so as usual, shopping around pays. Check several places for the best auto loan including banks, credit unions, dealerships, and websites such as: bankrate.com, eloan.com, and lendingtree.com. Credit unions frequently have the best rates. When you find a good loan, try to get "pre-approved" so that you know your interest rate, how big a loan you can handle, and your monthly payment. To get pre-approved, you supply the requested financial information so they can review your income, debts, credit rating, and other financial information to know what rate they will offer you and how big a loan you can get. The better your credit score based upon your credit history, the better rate you will get. Borrowers with a short credit history may not qualify for a loan from a bank, but might still be eligible for a loan from the car company.

After you have agreed upon the price, then discuss financing. Never end up at a dealer's financing desk without already knowing what rate you could get elsewhere. Be ready to negotiate with the dealer to see if they can beat your pre-approved loan. Compare the dealer's rate and terms with your pre-approved loan from your bank or credit union. Dealers' financing rates are negotiable unless they are part of a current special offer. Consider these financing options to lessen the amount of interest you pay (and the true cost of your shiny new car):

- Pay at least 20% of the cost up front, even if the lender does not require it (unless you have higher rate debts elsewhere such as credit cards).
- Agree upon the shortest term possible, preferably, four years, five is acceptable, but avoid seven. The longer the term not only means paying more interest, but also that soon your car will be worth less than the amount you still owe on it. Many web loan calculators and smartphone apps will let you compare the monthly payment, amount of interest you will owe, and differing loan lengths.
- Sometimes a bigger down payment and/or shorter term will qualify you for a lower interest rate.

- Avoid paying interest rates that are significantly above the local average, especially at used car dealerships. If you have a poor credit history and are unable to get an affordable rate, it's probably better to save up more money and/or get a less expensive car. An older, less expensive car does not always have more problems than a newer, more expensive vehicle. Just put away some savings for repair bills.

Buying tips

Try to negotiate to less than 5% above the invoice price – sometimes it's even possible to get near the invoice price because the dealer is still making money from the manufacturers incentives. Take advantage of sales such as Presidents Day that traditionally kick off the post-winter, car-buying slump. In the fall, look for bargains among current year models as dealers try to clear their old inventory for the new model year. Shop near the end of the month when sales people may still be trying to meet their sales goals and monthly bonuses.

Look for manufacturer and dealer incentives such as cash-back, rebates, or zero percent financing. You usually can't get them all so use a web calculator to decide which is best for you: http://autos.aol.com/calculators/rebate-incentive-calculator/

Most experts advise against extended warranties for most products, but it could be worthwhile when you plan to own a car for more than 4-5 years. In addition to covering repairs beyond standard warranties, they often include extras such as roadside assistance or free rental cars while yours is in the shop. Like nearly everything else, the price of the warranty is negotiable. Indeed, friends have reported that they called several dealers to get a warranty quote and then successfully asked their dealer to match it.

Skip the negotiating

If all this sounds like too much hassle, there are actually individuals and companies that will do much of it for you while promising to save you money. "Buyers agents" work for you for a fee, while "auto brokers" work for you, but also get a fee from the dealer. Some agents and brokers are former sales people and know all the dealer tactics, but this time used on your behalf. Many organizations that you may be a member of, offer car buying services that promise to make car buying easier and save you money including AAA, Costco, other warehouse clubs, credit unions, insurance companies, and plenty more. Indeed Costco is getting to be one of the nation's biggest car sellers thru arrangements with local dealers. Find more online by searching under "car buying services". They provide various services including searching for the car you want, showing prices from favored dealers, negotiating with the dealer, reviewing options packages and warrantees, or even delivering the car to your door. They may reduce or eliminate haggling by searching for the best deal with affiliated dealers and providing you a certificate to print to take into the dealer with the price. They may save you money, not only by doing the comparison shopping, but also by having arrangements with certain dealers to give you part of the dealer incentives from the manufacturer. Some services charge a fee and some are free because they get some type of referral fee from the dealer. You should still do some basic research about the type of car you want, average prices in your area, and satisfaction policies for the car buying service, agent, or broker.

http://www.checkbook.org/ - This is one of many services that, for a fee, aim to make the car buying process easier for you by doing much of the price searching and haggling for you. This is probably one of the best as it is a service of the nonprofit Consumers' *CHECKBOOK*.

Another option to avoid some negotiation hassles -- after completing your research and test drives, email the "internet manager" at several dealers, let them know you are shopping around, and ask them for their best deals on your desired car. Avoid the showroom showdown and do the back and forth over the internet with multiple dealers until you select the best offer.

When to trade it in

Deciding when to trade in your clunker or beloved friend for a shiny new car is not always easy. Plenty of cars can last for more than ten years or 100,000+ miles and it sure is great owning a car that is already paid for. But at some point the cost of repairs starts to add up and buying a new car makes sense in the long term. Here are some tips for deciding. Even expensive repairs can cost less than just the sales tax on a new car. If you still owe more than your car is worth, it is going to be expensive to trade it in. How frequent and expensive are the repairs in the recent past? How likely is it that this repair will be the last for a while? Consider trading it in when the repair is nearly 30% of the value of your vehicle, it may be unsafe, or you fear it will leave you stranded despite many repairs.

Buying used cars

New cars aren't your only choice and frequently aren't your best choice. As soon as you drive your new car off the lot, it becomes a used car and loses value. Prices of used cars depend not only upon depreciation, but also "supply and demand" so prices depend upon such factors as the availability of models, what's hot, the economy, gas prices, and aggressive pricing of new cars. Used cars not only are more affordable, but also may have the best value. Buying a pre-owned vehicle may be the best way to step up a level of luxury and remain within your budget *Consumer Reports* magazine recommends buying a used car 1-3 years old, and notes that many recent model cars can get up to 200,000 miles without major problems. However, buying used vehicles does require a few extra steps to increase the chance you are not getting a lemon or even worse – a car that has previously been in an accident or natural disaster.

Start your search at one of these websites:

- http://consumerreports.org/cro/cars/index.htm - Consumer reports provides reliability and other important data on used models. The monthly subscription is worth the information.
- http://www.safercar.gov/ - Check for recalls, crash test ratings, and other issues at this government website.

See average prices for dealers, private sales, and certified pre-owned:

- http://www.edmunds.com/used-cars/
- http://www.kbb.com/
- http://nadaguides.com/
- http://www.cargurus.com/

These provide average prices and enable you to start hunting for your best deal, which is not only the lowest price, but also the best options, lowest mileage, and best condition. Low mileage vehicles are usually best, but you can get a lower price on high mileage cars, and newer cars are more reliable than ever. Most powertrain warrantees, for example, cover up to 100,000 miles. After getting the "average" price from a website, start your bargaining 10% below that. Bargain harder for cars that have been on the dealer's lot for more than 30 days. (Carfax.com and cargurus.com should show this.)

You have many places to shop for used cars including local automobile dealers and many websites. If you want to cut out the middleman, try these:

- http://www.craigslist.org – Craigslist is more likely to list vehicles from individual, local owners.
- http://www.ebay.com/motors - Buying a car on eBay can require some faith and extra delivery charges, but tens of thousands of people do it successfully every year. Read below for how to reduce the risks.
- Rental car companies websites – They sell their cars after about a year, usually in the fall. They have many miles, but are generally well maintained.

Certified Pre-Owned

There is even a premium class of used cars called "certified pre-owned" which are late-model cars with low mileage that have been inspected by factory technicians and include extended warranties. Each automaker's certified program is different, so you can find the details here: http://www.autotrader.com/research/certified-cars/compare.jsp

The cost of certified cars can be $500-$3000 higher, but in addition to peace of mind and extended warrantees, you might get extras such as special financing from the dealer or lower interest rates from a bank. Verify that you are getting a certified car from the manufacturer's program rather than the dealer's which may only have an extended warrantee and little inspection. Note that sometimes one year old, used cars can be more expensive than new cars if the new car has lower interest rates to finance it, so here is another example where it pays to do your research.

Things to Look For

If you are not buying a certified pre-owned car, then you should reduce your risk by taking the following actions.

1. Have a trusted mechanic evaluate the vehicle or get a detailed inspection from services such as: http://www.aimmobileinspections.com/
2. Get a car history from one of these websites:
    a. http://www.carfax.com/entry.cfx
    b. http://www.vehiclehistory.gov/
    c. http://www.autocheck.com/
    d. http://www.nicb.org

These vehicle history reports aren't perfect and certainly do not mean that the vehicle is without any damage or defects, but it is an easy, inexpensive, and reassuring step. Most dealers provide them. Always ask for them, even from private sellers.

You can sometimes get a better deal when buying a vehicle that is not local to you and have it shipped. You can use middlemen to facilitate the purchase. Carfax and eBayMotors list mechanics that will inspect vehicles and provide you a report. Mutual transfer of payment and title can be assured by using an escrow agent such as Escrow.com for a fee.

Owning a car

I recommend you aim to own your car for at least several years after you have finished paying for it. It's a great feeling when you make that last payment, but consider continuing to make that payment into a savings account so you will have at least most of what you need when it's time to buy the next car – unless you have credit cards to pay off.

Buying or leasing an auto is only the first of many expenses to keep that beauty running. Now let's review how you can save money doing it.

Gas

We can't do anything about the price of gas, but there are plenty of ways to reduce how much we use and spend for it.

- Use the *Gasbuddy* mobile app to find the cheapest gas near your location. Available for PC/smartphone/tablets.
- Fill-up with "regular" instead of "premium" unless your car's manual specifically says to use premium gas.
- Fine tune your driving habits to accelerate evenly and moderately, brake less, and coast to a stop more.
- Limit your speed over 60 mph as each 5 mph uses 5-10% more gas.
- Turn off your engine while idling to avoid throwing pollution and your money into the air.
- Carry less stuff in your trunk as each 100 pounds can increase gas use by 2%.
- Get regular tune-ups, which helps with both gas mileage and a trouble-free car.
- Inflate your tires to the pressure listed on the side of your door.

- Keep your windows and sunroof closed when driving on the highway.

Auto Insurance

Auto Insurance is one of those required insurances, but paying a lot isn't necessarily so, unless you have a bad record or are a young male.

- Review competitors rates every year or two. Rates can vary widely among different companies. Always shop around for at least three quotes. Online rates may be cheaper and you have many choices.
- After reviewing premium rates, check the company's complaint ratio at the National Association of Insurance Commissioners website: https://eapps.naic.org/cis/ .
- Get a high deductible amount ($500-$1000) and save on premiums. Most people never have to submit a claim and many choose not to for small amounts to avoid increasing premiums. (You do have your emergency fund for emergencies like this don't you?)
- Bundle your auto insurance with other insurance such as homeowners, life, or renters insurance from the same company to get a discount.
- Ask how you can get a discount. Some companies offer them for things such as taking driver-improvement courses, having anti-theft devices, driving less than 10,000 miles per year, or being a member of the military, professional, or alumni organizations.
- You rates may go up after a driving incident, but you probably have to ask for them to come back down after they drop off your motor-vehicle record.
- Seeing the rate increase after adding a teen to your policy can be as scary as handing them the car keys, but there are things that can minimize the increase including having at least a 3.0 GPA, taking a drivers course, and being in college more than 100 miles away without a car.
- Raise your credit score to get a discount from some insurers.
- Consider a new type of plan offered by some insurers that may give you a discount if you let them install a temporary device in your car to monitor your driving habits. You could get as much as a 30% discount if the devices reveal you to be a safe driver.
- Tell your insurer when you decrease your driving from such things as losing or changing to a closer job.

- See if your insurer offers discounts for getting paperless billing, paying your premium in a lump sum, or using automatic payments.

Maintenance and Repairs

Newer cars are more well-built than ever before and *Consumer Reports* magazine says many cars can last for more than 200,000 miles if properly maintained. In any event, you can save tens of thousands of dollars by planning to keep your car for at least ten years and/or 100,000+ miles. This is one of the biggest places you can save big money – a lot more than giving up that morning muffin. There is no longer a reason to trade in your car every 3-5 years to avoid big repair bills. Owning a car past the time when payments are done is a fantastic feeling. Try it, you'll like saving all that money, too. Imagine what you could do with an extra $300-$700 per month, but don't forget to start with paying off credit cards and increasing your savings.

To do this, you must maintain your car well. That means copying the pages in your car manual on when to do which maintenance, and then doing them on time. Skipping the oil change is not saving money; it's contributing to more expensive problems down the road. Few recent cars need that oil change every 3000 miles that your shop or dealer is pushing for – check your owner's manual to know your *manufacturer's* recommended schedule. The maintenance schedule will tell you how often to replace important fluids, belts, filters, etc., and when to rotate your tires. Many local shops likely can do this for you inexpensively. Look for coupons, Groupons, and web specials. Next, keep your car clean inside and out. This not only makes it a nicer place to be and look at, it can also extend the life and value of your car by preventing rust, fading, stains, and premature wear and tear.

Eventually, repairs will be necessary. New cars are increasingly computerized with plenty of warning lights to alert you to problems. Delaying maintenance and repairs can make the problem worse, more expensive, or even unsafe. If the repair isn't under warranty, independent repair shops may be less expensive than your dealer. If you feel like you are being pushed into unnecessary repairs, get a second opinion. There is plenty of debate about whether "third party replacement parts" are as good as the manufacturers, but they can save you money and insurance companies seem to push them heavily. For an accredited repair shop, look for the Motorist Assurance Program (MAP) label that can give some peace of mind that an accrediting agency has reviewed the shop. Use these websites to find reputable repair shops and get repair estimates before you go.

- http://www.automd.com/repaircost/ - Get repair estimates and do-it-yourself guides.
- http://www.cartalk.com/mechanics-files - Find mechanics with customer ratings.
- http://repairpal.com/ - Find mechanics, see local prices for common repairs, and track your car's maintenance.
- http://www.carmd.com/ - You can see for yourself what the car's computer is telling you just like the mechanic with a relatively inexpensive diagnostic tool from CarMD. It also gives you information about the likely fix and repair costs.
- http://carcare.org/ - Get car care information, maintenance schedules, email reminders, and repair shop locations.

More information

These smartphone/tablet apps are handy for car owners.

RepairPal – Keep track of your auto repairs and maintenance schedule, find local repair shops, and best of all – gives you repair estimates for a variety of common repair costs.

Gas Buddy – Probably one of the most downloaded apps – helps you find the cheapest local gas prices.

iWrecked - This is an auto accident assistant for easily logging all details, photos, and info after being involved in an accident.

Summary

- If you only need a car occasionally, save money by "car sharing" instead of leasing or owning.
- Leasing a car is like renting it long-term – you own nothing to show for those payments. But leasing may be useful if you always want a new car, want the lowest car payments, or need one for only a short period.
- Use the internet to research potential makes and models, reviews, safety reports, comparisons, prices, how much others are paying, trade-in value for your current car, financing, incentives, dealers, payment calculators, and car buying services. Get quotes from multiple dealers and search their inventory.

- The time to buy a "green" car is when gas prices are low so you won't have to pay a premium amid intense competition.
- The keys to negotiating are to do your research, know your facts and data, comparison shop, and have multiple dealers compete against each other rather than you. Aim to pay around $500, or less than 5% above the dealer's invoice.
- Research your financing before going to the dealer. Compete what a bank will offer you against what the dealer can offer. Only discuss financing and trade-ins after you have agreed upon a price.
- If you want to avoid dealing with a salesperson, but still save money, hire a car buying service, buyer's agent, or car brokers to handle it for you.
- Buying a used car may often provide the best deals and you have many options including "certified pre-owned" cars. Many of the same research principles and options apply as for buying new cars.
- One of the easiest ways to save money is to keep your car for many years after paying it off. Many newer cars can last for at least ten years or more than 150,000 miles with good maintenance. This is easier when you buy a lifetime warranty with your new car.

Chapter Eighteen

Buying a Home

- Getting a home loan
- Buying a home
- Selling a home
- Owning a home

The biggest expense most people will ever have is their home, whether they rent or buy. Owning a home has long been part of the American Dream even though there are plenty of circumstances where it makes sense to rent. In the long-term, ownership forces you to convert spending on a place to live into equity in your home that increases your net worth and can be used, if needed, in a home equity loan, reverse mortgage, or sale. Once your mortgage is paid, all you will need to pay for housing is insurance, property taxes, and maintenance which is still less then renting. Eliminating rental or mortgage expenses before you retire makes retirement income go much further.

Getting a home loan

- Getting the down payment
- Qualifying for a loan
- Finding a loan
- Refinancing a loan

- Home Equity Loans
- Paying a loan early

Getting the down payment

One of the hardest parts, but only the first step, to buying a home is saving that big, huge, gigantic down payment. Most people need to set that as one of their savings goals – after an emergency fund and simultaneously as you are saving for retirement with at least an amount large enough to get the company 401(k) match. If you plan to reach this savings goal within five years, save this money in a safe investment such as CDs that you "ladder" with ever shorter terms to match your goal time frame.

However, other sources can also contribute to your down payment. For many people, that means their big pile of money growing in their retirement accounts. As usual, there are pros and cons to this tempting source. First, only consider it if you are far enough from retirement that you can replenish your retirement savings before retirement. Different types of retirement accounts have different rules for withdrawing money for a mortgage down payment. Verify what rules are in effect for retirement accounts before withdrawing from them, as mistakes can be costly.

From a 401(k) type account, you can usually borrow half your savings up to $50,000 and avoid penalties if you repay within 5 years for any reason or 15 years for a home. These withdrawals won't be counted against your credit history scores nor when lenders calculate your "debt-to-income-ratio" when applying for the mortgage. However, if not repaid, you will have to pay taxes and a 10% early withdrawal penalty if under age 59 ½. If you leave your job, you will only have 60-90 days to pay it back without penalty. Even though you will be paying your 401(k) back with interest, your retirement savings may still take a hit because it won't be earning the compound growth it could have.

From an IRA, first time homeowners can withdraw up to $10,000 ($20,000 for couples) for a home without suffering the 10% early withdrawal penalty, but you will still owe the taxes you have previously avoided. As usual with a Roth IRA, you can withdraw your contributions tax and penalty-free since you have already paid taxes on it, but for a house, you can withdraw up to $10,000 in *earnings* tax-free, after you have had the account for at least five years. Of course, robbing your IRA accounts will hurt your retirement income.

The usual recommended down payment amount is 20% of the sale price. This gives lenders confidence that you have invested enough to be a safe risk and will pay them back. This will earn you the lowest interest rate, avoid PMI (private mortgage insurance), and lower your monthly payment amount. Twenty percent was common before the housing bubble and credit crunch when many low or no down payments were allowed. That turned out badly for many and most of those programs are history.

Nevertheless, it is possible to get loans with less than 20% down. The USDA may have zero down payment loans for borrowers in rural areas and the VA for veterans. Check to see whether Fannie Mae still has "homepath" mortgages on foreclosed homes for 3% down payments. The FHA provides loans with only 3.5% down, but you will be stuck paying PMI indefinitely, instead of only until your equity reaches 22%. Lenders may also offer other down payment options such as 5-10%, so review you options when you are ready. It's even possible again to find loans with 0-3% down payments, but lenders claim to have learned their lesson from the last mortgage mess, so expect to have stellar credit, low debt, and thorough income documentation to qualify.

If your down payment is less than 20%, your monthly payment amount will be higher because your loan will be bigger, you likely will owe monthly PMI mortgage insurance (0.5-1.5% of loan amount each year), and the lender may charge you a higher interest rate. Once the home equity (home value minus remaining loan balance) exceeds 20% of your home's current value, you should request your lender to drop your PMI (unless it's an FHA loan).

Qualifying for a loan

When you think you have saved enough for a down payment, the next step is NOT to start shopping for a home, but rather shopping for a loan to pay for the home. This enables you to know how much home you can afford, how much your monthly payment will be, and how well it will fit within your budget. This ensures you will have completed your comparison-shopping and been pre-approved for a mortgage before you are ready to sign for a home

After mortgage abuses contributed to the Great Recession in 2008, the U.S. government has pushed reforms. Approval standards change over time and among lenders and types of loans, but here are some guidelines to help you determine whether you might qualify for a mortgage or refinance loan and how big of a loan you may qualify for. Basically the lender will need to know and verify your monthly income, monthly debt payments, credit score, and amount of down payment.

- You need a solid credit history going back two years.

- Acceptable credit scores change over time, but generally you will need at least 620-650, or 720-750 to get the best rate (lower for FHA loans). Lenders will generally take the lower of yours or your spouse's scores. Check your estimated credit score for free here: https://www.creditkarma.com/dashboard
- You need a solid work history going back two years.
- The amount of your monthly debt payments (including your new mortgage) cannot exceed 43% of your monthly income. If your income fluctuates, you will need an average of two years. Be prepared to submit two years of tax returns. In high home price regions, you may be able to find "non-qualified" mortgages that let people with good credit histories exceed the 43% rule.
- Guidelines suggest your monthly home payment should not exceed 28% of your gross monthly income. When calculating your new mortgage payment, include principle, interest, taxes, insurance, PMI, and homeowners association fees. This will determine how big a loan, and how expensive a home, you can look for.
- You may need enough savings to cover the down payment, closing costs, and two months of mortgage payments.
- If you are refinancing your existing mortgage, you likely will need 10-20% equity in your home, meaning that an appraiser puts the value of your home 10-20% greater than the amount of the new loan you are seeking.

When you apply for a mortgage or refinance, be prepared to submit this documentation: current pay stub, two years tax returns and W2s, employer's contact information, bank and retirement account statements, and other verification of income. Your credit report will show the lender your other debts.

A loan is generally the sale price minus the amount of your down payment, plus closing costs to pay for the loan, plus any "points" you may choose to pay upfront to get a lower monthly interest rate. Use these web calculators to determine how much home you can afford and your mortgage amount, payment, and qualifications:

- http://www.bankrate.com/calculators/index-of-mortgage-calculators.aspx
- http://www.mortgagecalculator.org/calculators/index.php

These calculators and guidelines can guide you to the maximum loan or payment someone will lend to you, but you must decide how much you can actually afford to still stay within your budget, pay other debts, save for your goals, and maintain your financial security. Remember to budget for utilities, maintenance, and repairs. Adjust your emergency fund to accommodate any new expenses.

Finding a loan

When you have found that dream home, the real estate agent or developer will probably be ready to refer you to a favored mortgage broker or lender so you can immediately apply for a loan, However it's much better if you have done your comparison shopping in advance so you can take your time and ensure you are getting the best deal for your situation. In fact, you should go ahead and get pre-approved by a lender of your choosing before you start home shopping. Then you not only know how much home you can afford, but you also have this big step out of the way before the pressure and excitement of searching for and committing to a specific home.

Here is what you should know about mortgages.

- **Term** – Time it will take to pay the loan. The most common terms are 30 and 15 years, but you can get other terms such as 10 or 20. The longer the term you take to pay the loan, the lower the monthly payment will be which is why 30 years is the most popular term. However, I highly recommend you also consider a 20 or even 15 year loan, especially if this is necessary in order for the loan to be paid before you retire. You will pay tens of thousands of dollars less in interest, obtain a lower interest rate, and get rid of that huge budget expense much earlier. In return, you may find that the monthly payment isn't that much larger than a 30 year loan and may still fit within your budget and 43% debt to loan ratio. Alternatively, you could opt for a 30 year loan and promise to pay extra each month in order to pay it off sooner. After all, mortgage interest is the cheapest money to borrow, but are you really going to pay extra as you vowed? Here is an example to illustrate with a $100,000 loan.

	30 yr	**20 yr**	**15 yr**
Monthly payment	$466	$580	$700
Total interest	$67,745	$39,190	$26,043
Interest rate	3.8%	3.5%	3.2%

- **Rate** – The percentage of the loan balance you will pay each year in interest.

- **APR** – The "annual percentage rate" is the interest rate plus loan fees. The APR makes it easier to compare loan offers because it combines the interest rate and fees of a specific loan offer.

- **Points** – A fee borrowers may pay in order to get a lower interest rate. One point equals 1% of the loan amount and is paid at the home closing. This will be factored into the lender's APR.

- **Principle and interest** – Loan calculators will show you how much your monthly payment will be for the principle (amount of loan you are repaying each month) and interest (amount you pay to the lender for the right to borrow their money). However, you will also have to pay property taxes and homeowners insurance each month of at least several hundred dollars. In addition to the term and rate of a mortgage, you can choose from several types of mortgages based upon what happens to the interest rate. Any lender's website should show you their mortgage options in a nice table or two.

- **Fixed** – The interest rate does not change. This is the most popular and gives you the same payment to budget over the entire life of your loan. (The amount of your taxes and insurance will increase periodically.) If interest rates go up, yours doesn't; if interest rates go down significantly in the future, you can refinance to a new mortgage with a lower rate.

- **Variable** – (5/1, 7/1, etc.) The term is typically 30 years, but the interest rate will change with a variable rate mortgage. It typically begins with a low initial rate, but may be changed higher or lower afterwards. The first number shows how many years the initial rate will be in effect and the second number shows how often the rate can change after that, based upon a financial index your rate is pegged to. Find out what your variable rate "caps" will be. There is an annual cap specifying how much the rate can rise or drop when changed and a lifetime cap for the total allowable change. Variable mortgages may be beneficial if you expect to move or refinance within the time period on your low, introductory rate. However, you should ensure that your budget can handle any future payment increase if you do still have the variable rate mortgage when the introductory rate changes. If you expect to refinance, know if your loan contains a "prepayment" penalty fee.

- **Jumbo** - A jumbo loan is larger than what is known as the "conforming loan limit" used by Fannie Mae and Freddie Mac. The conforming amount changes periodically, and in 2017 was $424,000 in most of the continental U.S., but higher in some expensive urban areas. In some metropolitan areas, homes are simply more expensive so they require a jumbo loan. Specifics vary among lenders at any given time, but jumbo loans may require/allow a higher interest rate, credit score, emergency funds, down payment, and debt-to-income ratio. Not just rates, but also approval standards vary among lenders, so it pays to shop around as usual. Your choices include websites, banks, and mortgage brokers.

- **Web quotes** – Many websites enable you to enter your information and receive interest rate quotes from several lenders. These sites vary as some give you instant quotes and some let you do it anonymously. Do not provide your SSN at this stage. This should give you basic information on rates, fees, and types of loans even if you also talk to a bank or broker later. You may have noticed by now that I start my research for practically everything on the web. (It's hard to remember how I accomplished anything before there was an internet.)

- **Banks** – Big banks dominate the mortgage arena, but also check out local banks which may provide more flexibility and credit unions which may offer better rates. Most bank websites will provide valuable information about their types of loans, rates, fees, and possible promotions and even let you apply online. However, if all this is new, you may wish to actually visit a bank and talk to a real person who can review your options, calculate your numbers, and answer your questions (if possible, try to avoid busy Saturday mornings). Don't forget to start with your own bank and/or credit union as they may offer incentives to keep your service or offer rate discounts for direct debit from your checking account.

- **Mortgage brokers** – Mortgage brokers can help you thru the mortgage search process and may be able to find a lower rate than you can. They are useful if your situation may be more complicated than usual. You will know if you are getting a good deal, if you have done your web or bank research in advance. However, avoid ones that are paid by the banks with an incentive to give you a higher rate. Find a broker that works for you for a set fee at this site: http://www.upfrontmortgagebrokers.org/

When going thru the search process, you will pay a fee for the lender to pull your credit report, but do not pay any application fees. After you select a lender and home, you may also need to pay an appraiser to value the property. Each prospective lender should provide you a "Good Faith Estimate" form (GFE) that lists the rates and fees so you can compare offers and know what you are getting into. Even after you apply for a loan with a lender, the rate could still fluctuate during the approval process unless you request that it be "locked".

If you have problems getting a down payment or qualifying for a mortgage, the federal and state governments offer mortgage programs to consider. The USDA and VA have programs that some people may qualify for, but the biggest program is from the FHA (Federal Housing Administration). FHA insured loans are particularly helpful for people with low income, poor credit histories, or small down payments (as low as 3.5%), but anyone can use them. FHA rates are generally comparable to conventional loans, but there are a variety of extra fees, both upfront at closing and in the monthly payments. If you are buying a condo with an FHA backed loan, the condo must meet certain conditions; see the FHA website: www.fha.gov.

Don't trust -- be certain you know what you are getting into. During the worst of the housing crisis, many unscrupulous mortgage lenders and brokers got unsuspecting borrowers into loans they couldn't afford or that charged high fees. Government agencies have since been implementing new safeguards -- but it is still up to you to look after your interests. The best defense is to ALWAYS get at least three offers so you can compare them. Discuss them with someone you can trust. If you need to, hire an attorney or other professional to review and explain your paperwork and obligations. Don't let your excitement rush you into something you don't thoroughly understand and know will fit within your budget.

More information

- http://www.hud.gov/ - Some states have mortgage assistance programs. Find your state here. The HUD settlement booklet has information about the home buying process and example of the "Good Faith Estimate" form.
- https://www.mtgprofessor.com/home.aspx - Extensive mortgage information, calculators, articles, tips, and spreadsheets.

Refinancing a loan

Even after going thru all that work and expense to get a mortgage for 15-30 years, you are not stuck with it. You can refinance your old mortgage loan with a brand new loan. It's basically like getting an all new loan, so why would you want to?

- The most common reason is to get a new lower interest rate than what you currently have. When interest rates have dropped 1-2% lower than yours, you may wish to see if it can save you several hundred dollars per month in lower payments. It's doubly beneficial when you can combine lower rates with another reason below.
- Borrowers can convert an adjustable rate loan into a fixed rate loan to get a payment amount that won't change for the life of the loan.
- When rates have dropped, you may be able to exchange a 30 year loan into a shorter-term loan such as 15 or 20 years for not much of an increase in payments, while savings tens of thousands of dollars in interest. Most of the increase you will pay by shortening the term period might be offset by savings you would get by combining a new lower rate with the extra low rate charged to borrowers with shorter-term loans. (Rates for 15 year loans may be around one-half percent lower than rates for 30 year loans.) In fact, whenever you refinance, I highly recommend you consider going to a shorter-term loan so you aren't simply extending your mortgage payments farther and farther into the future. Note that websites may only list 15 and 30 year mortgages, but you can also ask for other terms such as 10 or 20 year loans. This is a great way to ensure the mortgage will be paid off before retirement or the kids go to college. See more below under, "Paying a loan early".
- Sometimes people want more cash in their pockets right now and will refinance a new 30 year loan on their current lower mortgage balance. Since part of their original loan has been paid off, they will be borrowing less for the new loan, resulting in lower payments, but have to start all over on a new 30 year term. Think carefully before doing this as you probably don't want to extend your mortgage payments into your retirement.
- Borrowers can get cash back from refinancing to use for other things such as paying high rate credit cards, remodeling, or the kids' college. If the new loan is less than 80% of the home value but more than the balance of the old mortgage, you get the difference in a nice big check at settlement. But this increases your monthly payments. Mortgage interest is about the cheapest way you can borrow money and this was popular when home prices were soaring and people were living beyond their budget. But when home prices crashed, foreclosures were rampant, and many people found themselves owing more than their home was

worth. The new reality caused many people to stop seeing their home as a cash cow and start living within their means.

You will need to compare the amount you save from lower payments with the fees and cost to refinance. The refinance calculator on zillow.com shows you both: http://www.zillow.com/mortgage-calculator/refinance-calculator/. The larger your mortgage or the longer you will have the loan, the more likely you will see a significant benefit to refinance. Sometimes no or low cost refinancing is available, so check several banks, websites, or mortgage brokers for promotions – especially your current lender.

People who refinance have mostly the same process and issues as getting a first mortgage. You need a good credit score to get the best rate, home payments and total debt must still be below the income thresh-holds, and you will need plenty of documentation. But refinancers may face a couple of extra hurdles. If you have a second mortgage, you have to pay it off, or you have to include it in the refinancing. If your current mortgage has a prepayment penalty, you could be paying thousands more in costs. To refinance, you usually need at least 90% "equity" in your home – 80% is better to get a lower rate and avoid PMI.

Get an *estimate* of what your home is worth from one of these websites:
- http://www.redfin.com/
- http://www.trulia.com/
- http://www.zillow.com/

Home equity loans

Another type of home loan you can get is a "home equity" loan. You can get this after you already own a home and need to borrow money. Mortgage and credit card debt are two of the largest categories of debt in America. Home equity loans (HEL) and home equity lines of credit (HELOC) are a combination of these. You have great flexibility in using these loans, but your home is the collateral to ensure the bank gets their money back. Unlike credit cards, this means if you don't pay this back, the lender can foreclose on your home and bankruptcy is no protection.

How it works

There are two main differences between HELs and HELOCs. Home equity loans are for a fixed amount, interest rate, and term length that does not change. For example, you may get a lump sum for $50,000 and pay it back monthly for ten or fifteen years at 7%

interest. Home equity lines of credit usually have variable interest rates that can go up or down following a financial index and economic conditions in the country. Rather than a fixed loan amount, HELOCs have a credit limit like credit cards and you can use any amount between zero and your credit limit at any given time. You pay a monthly payment for however long it takes until it's paid off, but the line of credit still exists for future use. Therefore, HELOCs give you greater flexibility in borrowing and paying, but eventually the interest rate is going to rise.

The amount of your home equity loan or line can be up to 80% of the equity in your home. Example:

$300,000 - home's current value

- 100,000 – amount owed on your mortgage(s)

$200,000 – equity in home

X   80%

$160,000 – maximum amount of your loan

Advantages

There are two main advantages of HELs and HELOCs over credit cards: you can deduct the interest on your income taxes and they have much lower interest rates. You can deduct the interest on your taxes up to a loan amount of $100,000 and up to $1,000,000 if used for home improvements. For example, if you paid $1000 in interest and were in a 25% tax bracket, your taxes would be reduced by $250. But of course, HELs and HELOCs also have a flip side; since your home is the collateral, you could lose your home if you lose your job and can't make payments on your home equity loan or line, which would not happen with credit cards. HELs and HELOCs usually have large up-front fees, similar to a mortgage, so when you shop around to banks and credit unions, compare both interest rates and fees. Remember the *APR* rate combines the interest rate and fees to make comparison easier. Some lenders will give you a lower rate in return for direct debit of your payments or free closing costs if you don't close the loan within a certain number of years. So by now you should know the drill -- shop around starting with your current bank to see if they will give you a deal.

Home equity loans and lines should not be used to live beyond your means, but are a reasonable way to transfer higher interest loans. HELs are best for one-time large expenses such as remodeling. HELOCs may be best to keep available to handle emergencies, medical bills, or college costs. So equity in your home is not wealth to spend, but financial security and flexibility if needed.

Paying a loan early

There is an alternative to refinancing that still enables you to pay off your mortgage early and save thousands in interest. You can make extra payments on your existing mortgage at any time, but should you? The fact that this is a never-ending topic of discussion shows its high level of interest and that there is no conclusive answer for everyone's situation. One example with a 30 year, $150,000, 5% fixed rate loan – paying an extra $100 per month would save you around $35,000 in interest and 80 months of payments. Saving interest and getting out of debt early contributes to financial security and peace of mind, but here are alternative numbers. Investing that same $100 per month for the same 23.2 years, but at 7% return, would yield you $69,000 – almost twice as much as the mortgage savings. So this question involves both emotions and cold cash. Let's examine some details to help sort this out.

You may have a lot of competition for that extra cash, so establish priorities. First, pay off higher rate debt such as credit cards. Ensure you have an emergency fund that will give you more flexibility and financial security than "locking" money up in your home. Raise your retirement savings rate to 15% which is usually yielding you more than your low mortgage interest rate. Consider increasing the kids' college fund that is usually yielding more than your mortgage interest rate and is a nearer term problem. If you are deciding between paying off student loans or the mortgage, go for student loans with a higher interest rate, otherwise the mortgage, which increases equity in your home.

There are many ways to pay extra on your mortgage including a set amount per month, lump sum, annual bonus, or bi-weekly which forces you to make two extra payments per year, but don't pay your lender an extra fee to do so, which is all too common to join a formal, bi-weekly payment program.

Use these prepay calculators to help you decide:
- http://www.dinkytown.net/
- http://www.hsh.com/calculators.html

Buying a home

You saved a down payment, shopped for a loan and got pre-approved, know what size home you can afford, and reviewed your budget to decide how big a loan payment you can actually afford. Now comes the fun part – shopping for a home you can call your own. You can begin your research and narrow down your neighborhoods with many websites that will show you homes, prices, location, and features. Then evaluate schools, commuting to work, shopping, and neighborhoods you can afford. Visit open houses to see which features, sizes, styles, and neighborhoods match which prices.

Or jump directly to picking a real estate agent that can help narrow your choices, show you properties, help negotiate, deal with third parties, and hold your hand all the way thru settlement. There is no reason for a buyer not to work with a real estate agent (unless you are only buying a new home from a builder) because the seller will pay your agent from the proceeds of the sale. Typically, the seller pays a commission of 5-6% of the sale price that is split between the buyer's and seller's agents. Follow the money and note that the interests of your agent and yourself don't necessarily coincide. Your agent is paid by the seller, their commission is bigger the more expensive home you buy, and in fact they legally work for the seller. Moreover, some sellers will pay a bonus to buyer's agents to increase the likelihood of their home being shown to buyers and sold quickly. To lessen this conflict, consider choosing a "buyer's agent" that has a fiduciary responsibility to work for you even though they are still paid by the seller. When you interview an agent, ask them to be a "buyer's agent"; many will even if it is not their usual business.

When you decide upon a home, your agent can help you make an offer and negotiate. Here are some factors to consider.

- Are you in a buyer's or seller's market?
- What have comparable homes sold for recently?
- What other comparable properties are currently on the market for what price?
- How motivated is the seller to sell quickly and cheaply?
- How long has the home been on the market and how many times has the price been cut?
- What is the condition of the home and neighborhood?

Discuss these with your agent to decide whether your approach will be to offer a low bid and hope to negotiate or offer a reasonable offer you are willing to pay and avoid possible bids from other buyers. You can also ask the seller for help in paying your closing costs or interest points to get a lower interest rate. Real estate agents love these options because they get you more money without lowering the price and their commissions.

After reaching an agreement on price, your offer may include "contingencies" that let you back out without penalty based upon you getting a home inspection, financing approval, sale of your current home, or an appraisal level consistent with the home offer. Some of these may be unattractive to sellers or you may need to work with the seller's contingencies for such things as when settlement will be – soon or after they have bought a home or received bank approval for a short sale. When you reach agreement, be prepared to pay the seller an "earnest deposit" to show your good faith which will be applied to the closing costs at settlement.

If it is a house, always get an inspection so you will know any defects with the home. If any are found, you can negotiate with the seller to fix them or give you a discount.

Settlement/Closing

Once you have a signed an agreement, you can apply for or finalize your mortgage loan with your lender. Depending upon how busy they are and how quickly you provide the needed documentation, you could get your approval within three to six weeks. Then the real estate agents can work with the buyer, seller, and a real estate settlement company to schedule the "closing" when all parties will meet and sign thousands and thousands of papers written by government agencies and lawyers in microscopic print. The settlement agent or attorney will briefly explain each one and ask if you have any questions, but you won't have time to read all those pages. My favorite is one that informed me that there was a helicopter-landing zone in my area – or maybe that there wasn't one.

Concentrate on the most important document – the Closing Disclosure (formerly the HUD-1) that explains all the charges and credits to both the buyer and seller. This is the bottom line that shows who owes how much to whom, and it should not be much of a surprise because you can compare it to the "Good Faith Estimate" (GFE) that you received earlier from your lender showing how much you would owe for the loan, closing, and monthly payments. The GFE is only an estimate, but if the Closing Disclosure differs significantly, question the lender and settlement agent closely about it.

The financial crisis revealed that many people were put in loans they didn't understand. Don't let this happen to you. The time to understand your loan and payments is when you get the GFEs from at least three lenders so you can compare them. Discuss them with several of these people: lender, real estate agent, someone you can trust, settlement agent, or even consult an attorney or financial advisor.

In order to FULLY understand it and compare the Closing Disclosure with the GFE, you should get the Closing Disclosure from the settlement agent at least three days before the closing. You don't want the added pressure of reviewing all those details only when you are sitting at the signing table. In my experience, they are usually so busy that it's not ready until the last possible minute. Don't settle for this. Tell them you want the Closing Disclosure the day before closing. They can fax or email it to you. If it looks like you won't get it in advance with enough time to review it, call the settlement company and tell them if you don't get it in advance, the closing will have to be rescheduled because you won't be coming. Once, I noticed that my Closing Disclosure needed to be corrected to account for all the terms of agreement between the buyer and seller. It was much easier to spot and correct in advance than when everyone in the room is staring at you and waiting for you to sign.

In addition to a loan down payment, you will need 2-4% of the sale price for a wide variety of closing costs that will be detailed on the Closing Disclosure. Sometimes you can get some of this rolled into the mortgage amount, or negotiate to get the seller to pay for you. Some of the closing costs paid to the lender can be negotiated with the lender, so when you are shopping for the best loan, review fees as well as rates.

Details about settlement procedures and charges vary by jurisdiction and time period, but the Closing Disclosure itself will be the same across the US. Let's review a few highlights and tips.

- Title insurance – Insurance to protect the lender and you against claims from others against your home. You could save a few hundred dollars by comparison shopping here: http://www.entitledirect.com/. Do this before you agree to a loan when the lender will pick their favored company. Ask for a discount "reissue" rate if you are refinancing.
- Lender and settlement fees – One of your biggest charges is the "origination fee" you pay the lender and for which you comparison shopped among lenders. But there are plenty of other so called "junk fees" that nickel and dime you, as well as fees to third parties for appraisals, inspections, etc.

- Government taxes and fees – These vary by jurisdiction and no, they are not negotiable.
- Escrow – You prepay escrow to the lender so they can pay your insurance and property taxes when they come due once or twice per year. In addition to principle and interest, your monthly mortgage payment will include an escrow amount for these as well. This amount will change slightly every year.
- Interest – You owe the lender interest between the date of settlement and your first payment. **TIP:** I usually try to close near the end of the month so this interest amount will be as low as possible. If you settle near the beginning of the month, your interest could be hundreds or even a couple of thousand extra dollars you will need to pay.

Once you finish signing that pile of papers and asking your last questions, the buyer gets the keys and the seller gets a nice big check.

Selling a home

You may have one advantage when it comes time to sell your home, but it's no less stressful. Selling is the flipside to buying and you have gone thru the buying process before. If you are both selling your current home and buying a new one, it is usually easier to sell your existing home first and then buy your new home. This can make it easier to get your down payment and new mortgage pre-approval. Selling a home can be more difficult and take longer than buying and you want to avoid making two mortgage payments. If you do buy a home first, you can request a contingency to sell your current home first, but the seller might balk at the delay. If you do have to proceed and need funds to bridge the gap between buying and selling, you can try to raise the funds thru a home equity loan (watch for prepayment penalties) or look for a lender that offers "bridge" loans for just these occasions.

The appearance of your home is important in determining how close to your asking price you will get. Unless you are selling and pricing it as a "fixer upper", you should paint, repair, landscape, de-clutter, and de-personalize it. It must be kept clean to show at a moment's notice. You want your home to appear as nicely as possible. Removing as many of your personal items as practical, not only makes it show better, but also helps the potential buyers visualize it as their's. I can't say how many homes I have looked at where I couldn't get a good impression of the home because I couldn't see past the mess or clutter. Consider getting your own home inspection and termite report to immediately allay any buyer fears about hidden problems.

You can select a full service real estate agent, get a fee-for-service agent, or try to sell it yourself. As the seller you will be paying the real estate agents' commission, typically 6%, split between the buyer's agent and your's. You can also try ZipRealty which only charges 5% or Redfin which uses salaried agents with fees as low as 4.5%. A fee-for-service agent will split duties with you and charge a-la-cart for specific services, plus the buyer's agent commission, but could save you thousands. You can interview agents about their experience, marketing plans, and services. You and the agent specify a time limit for the agreement, for example 90 days, after which you can continue or move on.

A real estate agent has a lot of time, expertise, and resources you don't have such as listing, marketing, and showing your property as well as helping you with the other buyer/seller and closing company. Perhaps the most important is pricing your home right. Agents will conduct a competitive market analysis to determine what similar homes have sold for recently and price yours after taking into account the condition, features, competition, and all important location. Frequently, agents want to price it to move quickly and suggest a price slightly under the competition while sellers want to wring every last dollar they can and insist on starting with a high price. Regardless, you must be realistic and flexible. If you aren't getting showings, then you know the price is too high. You may even need to lower the price several times. Alternatively, you can offer a $1000-$2000 bonus to the buyer's agent that should prompt more agents to show your property to their clients. If you get showings, but few offers, then something may be off with the home, or the price is still higher than the competition. If you are still not selling, you must lower the price further and the agent will suggest when. If the home is on the market too long, then buyers start to wonder about it or drive a harder bargain.

Once you attract buyers, then the negotiations begin. The agent can give you vital information about what kind of market you are in – do buyers or sellers have to compromise more. The agent can also help work thru the bargaining, different ways to structure a deal to meet the buyer's particular needs, and possible contingencies for things such as the buyer getting a loan, selling their home, or getting a home inspection of your property.

For sale by owner

When selling your house, you can trade thousands of dollars in savings for dozens of hours of extra work by trying to sell your house without using a real estate agent. This is known as "for sale by owner" (FSBO), a route taken by an estimated 10-20% of owners each year. The savings can be significant because you don't have to pay the commission to the seller's real estate agent and can decide whether to pay one to the buyer's agent or not (but if you don't, the buyer's agent probably won't show your property to their clients). For example, on a 300,000 home, you could save $9000 on the seller's commission or $18,000 on both.

You will have to commit to a lot of time and effort to get those savings. Be prepared to stage open houses on the weekends, show the home any time you get an inquiry, and learn the basics of being your own agent at every step of the process. But you don't have to do it all on your own. Plenty of services, professionals, and websites will help FSBOs for a fee.

In addition to the issues covered above, FSBOs need to focus on the following. You will need to be objective in determining a price slightly above what you think you can actually sell your home for – too high and you won't get offers, too low and you lose some of your savings. You can set the price yourself by reviewing comparable properties that have sold previously or hire an appraiser for a few hundred dollars. You can pay to have your home listed in the MLS (Multiple Listing Service) that real estate agents use as well as web listings specifically for FSBOs. Get a real estate attorney to help complete forms and contracts, evaluate offers, handle escrow, advise on contingencies, help with closing, and help look after your interests. Remember that closing on real estate involves lots and lots of legal forms designed by real estate lawyers.

Whether you sell your home yourself or with an agent, you will need to sign a huge pile of papers before you can exchange your home title for a nice check, likely in a closing/settlement similar to what I described with the buyer. If it is your main home, you do get tax breaks for any capital gains below $250,000 ($500,000 if filing jointly), but you don't get to deduct any losses. See the IRS website for whatever rules are in affect at the time of your tax reporting:

http://www.irs.gov/Businesses/Small-Businesses-&-Self-Employed/Sale-of-Residence---Real-Estate-Tax-Tips

Owning a home

Financial security comes from being financially prepared for life's potholes and opportunities, rather than just reacting to them. Owning a home that fits within your budget contributes to your financial security because you get stability, forced savings that builds your wealth, growing equity that can be tapped in an emergency, and comfort from knowing that one of these years your mortgage payments will end. However, you must be prepared for the inevitable expenses and responsibilities that come with your home. Let's cover several you should be prepared for.

Insurance

Yes, there are many types of insurance you are required to get and home owners hazard insurance is one of them, at least while you are paying a mortgage. It's so important, that your lender will collect the money from you in your monthly payment and pay the insurance company for you when the premiums are due. Premiums depend upon your state, credit score, claims history, the claims history of the house, amount and type of coverage, and whether you live in a coastal or flood plain area. You do get to choose your insurer and here are ways you can save:

- Of course, the top of the list is to comparison shop since rates can vary widely. You should do this every few years because rates, coverage, and policies can change. You can check directly with specific companies or many websites to get multiple quotes.
- Bundle your homeowners and auto insurance with the same company and you could save 5-15%.
- Include a high-deductible. Going from $500 to $1000 could save 20-25%.
- Avoid making small claims to avoid price hikes of 5 -15% or even being dropped for too many claims – some say even inquiries about potential claims. Raising your deductible and paying small claims yourself give a double savings on premiums.
- Maintaining a good credit history is important for so many things including getting the best insurance rates. Check your credit history periodically and correct any errors.

- Adding safety upgrades to you home can reduce premiums. Ask your insurer about things such as dead-bolt locks, security monitoring systems, and smoke alarms.

Not everything is about just saving money. When you talk to your insurer, discuss coverage such as a correct replacement value to rebuild your home, liability coverage in case someone sues you, identity theft coverage, and flood insurance. Document your belongings with an inventory, video camera, and receipts.

- http://building-cost.net/ - calculate the cost to replace your home.
- https://www.knowyourstuff.org – Use an online system and/or smartphone app to keep an inventory of your belongings.
- http://www.floodsmart.gov/floodsmart/ - Enter your address at this government website and get your flood risk, estimated flood insurance premiums, and list of local agents.

Maintenance

Homes need maintenance, big and small, plumbers and new roofs, routine and emergency. You don't see it so much in condos because you pay that monthly fee to take care of the big stuff, but you still occasionally need plumbers, paint, new appliances, etc. Financial security means planning for maintenance expenses in advance, preferably with an emergency fund, possible with a home equity line of credit. The biggest way to save money on maintenance expenses is not to postpone it (too often that makes it worse), but to do as much of it yourself as possible. Painting is the easiest way to save big bucks, although I hire out second story jobs. You can rent a wide variety of tools such as chain saws, power washers, and carpet cleaners that will still save you good money over owning or contracting out.

Do-It-Yourself

The biggest surprise to me is how much money we can save by repairing things ourselves – even things we know nothing about. I count the internet as one of the most life-changing inventions of my lifetime and one of the most wonderful examples is the capability to look up almost anything. This includes a surprising number of maintenance and repair problems. I highly recommend that your first stop for repair problems is not the phonebook, but the internet to search for your problem. Chances are very good that you will find someone else who has encountered the same issue, has provided a solution, and even uploaded a video showing how to fix it. Obviously, not all internet information is equally good, but I'm continually amazed at how often this works.

A recent example involved my refrigerator that sprang a leak from the water dispenser. I know nothing about repairing appliances, so I quickly called a repairman and learned that the cost would be at least $250 plus parts. Next, I searched the internet for my model and problem and found plenty of information about it, including a common consensus of the solution – I needed a replacement valve. I quickly found I could order the part for only one fifth of the cost of a repairman, but was still dubious that I could install it myself. Then I found several YouTube videos that showed exactly how to do it. Vindicated for my do-it-yourself, cost-saving labors, I ordered the part, re-watched the video, installed the valve, and barely contained my glee that it worked, saving over $250! My family considered it just another routine fix, but I walked around with a swelled head for days. I discovered this also works for electronic control panels found in new appliances.

When you do need a repairman, learn what they do. I quickly discovered that I could save big electrician costs by replacing my own failed circuit breakers, light switches, and light fixtures for just a few bucks. Save plumbing costs by unclogging your own toilets, not with plungers, but with a plumbing "snake". Know that replacement toilet parts cost under $20, take minutes to replace, and have numerous YouTube repair videos to watch, compared to a plumber costing $250+There is a good reason why Home Depot, Lowes, and hardware stores are packed these days – even by women.

Contractors, handymen, and repair persons

Of course there are plenty of times when you will need to hire a repair person, handyman, or contractor. I recommend two ways to find a good one. First, ask friends and neighbors for a recommendation. My community has a list-serv/email group that we use to exchange information and request recommendations. Second, consider websites such as these:

- http://www.angieslist.com
- http://www.checkbook.org/
- http://www.yelp.com/
- http://www.thumbtack.com/

When you find a good one, keep them in your contacts and share with others.

Warranties

Because repairs can be expensive, it is sometimes tempting to consider home warranties that promise to cover some of the repair costs and replace broken appliances. Most often sellers provide these to attract homebuyers worried about problems soon after they buy. Most experts advise against them since you usually don't save your costs back, you don't get to choose repairmen or replacement appliances (if they do pay for them), and the warranties have so many "escape" clauses in the fine print. I can say I did appreciate warranties when the seller paid for them and sometimes saved a couple hundred dollars from repairs. However, I would rather have had the money applied to my closing costs. Dealing with the warranty company was always a hassle, and I never saved enough money to cover the costs. Despite this, one time I did choose to extend a warranty I got from a seller because the HVAC system was *ten years older than the normal life expectancy*. Sure enough, the ancient HVAC system did expire during the coming year and – surprise, surprise – the warranty company refused to fix or replace the $4000 system they had warrantied. Thus, my experience with several companies is that they will readily send a repairman that looks after their interests – not yours, but they are more than ready to find any excuse not to replace an appliance or system, so you don't even buy peace of mind. Save your money and avoid these home warranty companies – remember their entire business model is based upon very few customers getting back what they paid in.

More information

- http://www.makinghomeaffordable.gov   - Talk to a HUD-approved housing counselor to help you understand your options, prepare your application, and work with your mortgage company.
- http://www.decisionaide.com/ - More home calculators.
- http://portal.hud.gov/hudportal/HUD?src=/topics/avoiding_foreclosure -Tips and assistance for avoiding foreclosure.

Summary

- Renting is often a better short-term solution while you save a down payment, find a steady job, qualify for a loan, decide where to settle down, or expect to relocate. In the long-term, ownership forces you to convert spending on a place to live into equity in your home that increases your net worth and can be used, if needed, in a home equity loan, reverse mortgage, or sale.

- The commonly recommended home down payment is 20% and is often an early savings goal. This will lower your monthly payments and avoid PMI fees. However, you may have other options for getting this down payment or getting loans that allow a lower percentage, especially thru government programs with the VA, USDA, and FHA.

- Shop for a loan before a home. This enables you to know how much home you can afford, how much your monthly payment will be, and how well it will fit within your budget.

- Guidelines recommend home payments be less than 28% of your income and total debt less than 43%.

- Don't trust -- be certain you know what you are getting into. It is up to you to look after your interests. The best defense is to ALWAYS get at least three offers so you can compare them. Discuss them with someone you can trust. If you need to, hire an attorney or other professional to review and explain your paperwork and obligations. Don't let your excitement rush you into something you don't thoroughly understand and know will fit within your budget.

- Start your house hunting by driving thru neighborhoods and researching on the web, but a real estate agent can help narrow your choices, show you properties, help negotiate, deal with third parties, and hold your hand all the way thru settlement. Real estate agents are paid by the seller, so get you a "buyers" agent with a fiduciary interest to serve your interests.

- Insist upon reviewing your Closing Disclosure before going to settlement, which explains all the charges and credits to both the buyer and seller. This is the bottom line that shows who owes how much to whom, and it should not be much of a surprise because you can compare it to the "Good Faith Estimate" (GFE) that you received earlier from your lender.

- Consider refinancing an existing loan when rates are more than 1% less than yours, you want to convert a variable rate to a fixed rate loan, or you can get a shorter term loan for not much more money. Use refinancing to get cashback as a last resort.
- When selling your home, the appearance is important in determining how close to your asking price you will get. Paint, repair, landscape, de-clutter, clean, and de-personalize it. It must be kept clean to show at a moment's notice. You want your home to appear as nicely as possible.
- Financial security comes from being financially prepared for life's potholes and opportunities, rather than just reacting to them. Owning a home that fits within your budget contributes to your financial security because you get stability, forced savings that builds your wealth, growing equity that can be tapped in an emergency, and comfort from knowing that one of these years your mortgage payments will end. However, you must be prepared for the inevitable expenses and responsibilities that come with your home including insurance, repairs, and maintenance.
- Save serious money by learning to do as much of your maintenance and repairs as you can. Use the internet to see videos and order replacement parts for many types of repairs and maintenance.

Chapter Nineteen

Paying For College

- The college maze
- Scholarships and grants
- Paying for college
- Loans
- Saving on campus
- More information and calculators

College may be the second most expensive thing many people elect to pay for, after a home. The College Board reports that in 2016-17, the average cost of an in-state public college was $20,090 and a private college was $45,370. Repeat this for four or more years and the cost of a college education can appear staggering. Indeed college costs have skyrocketed since many of us parents went to college, with education costs rising much faster than inflation and states' aid to colleges plummeting since the recession. Moreover, it's much harder for students to work their way thru college considering that the minimum wage has risen much less than inflation and college costs much more than inflation.

Despite this tremendous cost, let's review why college is still so important. This 2016 data from the Federal Bureau of Labor Statistics show that college graduates earn more and have a lower unemployment rate than the average worker. See the current data on their website: http://www.bls.gov/emp/ep_chart_001.htm

Unemployment rates and earnings by educational attainment, 2016

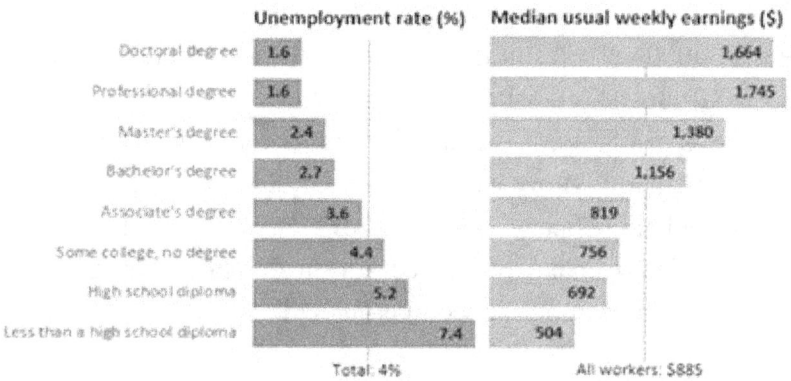

	Unemployment rate (%)	Median usual weekly earnings ($)
Doctoral degree	1.6	1,664
Professional degree	1.6	1,745
Master's degree	2.4	1,380
Bachelor's degree	2.7	1,156
Associate's degree	3.6	819
Some college, no degree	4.4	756
High school diploma	5.2	692
Less than a high school diploma	7.4	504
	Total: 4%	All workers: $885

Note: Data are for persons age 25 and over. Earnings are for full-time wage and salary workers.
Source: U.S. Bureau of Labor Statistics, Current Population Survey.

A 2014 study by the Federal Reserve Bank of New York found that graduates with a Bachelor's degree earned $1 million more than those with only a high school degree. So despite the rising costs, a college degree is still the best investment to increase your future earnings. Thankfully, there are many ways to pay for college and this chapter will help navigate us thru the maze.

Sallie Mae, the student loan corporation, published a study showing how Americans pays for college, http://news.salliemae.com/case-study/how-america-pays-college. It shows that families have been finding ways to reduce their college expenses including eliminating schools based upon costs (67%), living at home (57%), accelerating course-work (27%), and going to community colleges.

Here is how the average family paid for college in 2013:

30%	Grants and scholarships
27%	Parent income and savings
11%	Student income and savings
18%	Student borrowing
9%	Parent borrowing
5%	Relatives and friends

The college maze

There are more than 4000 colleges in the United States, and there are many things to consider when choosing your short list. Navigating the college admissions maze can seem daunting, but help is available. You can hire professional financial aid consultants for big bucks, but better advice is to consult with your student's high school guidance counselor, college financial aid officer, library, and of course the internet. But first, read on as this chapter is intended to make you successful in researching schools, paying for college, getting financial aid, comparing competing aid packages, and saving money while attending college.

Estimate what you will have to pay

We all know that college is hugely expensive, but what we really want to know is how much of that we will have to pay and borrow. That depends upon the cost of the school, family income and assets, and amount of financial aid you get. In determining the amount of financial aid you will get, all schools use the same federal formula to first determine your family's "*expected family contribution*" (EFC) amount. The EFC is based upon the parents' and student's income, assets, and expenses along with other factors such as parent's age (and time to retirement) and number of children attending college. Families are expected to pay this amount from savings, income, or loans. Schools subtract the EFC from the cost of the college to determine the family's "need" and use this to determine how much financial aid to offer. Schools can offer anywhere from nothing to the full amount needed, and financial aid can be any combination of grants, scholarships, work-study, and loans.

Thankfully, there are internet calculators to help. Start with the general calculators that estimate how much your family is expected to pay and how much financial aid you might qualify for based upon your family income, assets, and size:

- https://bigfuture.collegeboard.org/pay-for-college/paying-your-share/expected-family-contribution-calculator - Estimate how much the student's family will be expected to contribute to college in general.
- http://studentaid.ed.gov/fafsa/estimate - The federal website calculator estimates federal grants, work-study, and loans you might qualify for based upon your assets and income.

Then get estimates about specific colleges by using the "net price calculator" on most college websites. It will estimate what a typical family in your situation may receive, pay, and borrow at that particular school. These are only rough estimates and the accuracy can vary widely. The more detailed questions the calculator asks, the better the results are likely to be. If you choose to provide your contact information, many schools will send you more detailed information aimed at your specific situation.

Search for colleges

Picking a college is unlike any other purchase you'll make. Despite the humongous price, you are not looking for a bargain. You are looking for a school that has good *four-year* graduation rates, is affordable in your situation, offers a good aid package, and is where the student can do well. Be realistic about which schools you apply to. Match your student's academic achievements and interests, likelihood of getting financial aid, and financial situation to the appropriate schools. Local community colleges, in-state public universities, out-of-state public universities, and private colleges each present a new level of magnitude in costs and, potentially, academic levels. Within each of these categories, you may have many choices. Thankfully, the internet has many college search tools to begin your research. Here are a few:

- http://nces.ed.gov/collegenavigator/
- http://college-insight.org/
- http://costoflearning.com/
- https://bigfuture.collegeboard.org/college-search
- http://collegecost.ed.gov/
- https://collegeprowler.com/

Many organizations offer rankings of the best colleges – search "best college rankings". Here are a few:

- http://colleges.usnews.rankingsandreviews.com/best-colleges
- http://www.kiplinger.com/article/college/T014-C000-S002-kiplinger-s-best-college-values-2017.html
- http://www.princetonreview.com/college-rankings.aspx
- http://www.ruggsrecommendations.com/index.html
- http://new.time.com/money/best-colleges/

These search tools provide a lot of useful information to help select colleges that are right for your student. But even with nice search tools, narrowing 4000+ schools down to less than ten or so can be daunting.

Select your short list of colleges

There are many ways to choose a short list of colleges and different factors will be important to different students. I suggest you consider the following areas:

- Students grades, test scores, and major
- Quality of the school
- Financial circumstances
- Right fit for the student

Student grades, test scores, and major

Some majors are only offered at certain schools, so this might be the first filter in the college search tools. Then filter for schools that match the student's grade point average and SAT or ACT test scores. Schools with average rates above your student may be good schools, but harder to get into. These are called "reach schools" and you may want 1-2 of them in case you get lucky and your student is selected for reason other than grades. Schools with average rates similar to your student will be easier to get into, be a better academic fit, and more likely to offer financial aid. A handful of these schools on your list will more likely ensure you have several acceptances to choose from. Some students also apply to a "safety" school with average test scores and GPA lower than their student's which they will almost certainly be accepted into – just in case.

Quality of the school

You may be looking for the best schools that your student can get into. It's easy to know the quality of the Ivy's, the big state schools, and the expensive private schools, but how to you determine the thousands of other schools? Some of this is subjective; some you can get from the various college rankings; but you can also filter data with the college search tools.

- Higher average test scores and GPAs for admitted students mean more bright students are admitted.
- Lower "selectivity" rates mean that a smaller percentage of people that applied were admitted.

- Higher "graduation" rates mean that a higher percentage of the school's students actually graduated in 4 or 5 years. This is the school's success rate and can reflect efforts to help students succeed. Regardless which types of schools the student is considering, you should seriously consider this as a prime filter and aim for schools with rates above 40% or 50%.

Financial circumstances

An affordable education for the student is a prime consideration, but what this means depends upon a number of family, financial, and academic circumstances. The price of the school you are interested in is the "net price" after financial aid, so the amount of financial aid you will receive is as important as the sticker price of the school. Most aid is based upon merit or financial need. Thus, it primarily goes to students with the best academic or athletic attraction to the school and lower-income families. This is a big topic and I will discuss it in more detail below, but for now, this can be one of your college search filters. Low cost schools are a prime filter if you are not expecting much merit or need-based aid; less so if you can get enough aid to cover most expenses regardless how expensive the school is. Of course in-state tuition is much more affordable than out-of-state tuition (generally one-third to one-half as much), so this may be another prime filter. You may want a mix of affordable schools in case you don't get much aid and expensive schools in case you do get nice aid packages.

Right fit for the student

Using the data above, you should be able to use the college search tools to filter thousands of college down to a manageable list to consider. But there are a host of other factors that also go into the decision about which schools would be the best fit for a specific student. Many of these can also be filtered such as size, setting, and location of the school and town. But there are also plenty of other considerations that can be better sorted out by visiting their website and campus. And parents, there are plenty of things a family can do to make this process easier, but remember the student is the best person to make the final decision.

Financial aid fundamentals

Your student stands a better chance of getting significant financial aid from a college if their grades, SAT/ACT scores, extra-curricular activities, community service, or intended major is attractive to that college. Consider choosing a school in which your student is likely to rank among the top 40% of students. This not only helps to ensure a student will fit in and do well, but likely will result in the highest merit aid which schools offer to attract the best students. Use this college navigator to find the range of SAT/ACT scores at a potential college to see where your student would rank. http://nces.ed.gov/collegenavigator/

Thankfully, there are any number of reasons why a particular school would find your student attractive other than just academics or athletics. Examples may include a desire for a diverse student body based upon gender, race, geographical residence, desired major, or extracurricular activities.

The good news is that most students do get some type of financial aid, especially lower income families and top-tier students. Schools may offer four types of aid: scholarships and grants that do not have to be repaid, "work-study" that provides on-campus jobs to students, and loans. Obviously, scholarships and grants are the best, but work-study jobs are nice too. They are usually more convenient, guaranteed, and sometimes more interesting than other private industry jobs such as fast food or waitressing.

While the sticker price of private colleges on average costs two to four times as much as an in-state public college, don't dismiss them without researching. Remember it's the *net* cost after financial aid that we are interested in and more than half of private college students get significant financial aid. However, think carefully whether a more prestigious school is really worthwhile if it costs you more than a few thousand above a less expensive school – *after financial aid offers are deducted.* Consider that for most majors, a prestigious college doesn't necessarily lead to any more job offers or higher starting pay, even if it means much higher loan repayments for ten years after graduation. (Okay, that might not be true for the *most* prestigious universities.)

When choosing colleges to apply to, remember that most financial aid is based upon need. The more expensive the college, the more the need to pay for it, and the more financial aid you would be eligible for. So it may be worthwhile to apply to a few expensive schools to see what amount and kind of financial aid you are offered. But always apply to a "safety" school as well that is less expensive and more affordable if you don't receive the aid you are hoping for. Some parents don't bother to apply for financial aid fearing that they earn too little to afford college or earn too much to qualify for aid, but it's always good to apply initially to see what happens. While all schools use the same federal financial aid formula, each school may also have their own aid amounts, qualifications, or eagerness to attract your particular student. The easiest to get financial assistance is a small "legacy" tuition discount for attending a school where a parent or grandparent is an alumnus – if your school offers it.

Remember that there are alternatives to traditional four-year colleges, including two-year associate degrees at community colleges and certification exams from for-profit schools. These are much less expensive, while being popular for nursing, business, information technology, and law enforcement.

Scholarships and grants

It's tempting for parents to put off saving for college with the hope that their child will get a scholarship, but the reality is that only a tiny portion get athletic scholarships or "full" merit scholarships that go to the top tier of students. Even full merit scholarships rarely cover room and board, which can be around $10,000 per year. Nevertheless, most students do get some type of financial aid. Scholarships are based upon merit or other qualifications and can come from colleges or private organizations. Grants are based upon financial need and can also come from the federal and state governments. Submit your financial aid applications to colleges as soon as you can – do not wait until the student is accepted. Larger scholarships tend to have the earliest deadlines, as early as November 1. Private scholarships have their own deadlines and rules.

Additionally, there are thousands of scholarships from organizations unrelated to colleges or governments. We all hope our students will get big scholarships and grants from colleges, but in many cases, your best bet may be to apply for many scholarships that have nothing to do with athletics, grades, or family income. This is especially true for families with income that make them unlikely to be eligible for much aid from colleges or for students that are unlikely to get much merit aid. This is unlikely to cover most of your college expenses because most scholarships are small, but many small amounts could add up to a significant amount. Your best chances result from applying early and to as many as you can. The real challenge is how many scholarship essays can you get your student to write, or at least apply for.

Free Application for Federal Student Aid - FAFSA

The first step for aid from colleges is to apply for the *"Free Application for Federal Student Aid"* (FAFSA) which is the basis for need-based aid, federal loans, and sometimes for schools' merit scholarships. Beginning with the 2017-18 college year, families can begin submitting it on October 1 and use the prior year's tax data. So not only can you submit it earlier, but you would use your previous tax returns rather than estimating your coming tax return. http://www.fafsa.ed.gov – Get information and apply online for financial aid.

The FAFSA is used to determine the student's need for financial aid and is based upon the family's and student's income, assets, and other information. The FAFSA is used to calculate the amount the family is expected to pay which is known as the *"expected family contribution"* (EFC). In addition to family income, the amount of financial aid depends upon such factors as family savings, student income and savings, and how many siblings are in college. 5.6% of parents' assets are counted towards the family's EFC including college savings accounts, but not retirement accounts. However, some assets are excluded based upon the oldest parent's age. This means that for each $1000 of parent's assets, aid may be reduced by $57. Students are expected to pay more, so 20% of savings in their name are counted. Earnings that exceed certain amounts reduce aid, although federal work-study earnings do not. Coverdell Education Savings Accounts are counted as student's assets. Grandparent's 529 savings do not need to be reported on your FAFSA, but any payments they make from their 529 accounts are counted as student income for that year. When grandparents pay college expenses directly to the college, it might reduce aid dollar for dollar.

If parents are divorced, the parent who has had custody of the student for most of the prior 12 months is the one whose income and assets are listed on the FAFSA, along with the step-parent, if remarried. Some colleges do also require financial data from both divorced parents when determining their own aid, even though the federal application does not.

Nearly everyone should submit a FAFSA, at least the first time, even if you think your family's income or assets are too high to qualify. Even if your student won't qualify for grants based upon need, you may still be eligible for subsidized Stafford or Plus loans, or merit scholarships. Colleges may also have their own financial aid forms to submit with their own qualifications in addition to the FAFSA. Check with each school that you are interested in for their deadlines and requirements.

Aid advice

Rates, amounts, and qualifications for financial aid change frequently, so it is important to check on current information. See the web links at the end of the chapter.

Colleges offer merit aid to lure the brightest students they can get. To get the most generous merit aid offers, apply to schools where your student likely will rank among the top 30% of students. Conversely, don't expect much merit aid from schools where your student's grades and SAT's are in the lower half. If a parent or grandparent is an alum, see if the college offers "legacy" scholarships. Colleges may reduce their aid offers when you receive private scholarships, but reductions can be from loans or grants. If they reduce your grants, call and ask if they will reduce the loans instead.

Colleges say they don't negotiate financial aid; after all everyone wants more money and the amount available for giving is limited. Nonetheless, most have an appeals process and you can sometimes increase the amount you get. If you think the amount offered really is low, talk to a financial aid official and ask how it was computed. Look to see if a specific financial circumstance was overlooked, not included on your FAFSA, or has or will change such as a particular family financial hardship. Let the financial aid office know if you get a better offer from a competing school and see if they will match it because you really want to come to their school. You may have better success if you let the student do the appealing or the student's data is among the college's top 25%. Some experts suggest waiting until near the acceptance deadline to accept an aid package in hopes it will be improved to better entice attractive students, while others say that the earlier you apply and accept, the more aid that will be available. Still the reality remains that the most desirable students to a particular college will attract the best financial aid offers.

Comparing offers

It can be hard to compare competing aid packages from different schools consisting of several types of aid, and most want an answer by May 1. Complaints about some award letters may include not showing the cost to attend the school, loan repayment amounts, whether the aid likely will be similar or less in future years, and most of all – what is the net out-of-pocket costs to attend the school after aid is deducted.

Comparing aid packages may depend upon your circumstances. If your income may rise in the future, this could lessen your grants based upon financial needs and make merit scholarships more attractive. But some students find it difficult to maintain the grade point average to keep merit scholarships, so need-based grants might be better. Many schools offer a higher percentage of aid as grants during the first years than the later years because freshman aren't allowed to borrow as much as upperclassmen. When you are offered financial aid, ask whether it will be the same each year assuming your financial situation stays the same.

Several organizations are trying to make it easier to understand and compare your financial aid offers and options. Until more colleges adopt these tools, you can complete them yourself to get a better understanding of your options.

- http://www.finaid.org/calculators - Award Letter Comparison calculators and advice.
- http://www.consumerfinance.gov/paying-for-college/compare-financial-aid-and-college-cost/ - Comparison tool from the federal Consumer Financial Protection Bureau.
- http://www2.ed.gov/policy/highered/guid/aid-offer/index.html - The Department of Education has developed a financial aid form they are trying to get colleges to adopt to make it easier to compare aid offers.

Finding scholarships

Scholarships are the goal of most parents and students since they reduce the amount you have to borrow or pay for college. Unfortunately, there simply isn't enough scholarship money to go very far, so it primarily goes to lower income families, top tier students, and students that colleges are eager to attract. Nevertheless, there are thousands of kinds of scholarships available for those who are willing to hunt and apply for them. Nearly everyone is eligible for at least a small amount if they search diligently, follow the qualification rules, meet the deadlines, and submit a good essay and other requested items.

There is no need to pay someone to find scholarships for you. The internet now makes is easy to search for scholarships including the many databases listed here. Use several of them, vary your search terms slightly, avoid promotional offers and spam for giving up others' contact information, and be prepared to spend time slogging thru many mismatches. Increase your chances of being selected by going to the sponsoring organization's website to see what they are most interested in and then emphasize your best qualifications that match. Many websites help you search for scholarships including these:

- https://www.collegeanswer.com/paying-for-college/free-money-for-college/default.aspx
- http://www.finaid.org/
- http://www.meritaid.com/
- http://www.petersons.com/
- http://www.scholarships.com/
- http://www.athleticscholarships.net/

Scholarships directly from colleges are the easiest to find because they will be considered when you apply for financial aid from the college, but there are billions of dollars in scholarships available from thousands of other sources. For these you need to hunt and apply for them. Apply for as many as you can since awards are usually small, but can add up. Focus your efforts on where you have the best chance. The big national scholarships may have 100,000+ applicants and award less than 1000. For the best chances, start with ones that are local, listed at the high school, offered by groups you are a member of, or match your student's interests and talents. Many fewer students apply for scholarships from local organizations, so you have a better chance. In addition to your high school counselor, find them at your local library and by doing an advanced web search, for example *"your locality scholarships"*.

Most states also offer grants, scholarships, work-study, loans, or loan forgiveness. Most are based upon need, but some are also awarded based upon merit, family membership in certain groups (minorities, slain police officers, etc.), or students who commit to pursue certain careers such as in education or health. Various states have their own rules for granting aid, which may differ from the federal rules, so apply for your state's aid regardless of whether you received any federal aid. Check your state's website or your high school.

In addition to scholarships based upon need, merit, athletics, and even arts, many private scholarships are aimed at students going into certain professions or members in certain groups including minorities, women, handicapped students, religious groups, localities, organizations, and many more. Veterans can research education aid at www.gibill.va.gov, including how to transfer education benefits to spouses and children. In return for future military obligations, students can get financial aid by joining the military "Reserve Officers Training Corp".

Spending time now will save you money and loans later. Start early, apply to many, be organized, and keep track of deadlines. Polish your essay so you standout for more than just good grades and reuse relevant parts as often as you can.

Paying for college

Education savings accounts

By the time a child is ready for college, parents have had 18 years to save for college thru 529, Coverdell accounts, savings bonds, and regular taxable accounts. (See the chapter on "*Saving for College*"). Hopefully you have a nice amount of savings built up that will save you big borrowing costs. After you know how much your student will get in financial aid, you will need to come up with the rest. First pay qualified expenses from a non-529 account to get the tax breaks, then use your 529 and other savings on *other* qualified education expenses. The IRS defines "qualified education expenses" as tuition, room and board, fees, books, and equipment, for example, computers. See *IRS publication 970, Tax Benefits for Education* for information about 529s, Coverdells, education tax breaks, American Opportunity Credit, Lifetime Learning Credit, education savings bonds, and more – especially how all these relate to each other.

Effect on financial aid

Don't worry – your savings won't hurt your chances of getting financial aid very much. Use these savings to cover the "expected family contribution" (EFC) amount that financial aid does not cover. You aren't expected to use it all before getting financial aid. When you apply for aid with the FAFSA, only 5.6% of the parent's savings are considered while grandparents' savings aren't considered at all. Additionally, money that parents use from their educational savings accounts does not affect the amount of potential financial aid, but grandparents' payments are counted as part of the student's income.

If your student was lucky enough to get big scholarships so you don't need to pay from your 529 account, you can withdraw from your 529 account up to the amount of the scholarship without paying a penalty.

Raiding other accounts

Parents may be tempted to withdraw money from their retirement accounts to pay for children's college. Refer to the chapter on *"Saving for Retirement"* for rules, pro's, and con's. Remember the famous saying, "You can get a loan for college, but no one is going to lend you money for retirement." Bottom line – don't even think about this unless you are many years away from retirement and can and *will* make it up, knowing that you are losing many years of compound earnings.

Tax breaks

It's in the national interest to have an educated citizenry and workforce so government has long fostered making college more affordable. In addition to financial aid, the federal government offers tax breaks. The main programs are the *American Opportunity Tax Credit* (AOTC) and the *Lifetime Learning Credit*. The AOTC provides for $2500 tax credits for couples earning up to $160,000 and requires you to pay qualifying tuition expenses from an account other than your 529 account, but you can still use your 529 account for other expenses such as room and board. Couples can also deduct $2500 per year in college loan interest if income is under $150,000. Despite the number of tax breaks, be aware that you generally can't take multiple tax breaks for the same expense in the same year. Thus, I can't emphasize enough how important it is to get the latest information about changes to these programs and how potentially tricky it is to coordinate between them in the same year and expense, so I'm repeating again, see *IRS publication 970, Tax Benefits for Education*: http://www.irs.gov/publications/p970/ for current details about tax implications while saving and paying for education expenses, especially how to coordinate the various breaks.

Student loans

After you have selected an affordable college; been awarded grants, scholarships, and work study; paid what you can from savings to get the tax credits; and used part of your education savings accounts – you are left to fill the gap with loans. Since most grants go to lower income families, most middle class families should expect to pay for college primarily with private scholarships, family savings, current income, and loans for the rest. You do have choices of loans: student or parent borrowing, public or private loans.

Type of loans

In fact, most college financial aid packages will include public loans for the student. Public loans thru the government are usually preferable with lower, fixed interest rates, more flexible repayment options, forgiveness for service options, and no requirement for parent's to co-sign. There are several kinds of federal loans: subsidized loans for under-graduates based upon need, unsubsidized loans for any student, and subsidized loans for parents. With "subsidized" loans, you don't have to pay interest until after graduation. The most common loans for students are called "Stafford" loans and are limited to $5500 for freshmen in 2015 and higher amounts for upperclassmen. These loan limits increase periodically. "Perkin" loans are for students with exceptional needs and are managed by the school. Parents can get public loans called "Plus Loans" that require minimal credit checks, have a relatively low fixed rate, don't require repayment until six months after graduation, have more flexible repayment terms, and can be forgiven if the student dies or parent becomes permanently disabled. Some federal loans can be forgiven after peri-ods of public service. Get more details and the latest information about federal student loans at the agency's website that manages them: http://studentaid.ed.gov/types/loans/

Some federal loans limit the amount you can borrow, so your next resource to fill the gap is with loans from colleges, Sallie Mae, or private lenders like banks and credit un-ions. Sometimes advertisements for very low rates on private student loans look tempting, but it's still preferable to review all your public loan options before exploring private loans. The lowest rates only go to borrowers with high credit scores and are usu-ally variable rates that will increase in future years. Private loans usually have higher rates, less flexible repayment options, and require a co-signer. If the student misses payments, even if unemployed, the co-signer is expected to make those payments or their credit score will be damaged. Unlike credit card debt, it is rare for student loans to be forgiven by declaring bankruptcy. Still, if you have a high credit score, you sometimes can get a good rate even better than the federal PLUS rate.

Finding loans

Don't forget to check your credit union when shopping for private or consolidation student loans. Several websites help you shop for student loans including:

- https://www.salliemae.com/
- https://www.alltuition.com/

- http://www.simpletuition.com/

Other sources of college loans may be your state, non-profits, or charities. Some states offer their own student loans with nice rates.

Parents may also wish to consider borrowing from home equity lines of credit (which do not count against your financial aid as regular home equity loans do), or existing whole life insurance. However, do NOT buy whole life insurance as a means to save for college which is much more profitable to the insurance agent or so-called "college financial advisor" than it is to you.

How much to borrow

Loans are your last resort, but most students do need them. The average debt for a 2016 graduate was more than $30,000, so you need to keep student loans under control. Total student loans should not exceed the student's expected starting salary. Parent loans should be able to be repaid within ten years or prior to retirement – whichever comes first. Another measure is to keep the student's monthly repayment amount to 10-15% of their expected first year's salary. Use the FinAid.org calculator to enter your major and other data to see how much your maximum, monthly payment could safely be. Finaid.org has a couple of dozen different types of student loan calculators for every imaginable situation http://www.finaid.org/calculators/.

Every time you get a new loan, know what your total debt repayment amount will be. Even as they grow, loan amounts may seem so huge and distant as to seem abstract. But once you convert that abstract loan amount to an amount you will have to repay every month for years and years, they may seem more real. Then you can calculate just how easily loans could be paid along with all your other expected expenses. Getting student loans means the ludicrous situation of borrowing money without actually knowing that you can make the monthly payments. Nevertheless, don't get any loan without knowing how much your monthly payments will be and that it will fit within your likely monthly budget based upon your expected salary after college.

Saving on campus

Now let's talk about how to save money while in college.

Graduate in four years

The biggest money saver is to simply **graduate on time**. They are called "*Four* year colleges" for a reason. Four years is how long it should take to get enough credits to graduate, but only 1/3 of public school students and ½ of private school students manage that these days! So how long does it usually take today's students to graduate from a *four* year college? No not five years – SIX! I have a big problem with this for two reasons:

1. I graduated with a Master's degree in only five years by testing out of five courses and taking an extra course in most semesters. Yes, I did too change my major, work part-time during most of those years, and still had fun. (Maybe I didn't sleep.)

2. Unless the student is living at home during all that time, they are running up an extra $10,000-$15,000 for each additional year in expenses or debt. This could add a serious and unnecessary handicap to the student's or parent's debt.

I recommend you review a college's graduation stats when choosing a college and discuss this with your student. Most colleges require around 120 credit hours to graduate. This means taking 15 hours per semester for eight semesters – NOT the *minimum* of 12. If you get behind or change majors, then you can take 18 hours, go to summer school, or test out of courses to catch up. Students should plan ahead for required courses and work out a schedule with an academic advisor. Take introductory, required courses that could work with several majors. If the student is too far along in one major when the notion strikes to change majors, consider staying the course, but changing their minor, or compromising on a new major that uses most of your courses and doesn't require adding another year.

Test out of college courses

Sometime you need to plan ahead as with "Advanced Placement" (AP) courses in high school for which many colleges offer full credit if you get a certain grade on the AP test. This could get you many college credits for free. Students can also get full credit at some schools by taking a test to demonstrate proficiency in different subjects. Find out more about two popular programs:

- http://clep.collegeboard.org/?navid=bf-clep – 33 exams from the "*College Level Examination Program*" *(CLEP)* and even download study guides.

- http://getcollegecredit.com/ - 38 exams offered by *DANTES Subject Standardized Tests* (DSST).

Start at community colleges

In recent years, local community colleges have become more attractive for saving college expenses. Many students attend their first two years at a less expensive community college and then transfer to a four-year university to get the same degree as someone who attended all four years at the expensive school. You not only can take your introductory/required courses less expensively, but probably can also live at home. Note however, that only a small percentage of community college students do actually go on to transfer and graduate. Improve your odds by seeing if there are any programs in your area that facilitate a transfer, talking to the admissions office at the four year school about transfer requirements, and getting good grades.

Room and board

Room and board can cost at least $10,000 per year, is rising faster than inflation, and can be half the total cost of a public college. Consider ways to reduce it:
- Live at home.
- Start with a cheaper cafeteria meal plan and upgrade it later if needed. (Most colleges offer several options and will let you upgrade, but not downgrade.)
- Save a couple of thousand dollars, if your college offers a "co-op" that requires a few hours of chores each week.
- After the freshman year, sharing an apartment with room-mates could save money if the students share most of the cooking rather than eating out.

Cars

Students may not need a car, especially at urban colleges with good public transportation and high parking fees. Students often get a break on public transportation costs. Use a car-sharing service like ZIPCAR for the occasional need at much less cost. Get a break on your auto insurance when your student goes to a distant college without a car – notify your insurer carrier.

Work part-time

Many students work part-time during the year and full or part-time during the summer. This can earn thousands of dollars, as well as lead to work and time-management experience. Work might be work-study, internships, or a wide variety of private sector jobs – especially as your know, in the food service sector. In addition to the usual job-search resources, students can get help from their college job-placement office.

Incidentals

Of course tuition, room, and board aren't the only expenses students have. Here are a few ways to save in other areas:

- Get a "Student Advantage Card" for 10-20% discounts at places like Amtrak, Greyhound, Target, AMC Theaters, T-Mobile, Toshiba, Lenovo, and other retailers. http://www.studentadvantage.com/discountcard/
- Students can get cheap software at the student store and online. Search "educational software".
- Buy used textbooks and comparison shop for them between the college bookstore, backpackbook.com, campusbooks.com, Amazon, eBay, GooglePlay-Books, Chegg.com, bookrenters.com, and other online textbook discounters. Get ebooks at CourseSmart.com.
- Limit the urge for munchies and pizza. Check out deal-of-the-day websites that offer deals on food like http://www.moocho.com/, http://www.groupon.com, and http://www.livingsocial.com.

Take responsibility for money management

When students begin college, they should also take responsibility for their money management. Regardless of whether students are getting money from aid, jobs, or parents, they should be learning and using the financial skills that will serve them well at college as well as later along life's financial journey. Even if you pay the big expenses for tuition, room and board, have your student manage their own expenses for textbooks, eating out, clothes, and entertainment. Students can complete the financial aid applications; practice balancing costs, aid, income, and loans; develop a monthly budget; learn to spend money wisely; know the pitfalls of running up a credit card debt; balance needs and wants; and live within their means. It is time for them to practice the sound financial principles we have been discussing that will help make the rest of their financial journey more successful.

Here are some suggestions for turning financial principles into cost savings. At the beginning of each semester or year, discuss how much money they will have available for living and miscellaneous expenses. Help students prepare a semester budget that balances needs and wants. Track income and expenses in a spreadsheet, notebook, or smartphone app. Learn to grocery shop, cook, and share with roommates to reduce eating out. Buy clothes at sales and discounters. Consider using a refillable prepaid debit card to keep spending within the budget. When the debit card is empty, spending for that month is over. *Kaiku.com's* monthly fee is only $2.00 per month and can be refilled each month from any bank account by the student or parent. Credit Unions or banks may have debit cards specifically for young adults.

Upon graduation, give your student a copy of this book and point them to *Chapter* 1 about handling student loans and starting out successfully along life's financial journey.

More information and calculators

- https://bigfuture.collegeboard.org/pay-for-college/tools-calculators - Calculators to search scholarships, loans, savings, aid, and costs.
- https://www.collegeanswer.com/paying-for-college/default.aspx - Sallie Mae's financial aid page has information and calculators for grants, scholarships, financial aid, loans, and planning.
- https://www.collegeanswer.com/planning-for-college/preparing-for-college/college-planning-calendar.aspx – Sallie Mae's college planning calendar. Know when your student should be doing what to get into college.
- http://www.collegeboard.org/ - College Board resources for college planning and searching. One of many nice features is the capability to search for colleges based upon "average percent of financial need met".
- http://collegecost.ed.gov/ - Federal website with information and tools to search colleges and costs.
- http://www.fafsa.ed.gov/index.htm - Federal government website with resources about financial aid.

- http://www.payscale.com/education/benefit-of-college-education - The "salary lookup" website includes research for which colleges and majors yield the best return on investment. See the starting salary you should have for repaying your student loans.
- http://www.sreb.org/page/1304/academic_common_market.html - Study in a specialized field at an out-of-state college, while paying in-state tuition rates.
- http://studentaid.ed.gov/ - Website with many resources of the federal agency that manages college financial aid.

Summary

- Despite the escalating cost of college, higher education still results in lower unemployment and higher salaries.
- Picking a college is unlike any other purchase you'll make. Despite the humongous price, you are not looking for a bargain. You are looking for a school where the student can do well, has good four-year graduation rates, is affordable, and offers a good aid package.
- Many internet calculators can give you an estimate of what you might have to pay for college in general. Get estimates about specific colleges, by using the "net price calculator" on most college websites that will estimate what a typical family in your situation may receive, pay, and borrow at that particular school.
- Your student stands a better chance of getting significant financial aid from a college if their grades, SAT/ACT scores, extra-curricular activities, community service, or intended major is attractive to that college. Consider choosing a school in which your student is likely to rank among the top 30% of students.
- The first step for any aid is to apply for the *Free Application for Federal Student Aid*" (FAFSA) which is the basis for need-based aid, federal loans, and sometimes for schools' merit scholarships. Submit it every year beginning October 1.
- There are thousands of scholarships available for those who are willing to hunt and apply for them. Nearly everyone is eligible for at least a small amount if they search diligently, follow the qualification rules, meet the deadlines, and submit a good essay and other requested items. Apply to many since most are for small amounts, but can add up to big amounts. For the best chances, start with ones that

are local, listed at the high school, offered by groups you are a member of, or match your student's interests and talents.

- See *IRS publication 970, Tax Benefits for Education*: for current details about tax implications while saving and paying for education expenses, especially how to coordinate the various breaks.

- You can get a loan for college, but no one is going to lend you money for retirement. So don't be quick to withdraw savings from your retirement accounts to pay for college unless you are many years away from retirement and can and *will* make it up, knowing that you are losing many years of compound earnings.

- After you have selected an affordable college; been awarded grants, scholarships, and work study; paid what you can from savings to get the tax credits; and used part of your education savings accounts – you are left to fill the gap with loans. Since most grants go to lower income families, most middle class families should expect to pay for college primarily with private scholarships, family savings, current income, and loans for the rest. You do have choices of loans: student or parent borrowing, public or private loans.

- Don't get any loan without knowing how much your monthly payments will be, and that it will fit within your likely monthly budget based upon the student's expected job. Guidelines suggest total debt should not exceed their expected first year's salary and monthly payments should not exceed 10-15% of their expected monthly income.

- One of the best ways to control college costs and debt is to graduate on time – within four years. There are many ways to do this, especially by planning your course requirements in advance and taking a full-time course load of 15-18 hours.

- When students begin college, they should also take responsibility for their money management. Regardless of whether students are getting money from aid, jobs, or parents, they should be learning and using the financial skills that will serve them well at college as well as later along life's journey.

- One of my favorite money management tools is a pre-paid debit card that limits monthly spending to the balance on the card. Refill it online once per month.

- Upon graduation, give your student a copy of this book and point them to Chapter 1 about handling student loans and starting out successfully along life's financial journey.

Chapter Twenty

Credit Cards

- Understanding credit and debit cards
- Choosing a card
- Paying a card
- Managing a card
- Avoiding the slippery slope

Many things such as autos, homes, and college are so expensive that most people borrow money to pay for them over an extended period of time. They have a fixed term so we know exactly when we will finish paying for them and can ensure they will fit within our budget. Then there is spending and borrowing with credit cards. The convenience of credit cards can be both a lifesaver and a curse. Regardless, they are undeniably a convenient way to make purchases – especially online. Studies show that paying cash is a good way to think about and reduce spending, but we are becoming more and more a cashless society. Credit cards help us avoid carrying around large amounts of cash, give us a detailed record of our spending, make it easy to setup recurring bill payments, and pay us rewards for using them. So in this chapter, let's review how to choose, use, and pay for credit cards so they are more a convenience with rewards than a facilitator to the slippery slope of debt.

Understanding credit and debit cards

Both credit and debit cards provide convenient means of paying for purchases without having to carry cash around. Credit cards, secured credit cards, debit cards tied to checking accounts, and prepaid debit cards each have advantages for different situations.

Credit cards

Many credit cards have a long list of benefits, but read the fine print to know which ones your card has:

- Rewards – Credit cards usually have much better rewards than debit cards.
- Fraud protection – Unlike debit cards, nearly all credit card companies will take responsibility for all unauthorized purchases. That's why some are overly zealous at declining your purchases when you are traveling out of country. (American Express, you know who I'm talking about.)
- Grace period – When you pay your balance in full, you get several weeks before you have to pay for it – up to four weeks until the end of the billing cycle and up to three more from the bill date to your due date.
- Extended warranties - Many cards will double your warranty period on purchases.
- Investigate disputes – If you have a dispute with a merchant over a purchase, credit card companies must investigate and you can't be charged while they do.
- Rental car damage coverage – Some cards will provide this so you can safely decline the collision damage waiver charge when renting a car.
- Build a credit record – When you pay on time *every* month, you establish and improve your credit rating which is used to determine whether you will get credit and the lowest interest rates, as well as an increasing number of other qualifications. Debit cards do not. See the chapter on *Your Credit Score,* in part five.

Watch out for merchants who charge a fee for using a credit card. They are trying to recoup the fee they have to pay to the credit card companies, but you might want to use cash.

Credit cards are best for people with big spending to earn nice rewards, who can live within their means, to build credit histories, or who need flexibility to charge expenses to even out irregular income.

Secured credit cards

Secured credit cards allow you to borrow up to the amount you have previously deposited on the card. Since you are borrowing against your own money, anyone can get one with no credit check. These enable people with bad or no credit history to establish a good credit history by paying on time. Just ensure that the card reports your payment history to all three credit rating bureaus in order to build your credit rating. After six months or so of reliably paying on time, you may be able to ask for an increase in your credit limit or apply for a regular credit card. Secured credit cards are best for people who can't get a regular credit card because of poor credit or people with no credit history such as college students.

Bank debit cards

Debit cards are tied to checking accounts so each time you make a purchase, it deducts the amount from your checking account. Thus, you don't have to worry about making future payments, running up debt, or interest rates. Some banks may offer extra checking or rewards perks, but they generally have fewer rewards, perks, and fraud protection than credit cards. Beware of the outlandish overdraft fees for making even small purchases that exceed your checking account balance. The news media was full of stories about multiple overdraft fees far exceeding the amount of purchases. So know your bank's policies, monitor your balance closely, and consider turning off overdraft protection so your purchase is declined rather than socked with a huge fee when overdrawn. Most banks now provide a mobile app for monitoring your balance.

Fraud protection rules with debit cards are different than credit cards and may vary more widely depending upon your bank's policies. You are subject to more liability the longer you wait to report a missing card. That's not unreasonable, but is not as good as with credit cards. Debit cards are best for people who need help to control spending, but still work best when you have at least a general budget and you monitor your money flow and balance.

Prepaid debit cards

Prepaid debit cards only let you spend what you have preloaded onto the card. They are the easiest way to control spending – no debt as with credit cards and no juggling money flow and overdrafts as with checking debit cards. Many prepaid cards have features similar to a checking account including direct deposit, online bill-paying, ATM access, and card-to-card money transfers. There is even a growing trend to add perks such as check writing, FDIC coverage, purchase protection, and other perks. However, prepaid cards don't have much consumer protection rules for unauthorized charges, although your bank may limit your liability if you report problems promptly. Some prepaid cards are notorious for a wide variety of fees including monthly, inactivity, ATM access, customer services, and activation fees. Nevertheless, growing competition is working its magic so comparison shop carefully, as there are plenty of good cards out there.

Prepaid cards are best for people who need to control their spending, don't have checking accounts, or can't qualify for credit cards. They are popular among parents who want to control children's spending including college bound students. I highly recommend them as the surest means to get control of your spending and live within a budget. Consider using your checking account for recurring expenses and filling a prepaid card with an amount you have left over for all other spending. This can help you remember the difference between "needs" and "wants" and spend accordingly.

Choosing a credit card

Like any other loan, the better your credit rating / FICO score, the easier time you will have to get a card with better terms. Innumerable banks, credit unions, retailers, hotels, airlines, and others offer credit cards. Additionally, numerous retailers and oil companies offer their own cards, but these are generally useful only for the introductory offer or if you shop there a lot and they offer ongoing rewards and discounts.

With this many choices, here is what you should look for when choosing a card:

- **Whether there is an annual fee** - Pay an annual fee only if the rewards that come with it are guaranteed to exceed the fee, for example a free hotel stay every year or free checked bag for frequent flyers.
- **The annual percentage rate (APR)** - If you do not pay your balance in full every month, then look for a card with the lowest interest rate.
- **The rewards that come with it** – After a good interest rate, look for a card with the best rewards. There are many rewards details, so consider cards that:
  - pay more than 1% of your spending as rewards (at least 1.25%),

- award additional reward points at places where you spend a lot of money, for example, 5 points instead of 1 for groceries, gas, hotels, airlines, etc.
- have rewards you are most likely to benefit from such as free gas, hotel stays, or even cash. Cash is usually best because it is harder for you to compare other rewards such as free hotel stays or flights and easier for companies to reduce the value of your points.

- **Best introductory offer** – Card companies are eager to get you if you have a decent credit score, so look for the best introductory offers that combine extra rewards, low introductory interest rate over a long period, or nice balance transfer terms (ideal is 0% interest for at least a year with only 1-2% transaction fee).

To find a card that is best for you, start by investigating ones at your credit union, local bank, union, or other member association. Then check out one of the many websites that offer more tips and card comparisons. There are many of these websites because they get very nice affiliate fees for anyone they can get to sign up. (Search "credit cards comparisons".) Perhaps because of this, the quality of their recommendations can vary widely, so use several sites and analyze the results carefully. Remember that getting anything new that involves significant money should mean comparison shopping and comparison shopping should mean at least three sources. You are going to have a long-term relationship with your card, so spend the time now to reap the benefits later.

Paying credit cards

- Pay on time to avoid penalties.
- Pay in full or at least as much as you can to reduce your debt burden.
- Pay before the due date if you carry a balance to reduce your interest.
- Pay more than the monthly minimum so it doesn't take forever to pay off the balance.
- Pay something every month, even if the bill offers to let you skip a payment, because you are still paying interest on the full balance.

Paying your credit cards in full, on time, every time, not only avoids nasty penalties, but also gives you a grace period to pay your balance with NO interest. Credit cards offer a grace period where they don't charge you interest on new purchases from the date of purchase until your payment is due. But if you carry even a $1.00 balance from the prior month, then you get no grace period and are charged interest on new purchases immediately. If you carry a balance and don't get that grace period, then remember to pay your bill as soon as possible so you lower the amount of interest you pay. Waiting until the due date to pay, only increases your interest.

Managing a card

Always pay on time - always

Yes, I'm going to repeat this yet again: the most important principle you need to know about credit cards is ALWAYS to pay them on time. The financial consequences are costly, not only resulting in late fees and a huge increase in your interest rate, but also damage to your credit score. The certain way to damage your credit score is to be late with credit card payments. Your history of on-time credit card payments is the biggest single factor in calculating your credit scores – probably 35%. Setup a monthly reminder on your calendar or text alerts at the credit card's website to ensure you avoid this costly mistake.

Pay more than the minimum balance

The next most important principle is to pay more than the minimum amount. Your billing statement will now show you how long it takes to pay your balance with only the minimum payment versus a three year schedule amount. Notice that paying only the minimum will cost more in interest and take much longer to pay off, up to 7-10 years. Don't take 7 years to pay off that pizza or jacket.

Balance credit and prepaid cards to manage spending

Use your credit and prepaid cards for different types of spending to help stay within your budget and still get credit card rewards and perks. Some people advise against using credit cards for everyday purchases because that makes it too easy to run up debt to finance your basic living expenses. However, my view is that the key is not whether you pay using debit or credit cards, but rather do you have the budget, plans, and discipline to manage your money? In fact, my view is that it is better to pay almost everything on your credit card to get the rewards, even autopay recurring bills like utilities, cable, internet, telephone, etc. Then calculate the amount you need to set aside every month to pay your typical credit card payment. Use your prepaid card for your "fun" money and discretionary spending on "wants," such as eating out, entertainment, and shopping so that you can't easily go over-budget on these. You can also use a second credit card with a *very low limit* for discretionary spending. When it is maxed out and not paid off, then fun spending is over until it is paid. Whatever cards you use, monitor them regularly with a mobile app or website to ensure you are on budget and living within your means.

Maximize your rewards

Credit card companies pay you 1%-5% to use their cards. Take full advantage of that. Maximize your rewards points not only by charging your monthly, autopay bills, but also by using the appropriate card to purchase items that you get extra points for. Most cards pay 1% for everything, but some cards pay more for certain categories. Take advantage of this. For example, many cards give 2-5 points for groceries, gas, or travel.

Here's a tip to further maximize your bonus by buying gift cards that you can use to pay for things that don't pay a bonus; for example, buy gift cards at drug stores with cards that pay 5% and use them at other locations that only pay 1%.

Carrying a balance

If you carry a balance, then pay close attention to the interest rate you are paying that routinely ranges anywhere between 10-25%. Miss a payment deadline and it could jump up to 30% and damage your credit score! If you make payments on time, then your credit score will be improved. The best way to take advantage of a good credit score is to get lower interest rates. Call and ask your credit card company for a lower interest rate – yes, I'm serious – most people with good credit who ask do get at least one reduction. I can verify this does work, but I don't try it every other month. If your credit card rate is in the higher range and you don't get a reduction, then request to speak to a supervisor, ask about switching to a lower rate card, switch from a variable rate to a fixed rate card, or shop around for another card – this is a competitive and lucrative market. Other things you can ask your credit card company for include waiving your first over-limit or late fee and changing your due date to a more convenient time of the month

Protect yourself against fraud

You can do several things to protect your credit cards against unauthorized or fraudulent use. Consider taking advantage of your card's push to get you to receive statements online rather than paper in the mail. They want you to "go green" to save them mailing costs, but you also benefit by not having to shred your paper bills or risk an identity thief intercepting it and making your life miserable. Review all your charges each month to ensure no one has snuck an erroneous or fraudulent charge on your bill. I have discovered erroneous charges numerous times and they are generally easy to dispute on the card's website. Notify your credit card company as soon as you lose your card or spot an erroneous charge. Avoid leaving your credit card information permanently with online merchants unless you really shop there frequently. Good websites will give you a choice whether to enter your credit card information for one-time use or stored for future use. Given the number of merchants that have been hacked, why take the risk unnecessarily?

Do not be tempted to use your credit card to get a cash advance at an ATM machine as this usually comes with extra fees and much higher interest than purchases.

Avoiding the slippery slope of debt

There are plenty of times when borrowing from a credit card is necessary. However, borrowing from credit cards can become a slippery slope to financial hardship because it is too easy to resort to them without ensuring payments will fit within our budget or knowing when the last payment will be. It's too easy to use them for wants more than needs and to live beyond our means – *for a time*. Credit card borrowing is very convenient, but we pay big time for that convenient borrowing as interest rates on credit cards can be 3-5 times higher than financing an auto, home, or even college.

Using credit increases the price of everything we buy. Even if we get a good deal on something, we are increasing its price by the amount of interest, which on credit cards can range from 10% to 29% per year. If we don't pay off those credit cards for good, we are paying that interest year after year. At 20% interest, we will have paid double the price in five years. Think how many of those things you charged that you no longer even use. Think of how many dinners out you are still paying for years later. Think about whether you would even have bought that item if you had realized the price you would be paying with interest would be 20-100% more.

If you are running up a credit card balance, called debt, take action. That means living within your means. That means reviewing your budget to see how much money you have to spend on *wants* after *needs* and *savings* are accounted for, but now add a debt repayment amount to your required expenses. Use a prepaid card for discretionary spending. Reduce your spending. Postpone major purchases. Devote extra money to your debt such as tax refunds, bonuses, raises, part-time work, etc. Ask the credit card company for a rate reduction or lower rate card. Get a zero-interest balance transfer to another card to get some breathing room and use the savings to pay down the balance. Keep extra money in a savings account to cover those times when credit card spending gets out of sync with the budget temporarily.

Getting and keeping control of your finances is not all about self-discipline. Don't rely only on will power – use the right tools to make it easier. Useful tools may include a budget, prepaid debit card for fun money, mobile apps for monitoring your various account balances, text alerts for bill due dates, autopay for recurring bills, emergency funds to avoid debt, and multiple savings accounts for multiple savings goals. Use what works best for you, but take action early.

It is amazing how credit cards are related to so many other financial topics, so review these other chapters for additional information:

- Part One, Chapter 1 – Starting Out
- Part Two, Chapter 6 – How to Save
- Part Two, Chapter 7 – Budgets
- Part Four, Chapter 21 – Debt
- Part Four, Chapter 22 – Spending Wisely
- Part Five, Chapter 25 – Your Credit Score

More information

- http://www.bankrate.com/calculators/index-of-credit-card-calculators.aspx - Use a variety of credit card, debt, and consolidation calculators.
- http://cgi.money.cnn.com/tools/debtplanner/debtplanner.jsp - Enter multiple credit cards to learn "When will I be debt-free".

- http://www.money-zine.com/calculators/loan-calculators/ - See several types of credit card calculators as well as other loan and debt calculators.

Summary

- Use self-discipline and a variety of tools to ensure that credit cards are more a convenience with rewards than a facilitator to the slippery slope of debt.
- Always pay your credit cards on time every single month to avoid late fees, increased interest rate, and damage to your credit score.
- Paying your balance in full every month avoids interest charges and debt, but also provides you a grace period between when you make the purchase and have to pay the bill.
- Always pay more than the minimum amount to lower your interest, debt, and time to pay off the purchases.
- Separate your required and monthly spending from your discretionary spending on separate cards. Consider paying almost all "needs" on your credit card to get the rewards, even autopay recurring bills like utilities, cable, internet, telephone, etc. Then calculate the amount you need to set aside every month to pay your typical credit card payment in full. Use a separate prepaid card for your "fun" money and discretionary spending on "wants" like eating out, entertainment, and shopping so that you can't easily go over-budget on these.
- Using credit increases the price of everything we buy. Even if we get a good deal on something, we are increasing its price by the amount of interest, which on credit cards can range from 10% to 29% per year. If we don't pay off those credit cards for good, we are paying that interest year after year even when the purchase is long since eaten or disposed of.

Chapter Twenty-one

Dealing with Debt

- Develop a plan
- Deal with severe debt problems
- More information

Too often serious debt problems can result from not living within our means. When you see you are sliding down this slippery slope, STOP before it's too late. But sometimes it comes from things over which you have less control such as losing your job or getting huge medical bills. Let's review potential remedies to consider that basically involve increasing your income and debt repayments and decreasing your spending and debt amounts. But to be successful, any of these must begin with developing both the will *and* plan for living within your means and paying more to debt.

Develop a plan

Getting out of debt is a multi-step process that involves psychology, discipline, strategy, action, and tools.

1. Change your attitude - You need to be ready to reduce your spending with discipline, strategies, and persistence.

2. Create a budget – Calculate your income and expenses. Ensure your spending is less than your income. Free up money to accelerate debt repayment.

3. Have a plan – Have a plan to pay off your debts: smallest DEBfirst or highest rate first.

4. Take action – There are many things you can do to reduce spending, increase debt repayment amount, and get debt free.

Change your attitude

As usual, step one is to recognize you have a problem and decide to deal with it seriously. There is plenty of advice about how to recognize when you have a debt problem, but in my view, it's when you are carrying or juggling credit card or medical debt on more than a temporary basis. There are many other types of debt and we have discussed many of them previously. I primarily see fixed-term debt as a problem only when they prevent you from meeting savings goals or living within your means. Whereas credit cards, other personal loans, and medical debts can more easily spiral out of control.

Getting out of debt may take many years and mean adjusting your life style, but that probably does not mean living like a monk. Trade your financially worrying stress for peace of mind knowing that you are on track to get control of your finances and get out of debt. Getting out of debt is truly liberating and makes many other things easier such as stress, family life, personal satisfaction, and peace of mind. Remind yourself often that it is well worth the sacrifices.

A psychological aspect of getting out of debt is to recognize the difference between needs and wants and to control impulse buying. All attempts to get spending under control must include a drastic reduction in impulse buying whether at the mall, web, home shopping channels, "As seen on TV" commercials, or even the grocery store. Advertisers are ingenious at finding new ways to get us to spend – even on things we never knew we wanted. The solution has two parts: psychology and strategy. See "Part One, Chapter 1, *Saving – How to Save*" for practical tips on how to reduce impulse spending.

Create a budget

To be successful, you must move beyond just psychological and will power issues. No matter how much you resist, it is absolutely vital that you create a budget so you know how much money you have for needs, wants, and accelerated debt repayment. When debt is a problem, use a budget to calculate how much money you have left over after subtracting *essential* bills from income. The remainder must be used for both wants and debt repayment so the more you cut *wants/discretionary spending* to the bone, the more you have to repay debts and the faster you will get out of debt. To free up the maximum amount possible for accelerated debt repayment, use the following action ideas in this chapter and the savings ideas scattered throughout this book. See especially in *Chapter 1 – Saving, Chapter 20 – Credit Cards,* and *Chapter 22 – Spending Wisely.* I discuss budgeting in Chapter 2 – *Budgets.*

- http://www.practicalmoneyskills.com/personalfinance/savingspending/budgeting/ - budget calculators, worksheets, and information.

Have a plan

Once you have the will power and have identified the maximum amount possible to devote to accelerated debt repayment, you need a plan. For those who still need more help in turning their will power into won't power, there are plenty of other fine financial books devoted to the psychological aspects of finances. I want to concentrate on giving you practical tools, ideas, and strategies so you don't have to depend upon only will power that is subject to relapses. Rather than the notion "the spirit is willing, but the flesh is weak", I suggest "the flesh is weak, but the plan is strong".

The first step is to know what debts you have. On a spreadsheet or paper, write down each of your debts with the company, amount owed, months to repay loan, interest rate, and minimum monthly payment. Add the total amount owed and minimum monthly payment columns to see where you stand.

Your goal is to eliminate each item on that list one-by-one. Your plan is to pay the minimum on most debts and devote every spare dollar you can to your priority debt. When your first priority debt is paid off, you devote that entire amount plus the minimum you had been paying to the second priority debt. When the second debt is paid off, you devote the combined payment amount from debts one and two, plus the minimum you had been paying to debt three. Continue until the last debt is paid. This cumulative effect makes paying the later debts easier and faster. In addition, you can see your progress, which should enhance willpower to sacrifice and continue.

You have two choices for selecting which debts to prioritize and pay off first: either the smallest debt first or the debt with the highest interest rate. Paying the highest interest rate debts first will result in paying the least interest and fastest repayment. However, many people advocate paying the smallest debts first because that method gives you a quicker psychological boost in seeing debts eliminated sooner, and keeping the will power strong is half the battle to keeping the plan strong. My suggestion is to start paying off a couple of the smallest debts first to show quick progress and then shift to the highest interest rate debts to free up more money to pay the big debts faster.

Take action

You have the will power, budget, and plan showing how to live within your means and free-up money for accelerated debt repayment; now let's discuss ways to get more money for faster debt repayment.

- increase your income
- free-up more of your current income
- decrease the minimum monthly payments of debts
- deal with specific types of debt
- avoid debt traps

Increase your income

Many people have second jobs and sometimes you can't be too picky about it. Alternatively, find a "work at home job". Many of these are scams or just too hard to actually earn much money, but some of them are for real. Real ones include jobs such as sales, telephone call support, typing, data entry, virtual assistants, cleaning services, accounting, and writing. See these websites for more information:

- http://www.reviewopedia.com/internet-marketing-guide/section1-intro-to-making-money-online.htm - great overview of your best options with many links to real jobsites
- https://www.upwork.com – bid on freelance jobs in many categories
- http://www.doughroller.net/category/make-money/ - ideas and links

Free up more money

I have frequently discussed ways to save money by decreasing spending, and the big chapter on spending wisely is next. You should scour your expenditures to find areas you can temporarily or indefinitely reduce to free more money for accelerated debt repayment. Being extra frugal to get control of your debts yields huge payoffs later as you are better able to meet all your financial goals including a better standard of living when debt free.

Inevitably, that raises the question about whether to suspend or reduce any of your savings such as emergency, college, and retirement funds. This is a controversial topic, so consider these points and your personal situation. Mathematically, it doesn't make sense to keep or continue savings that earn 0.01-10% while we pay interest of 10-29% on credit cards and consumer debt. On the flip side, saving goals represent more than just money, including peace of mind now and financial security in the future. As usual, I come down in the middle thinking that continuing some savings goals is important, but that it is vital to free every dollar we can to accelerate debt payments. So having some emergency fund is important for peace of mind and ensuring sudden expenses don't torpedo your get-out-of-debt plan, but you can't afford as large of a fund as you will when you are free of credit card and other high-rate debt. Keep a larger emergency fund if your job is not secure, your credit might be revoked when paid off, or you don't have access to other lines of credit for emergencies. Otherwise, keep only a small emergency fund for sudden repair and medical bills and devote every dollar you can to debt.

Reduce college saving to a minimum to keep the accounts open with the expectation that you can better handle college savings and expenses when debt-free or from student loans. Reducing retirement savings to a minimum could free hundreds of dollars per month to pay debts with the expectation that you will double down on retirement savings when debt-free. However, I repeat the admonition to ALWAYS contribute enough to any 401(k) retirement plan to get the company match which is FREE money that cannot be recouped in the future. Most important: beware that suspending or emptying savings without *also* getting your spending under control is doubly harmful to your current *and* future financial security. Emptying your savings funds simply to continue an unsustainable life-style just postpones and worsens the day of reckoning. Betting your future to satisfy your present is an ever-enticing, but rarely wise temptation.

Decrease minimum debt payments

If you can lower your minimum debt payments, this can free up more money that you can use for your accelerated debt repayments. There are many way to do this depending upon the debt.

Refinance to longer term loans which increases the time to payoff, but decreases monthly payments. I'm a big fan of 15 or 20 year mortgages because it lessens the total interest you pay and shortens the time you are in debt. However, shorter term loans mean you have to make higher monthly payments. If you refinance a 15 or 20 year mortgage to a 30 year term, it could free up hundreds of dollars that you can use to pay off priority debts. Once the higher interest rate debts are paid off, you can always make extra payments to the mortgage to pay if off sooner than your remaining mortgage term.

Lower your interest rates to pay less interest and use the extra money to pay debts. Methods include calling your credit card companies and asking, transferring balances to zero interest offers (*Chapter 20 - Credit Cards*), refinancing your mortgage if rates have dropped or your credit score has improved, and getting a home equity loan to pay off higher rate credit cards (*Chapter 18 - Buying a Home*). Beware that if you move credit card debt to a home equity loan without getting control of your spending, your home could be at risk if your credit card debt again balloons out of control and you can't make payments on your home equity loan.

Call your creditors, explain your situation, and ask for a lower interest rate or trading lower monthly payment for longer term payments. This does sometimes work because creditors do have an interest in keeping you paying something.

"Debt consolidation loans" are offered by some lenders to bundle many existing credit card and personal debts into one loan, interest rate, and payment. This can provide total lower debt payments thru a lower interest rate or longer term to repay. Just remember that anytime you extend the term of a loan to repay, you are increasing the amount of total interest you pay in the end.

Seniors can consider a "reverse mortgage" in which they receive payments based upon the equity of their home (See Chapter 23 - *Retirement > Reverse Mortgages*).

Types of debt including medical debt

We have discussed many types of debts previously, so see those chapters for suggestions on how to deal with them:

- Student Loans - Part One, Chapter 1, *Starting out*
- Autos - Part Four, Chapter 17, B*uying a car*
- Mortgages and Home Equity Loans- Part Four, Chapter 18, *Buying a home*
- Credit Cards - Part Four, Chapter 20, *Credit cards*

Another major source of debt (and the leading cause of bankruptcy) is medical bills. When medical bills do threaten to overwhelm your finances, try these strategies. First, review any bills carefully for errors, especially large hospital bills, and match them against your health insurance coverage. This may not be easy, as medical bills are not known to be user friendly. One of my recent bills for a broken leg illustrates this. The back of the bill lumped all the things they did for me under a single category they called, "medical services and supplies" while the front of the bill said, "Something new! Our updated bill is easier to read and understand." This is why some people hire medical claims specialists to review their lengthy bills in return for a percentage of any errors and reductions they can obtain.

As always, negotiate large expenses, including medical bills. Explain your financial situation and ask for a reduction. See if you can get a reduction for paying in a lump sum now rather than installments later. If not, ask about interest-free installments that will fit your budget or whether the provider or your state offers any financial assistance. Remember to take the medical deduction on your taxes when medical expenses exceed 7.5% of your income. Get more information about medical debt here:

- http://www.irs.gov/publications/p502/index.html - IRS Publication 502 covers medical expenses.
- http://claims.org/ - Hire a claims professional to help sort thru that medical jargon and see if you can save money. This may be especially useful after hospital stays or expensive care with long, complicated bills.

Avoiding debt traps

Merely moving debt around is not helpful unless you also take action to ensure your credit card balance does not reappear so you then have more debt.

Some of these suggestions involve moving debt from high-interest rate debt, like credit cards, to low-interest rate debt, such as home equity loans, so that you can lower your minimum monthly payments and free money to accelerate payments to your priority debt. Removing credit card debt could also improve your credit score and lower future interest rates available to you. However, this only moves debt, but does not lower the amount. It could be counter-productive if you fail to live within your means, pay off your priority debt, and keep your credit card balances from rising again. If you move the debt off your credit cards and fill them up again, then you now have twice the debt and are worse off than before. So we again see that any plan for getting out of debt, must also include a plan for living within your means and not depending upon your credit cards.

Dealing with severe debt problems

I hope you see by now that there are actions we can take to control our spending, live within our means, and get out of debt. Like so many things, debt is much easier to resolve when we deal with it early before it gets out of hand. Nevertheless, when debt becomes severe, there are other more radical steps available. At some point you may need assistance to get your financial mess under control including credit counseling, debt management, debt settlement, or even bankruptcy. See these websites for information.

- http://aiccca.org/ - Association of Independent Consumer Credit Counseling Agencies (AICCCA) represents non-profit credit counseling companies.
- http://nfcc.org/ - "National Foundation for Credit Counseling includes more than 700 community-based offices located in all 50 states and Puerto Rico. More than 3 million consumers annually receive financial counseling and education from NFCC Member Agencies in person, over the phone, or online."
- http://www.consumerfinance.gov/
- http://www.uscourts.gov/FederalCourts/Bankruptcy.aspx
- http://www.abiworld.org
- http://www.thebankruptcysite.org/

More information

- http://www.consumer.ftc.gov/topics/dealing-debt - Federal Trade Commission resources.
- http://portal.hud.gov/hudportal/HUD?src=/homeownerhelp - If you face foreclosure, see the resources on this federal website.
- https://www.readyforzero.com/ - Budgeting website aimed at people wanting to pay off debts faster.
- http://www.whatsthecost.com/snowball.aspx - Calculates how to pay off multiple debts.

Summary

- Getting out of debt is a multi-step process that involves psychology, discipline, strategy, action, and tools.
- Change your attitude, develop a new budget, develop a debt-repayment plan, and take action.
- Getting out of debt is truly liberating and makes many other things easier to deal with such as stress, family life, personal satisfaction, and peace of mind.
- It is absolutely vital that you create a budget so you know how much money you have for needs, wants, and accelerated debt repayment.
- List your debts, prioritize them, and apply maximum debt repayment to each in turn. Enjoy the snowball effect as debt payments get bigger with each one paid off and you combine the entire debt repayment amount from the previous debt with the minimum payment you had been paying for the next debt.
- Apply your plan by identifying the maximum amount you can pay by increasing your income, freeing-up more of your current income, decreasing the minimum monthly payments of debts, dealing with specific types of debt, and avoiding debt traps.
- Any plan for getting out of debt, must also include a plan for living within your means and not letting your credit card balances rise again.
- There are actions we can take to control our spending, live within our means, and get out of debt. Nevertheless, when debt becomes severe, there are other more radical steps available including getting professional assistance.

Chapter Twenty-two

Spending Wisely

- Avoid paying full price
- Frugal mind-set
- Spending strategies
- Practical tips for everyday spending

"A penny saved is a penny earned." Ben Franklin's proverb reminds me that being thrifty has been a goal throughout the ages, but something we may still struggle with today. Nonetheless, it is usually easier to save money than to earn more. Most of us have more control over reducing our spending than increasing our income. Rather than yearning for more money, spend more time learning to save. We have already discussed saving for a goal and saving on big-ticket items; now let's discuss saving while spending on all those everyday things that we need or want. Saving can mean cutting back or doing without, but spending wisely does not. In this chapter, I'm not talking about doing without or cutting back -- we do have to spend some money. Just make your money go further by spending wisely. Anyone can do it whether misers or shopaholics. This is a fun chapter about spending money and seeing how easy it is to save while doing it.

Avoid paying full price

Spending wisely starts with the basic rule, "Avoid paying full price," one of our fundamental principles. Following this rule makes nearly any other financial situation easier. The more money you save when spending, the more you have for other purposes whether saving, spending, giving, or investing. It is both a mindset and an endeavor. Whenever you think about spending, this should be one of the first things that comes to mind and then guides you towards your goal. Yes, there are plenty of times when we have to pay full price, but that should be a last resort – not routine. To follow this rule, we need three things: a frugal mind-set, spending strategies, and practical tips for everyday things.

Frugal mind-set

Before we get to the fun strategies and tips, we need to get into the proper mind-set. To some degree, I tend to gloss over the constant struggle about mind over matter and the psychological aspects of managing your money in favor of practical how to tips. But I think developing a frugal mind-set makes other financial issues easier. Before you take a financial action, you should think "frugally". The two notions should go together. Save frugally. Invest frugally. Spend frugally. Even live frugally. Frugal should become a habit, a way of life. This doesn't mean no shopping, fun, or indulgences in your life. Just do it economically, avoid paying full price, live within your means, and still save for your goals. Thinking and acting frugally is the foundation for your other financial goals and security.

Frugal, thrifty, penny-pinching, cheapskate – different views of minding your pennies, but a 2009 American Express study found that 84% of millionaires hunt for bargains. I know I'm not going to convince people to live frugally by such things as using both sides of a sheet of paper, so let's concentrate on a frugal rule that anyone can follow.

When you think about spending, think first about our basic rule,
"Avoid paying full price".

After savings successes, you should be rewarded with more than just extra money in your budget; you should feel the thrill of victory. After that comes the joy of the hunt itself. Change your mind-set from, "I don't have time to hunt for bargains" to "I like saving money, the joy of the hunt, and the thrill of victory." Enhance the joy of the hunt even more when you can get multiple savings together, such as a sale item with free shipping, no sales tax, and a coupon code! It's easier than you may think, so let's hurry on to the spending strategies.

Spending strategies

While our frugal mind-set reminds us of the basic rule, we need strategies to make it happen. Thankfully, there are plenty of them for nearly any occasion. Always look for savings opportunities and cheaper alternatives to full price products and services.

Comparison shop

The most important strategy for spending wisely is to compare prices for your item at more than one place. The more expensive your item, the more essential your comparison shopping. The prices of products and services can vary widely, so it literally pays to comparison shop. Even if it takes a little longer to do it, you likely will be paid for your time with savings.

The internet makes it easy to comparison shop, but of course, real stores have sales, deals, and good prices, too, plus you don't have to pay and wait for shipping. These smartphone apps make local shopping better.

- Redlaser - This app shows deals that are nearby, compares prices for local and online, and even enables you to buy items and have them waiting for you to pick up.
- http://shopsavvy.com/ - Find a product by scanning a barcode or searching for keywords, and get price, details, and reviews. Then it's up to you whether you want to buy online or local.

These web browser plug-ins will alert you whenever they find a lower price elsewhere for an item you are viewing:

- http://www.priceblink.com/webcpns/browser-add-on/
- http://www.ziftr.com/

There are so many good shopping comparison websites that I don't need to list just a few. I think these websites that find products, compare prices, estimate shipping, rate retailers, and include both local and web retailers have revolutionized comparison shopping. Try many, find several you like, and consider them the first stop on your comparison shopping.

Sales, coupons, rebates, deals

There are many strategies to avoid paying full price and these are your most common.

Sales

Sales are the simplest way to save, so whenever possible, delay your purchase until it is on sale. If you have to buy now, take the time to look for a sale with your newspaper circulars, internet comparison websites, email newsletters, and checking the websites of your favorite retailers. Everyone loves a sale, both customers and retailers; just remember why retailers love them – to get customers into the store and spend their money. So don't get carried away, don't exceed your budget, don't blow your savings, and do limit yourself to no more than one little impulse buy. If a sale item is out of stock, don't be shy about asking for a "rain check" coupon for a future item at the sale price.

Coupons

Images of couponers can range from penny-pinching to extreme hoarders, but in reality, sensible couponing is one of the easiest ways to avoid paying full price. Your goal is not to see how low you can get your grocery cost or how many boxes or cans you stock in your closet, but to save money by avoiding paying full price. Now it is easier than ever because you find coupons in so many places. Coupons for groceries and personal care items are the most plentiful, but coupons for chain restaurants are easy to get and make dining out more enjoyable when you aren't paying full price. Look for shopping "passes" for store discounts to make trips to the mall even better. Here are tips to make it easy.
1. **Find your coupons.** The best place is still the Sunday newspaper. You may remember or have heard of a newspaper that is delivered right to your home with

news, color comics, sales circulars, and in this case, coupons that pay for the newspaper many times over. The internet may be killing off newspapers, but at least it's not forgetting to replace its coupons. The web has many, many coupon sites and you can see a sampling at the end of this section. You can also trade your email address to your favorite retailers and chain restaurants to get coupons emailed to you. Many manufacturers will send you coupons when you send a complimentary letter to them. More retailers are sending coupons to your smartphone but details differ widely, so it might pay to find out the details for your favorites. Food coupons are especially plentiful around the November/December holidays, so stock up then.

2. **Get organized**. You will soon have fistfuls of coupons so you need to organize them. Keep the restaurant coupons in your car or purse so they will always be handy when the need or urge arises. Coupons are easier to use when you organize them into categories. You can buy a handy organizer at the grocery or stationary store, but I just use paperclips and an old bill envelope. Sometimes you can load online coupons onto your store loyalty card or smartphone app.

3. **Enhance your coupons**. Coupons are even better when you can combine them with other savings, especially the weekly sales and retailer loyalty rewards. Favor grocery stores that double or triple your coupons. See if your store will let you "stack" or combine a store and manufacturer coupons. Bagging the deal is even sweeter when you can combine a coupon, sale, and online saving coupon, such as https://savingstar.com/ that pays you cash when your online savings have accumulated.

4. **Be sensible.** Do not stock up on stuff just because you have a nice coupon – you may avoid paying full price, but are you really saving money on stuff that will take eons to use?

Online Coupon Codes

When shopping online, have you noticed that many checkout carts include a box for a "coupon or promo code"? You might get these from their email newsletters, but before completing your purchase, first do a web search for a code, for example, *"your retailer coupon code"*. You can also do a search on your favorite coupon code website. You can find many by searching "coupon codes". Yes, many of the codes have expired, but it only takes one minute to check. Note that even many airlines sometimes offer promo codes and they can add up to big money. They are usually found on their websites, email, or social media, but also do a web search.

- http://www.coupons.com/ - Printable coupons and codes.
- http://www.couponcabin.com/ - Coupon codes and sales, plus you can sign up for alerts for new deals you are interested in.
- http://www.couponmom.com/ - Includes additional ways to find coupons including by state, restaurants, and drug stores.
- http://www.freeshipping.org/ - Coupon codes for free shipping makes online shopping even better.
- http://www.retailmenot.com/ - Coupon codes and printable coupons.
- www.smartsource.com – Printable coupons, mostly for groceries.
- www.valpak.com – Coupons for local businesses.

Rebates

Rebates enable a company to advertise a great price knowing that many customers won't go to the trouble of taking advantage of that great price. Don't be one of them! Rebates are only a little more work than coupons, but the payoff is usually much bigger, commonly $10-$20, but sometimes $75-$100 on big-ticket itemsFollow the directions carefully, write legibly, double check to ensure you include all requested items, and act before the deadline. They will sometimes look for any excuse not to pay you without even notifying you, so photocopy your submission, enter a follow-up date on your email calendar, and check back after the recommended time. It's really sweet to get that check in the mail one day in the midst of all those bills, although many are now paying with a gift card which is really, really annoying trying to use the entire $20 card for a bigger or smaller purchase.

Much easier than rebates are "cash back" websites that pay you cash when you access online retailers thru their websites. Cash back normally equals 1-10% and pays you when your total reaches a certain level. The cash back websites commonly also include coupons and codes. Here are a few to check out:

- http://www.ebates.com/
- http://www.shopathome.com/

Deals

Let someone else find the deals and email you.

- http://bensbargains.com/ - Enables you to set email alerts for bargains you are looking for.
- http://dealnews.com/ - The website show deals daily on many different items from all over the web, but the best part is letting you create a search with any key word and it will email you when a deal is found on whatever you are looking for.
- http://www.gottadeal.com/ - Deals of the day from around the internet, plus coupon codes and forums.
- http://www.offers.com/ - Deals, coupons, store sales, and local deals organized into categories.
- http://slickdeals.net/ - Deals, coupons, forums, and mobile website.

Refurbished, used, auctions, swapping

You probably know that you can save big money if you buy stuff that is not new, but what may be surprising is how many ways you can do it. In addition to yard sales, thrift stores, and flea markets, you can save money by bidding at auctions, swapping your old stuff for someone else's stuff, renting instead of buying, and buying refurbished items. You can take advantage of these tips in person or online. The best time to visit thrift stores is December and January after many people have made their end-of-the-year donations. You may be pleasantly surprised at the nice things you can often find. Find thrift stores near you at: http://www.thethriftshopper.com/.

Refurbished

Buying refurbished items is probably one of my personal favorite ways of saving serious money when buying expensive products. Have you ever wondered where all those products go that people open and then return to the retailer? A big portion of them are tested, repackaged, and sold as "refurbished" at big discounts, especially electronics, gadgets, appliances, and tools. Sometimes they may also include overstock or dinged items. They usually come with a warranty, although not necessarily as long as a new item. Many retailers have special outlets or sections of their websites for these deals. It is well worth your time to look for them and see how much you can save. Sometimes, I take advantage of these deals to just save money; other times I "trade up" to the next level of options that I otherwise could not afford. For example, getting a *refurbished* 70 inch HDTV for the same price other people are paying to get a *new* 60 inch.

Auctions

EBay is the most famous online auction site, but there are others such as these:

- http://www.shopgoodwill.com/ - Goodwill's website.
- http://www.govdeals.com/ - Government agency auctions including big stuff like autos.
- http://www.policeauctions.com/
- http://www.usa.gov/shopping/shopping.shtml - More government auctions.

Swapping

Many websites help people swap things they no longer want for things they do.

- http://www.paperbackswap.com/index.php - Post your unwanted books, get credits when you ship one to a requester, and use your credits to request books from other people.
- http://www.swapacd.com/index.php - Post your CDs, get credits when you ship one to a requester, and use your credits to request CDs from other people.
- http://www.swapadvd.com/index.php - Post your DVDs, get credits when you ship one to a requester, and use your credits to request DVDs from other people.
- www.swap.com – Swapping or consignment selling of clothes and toys.

One of the biggest swapping areas is women's fashions. There are a growing number of websites and mobile apps that specialize in helping women clean out or rotate the stuff in their closets, either swapping or selling with online consignment shops. You can post your unwanted items for people to view and offer to trade items for a swap or digital credits. It's still early to know which of these sites will catch on, so rather than provide you links, I'll just say to search for "clothes bartering websites," and get you a whole new wardrobe the inexpensive way.

Freebies, memberships, birthdays

Let's rephrase Gordon Gekko's notion about "greed is good" to "free is good" - and possible. There is nothing like getting something for free, which is why advertisers know the power of the word "FREE!" It gets our attention and rightly so. Food always tastes better when free, right? It is possible to get stuff for free when you belong to certain groups or know where to look. You may need to join a group or already belong to one. This category changes regularly so rather than provide you the usual web links, I'm going to give ideas to search for so you can get the latest treats.

Some restaurants give away free food on Mother's day, Tax day, Donut day, Pancake Day, among others. You may already be a member of some groups that can get free stuff. Many restaurants and business offer freebies to veterans and military personnel on Veteran's day. Search "veterans day freebies". Other searches to consider include "freebies for . . ." teachers, moms, babies, twins, teens, and seniors. Find where kids can eat free here: http://www.kidsmealdeals.com/.

Before we are carried away with all that free stuff these websites and companies give away, it would be wise to remember that even free stuff isn't always *free*. Sometimes we need to ask how much does that free offer actually cost in the end. Other times we need to weigh how much personal information we are willing to exchange and how much we want our email inbox to expand.

TIP: I strongly suggest you get a second email address to use for all those commercial offers and newsletters you sign up for. Then you only need to check that commercial email occasionally without it distracting you from your friends' and family's email. Remember that when you get tired of junk email, newsletters, special offers etc., most email programs let you setup "junk" folders to automatically route junk email to. Then you can browse and delete that email folder even less often.

Now back to the freebies. Perhaps the best treat is to make your birthday extra special with freebies, discounts, or savings from a wide variety of restaurants, retailers, and businesses. Many websites cover this constantly changing universe, so find the latest with a web search for "birthday freebies".

It's also amazing how much free stuff you can get from people who are just giving stuff away. Check these places:

- http://www.freecycle.org/ - Offer and request *free* stuff from your local community. "It's a grassroots and entirely nonprofit movement of people who are giving (and getting) stuff for free in their own towns. It's all about reuse and keeping good stuff out of landfills."

- http://www.craigslist.org/about/sites - Look for the "free" category under "For Sale" at your local site.

Sometimes you just need to borrow something for free:

- http://localtools.org/libraries/ – Find tool lending libraries that let you borrow tools for free or membership fees.

Free is great, but discounts are good, too. Membership in many organizations provides discounts including AAA, AARP, USAA, unions, college alumnae associations, and many large businesses. Students and teachers can get discounted software; search "academic software". Join the rewards club of retailers and restaurants for which you like to get email offers of freebies and discounts, especially around your birthday.

Generics versus name brands

Hot brands may be cool, but they come with a premium price that may not be any better than their no-name competitors. Big brands can and do charge whatever they want knowing that there are plenty of consumers that will pay for cool. But the little brands have to compete harder – usually with a much better price. Maybe Apple and Samsung tablets do have some better features than the generic brands, but enough to cost twice as much or more? When you pay twice as much, do you use them twice as much?

Clothing is a prime example. Do you seriously want to pay extra so you can wear a company's advertising all day? Shouldn't they be paying *us* to do their advertising for them! Aren't almost all clothes made in the same overseas factories by people making 10 cents an hour? Young people are a prime target of the advertising to pay big bucks for something cool so I couldn't stop beaming the day one of my sons came home laughing at a classmate who had bragged that his pants cost $100! So yes, paying for something cool to one person can be laughable to others, even if it's behind your back.

Generic drugs are an obvious example. Drugs are drugs and the extra price you pay may mostly be for the extra advertising the big guys do. You know the ads that tell us one miraculous thing they do and twenty unfortunate side effects and we're supposed to leave thinking, "I can't wait to get that!"

Buying store brands is another area where you can save big, maybe not on each item, but it definitely adds up over dozens of items per week after week, month after month, especially at grocery, drug, and discount stores. Most people cannot taste or feel much difference between most store and name brands. If you find the exception, then pay extra for the name brand, but don't think the exception is the rule even for other products of that name brand.

When to buy

Sometimes we don't have much control over when we need to buy something, but whenever we can plan ahead, savings should result. The perfect example is knowing when is the best time of year to buy what. General guidelines include buying things out of season, last year's model when new models are due to arrive, and around certain holidays and annual events.

You don't have to buy Christmas gifts to know that December is a great season for sales, but even then remember that the best sales are the few days around Thanksgiving and the week before Christmas. December is also a great time to haggle for a car because auto showrooms are empty of people out shopping for other things. It's not just holidays; look for televisions around and after the Super Bowl, kids' clothes during back-to-school sales, and the traditional "white sales" in January.

Buying things out of season may not get the best selection, but usually gets the best savings. Examples include coats, sweaters, and space heaters after winter; camping and swim gear after summer; gas grills, sports equipment, and lawn equipment after fall; and china and flatware before the wedding season. The day *after* holidays is a good time to buy holiday items like Valentine chocolate, Easter candy, Halloween costumes and decorations, and Christmas wrapping paper and decorations. Stock up for next year – no not candy – wrapping paper.

Buying last year's model when new models are getting ready to come out is a great way to save on many gadgets and autos, but some items tend to come out at certain times of the year. Examples include new cars, bicycles, and appliances in the fall; TVs in March; and furniture in February and August.

Here are the best internet sites that keep track of the ever changing best times to buy for many more items.

- http://lifehacker.com/5973864/the-best-time-to-buy-anything-during-the-year   - Or just search their blog articles for "best time to buy".

Good timing means extra savings in other ways as well. The best time to bid on eBay and many other auction websites is when fewer people are biddingThis usually means holiday weekends when people are doing other things and during weekdays when people are at work.

Internet

We have discussed many strategies to spend wisely and avoid paying full price. Let's put it all together with a step by step strategy for pursuing a major purchase on the internet. The internet makes it easy to save money on purchases because it has so many shopping resources just a few clicks away, but it's still important to follow a strategy to ensure you get the best deals on major purchases.

1. **Research your item** – Many websites and blogs provide reviews on products, especially tech and cars. Search *"your item* reviews", for example "tablet reviews". After you know the main features you are interested in and have a few recommendations, get users' reviews on Amazon. Read several of the 5, 3, and 1 star reviews, but remember that people with gripes are much more likely to take the time to log in and post a review.

2. **Compare prices and look for sales** – Amazon is usually a great starting point to not only see user reviews, specifications, and good prices, but to also view prices for new, used, and refurbished goods. But remember to always go to at least three websites to comparison shop. The web makes this easy with numerous shopping comparison websites that will show you prices, multiple locations (online and stores), estimated shipping costs, and user ratings of the retailers. There are too many comparison choices to mention, but you can search, "shopping comparison sites".

3. **Get cash back** – You many think that when you know what you want and where the best price is that you are ready to purchase, but that is just being impatient -- you still have a couple more steps to go. The next step is to go to your favorite "cash back" website to see if your retailer offers cash back of 1-6%. This is only available by first going to the cash back website and then clicking thru to your retailer so your purchase can be logged for the cash back. Two popular choices include http://www.ebates.com and http://www.extrabux.com/. Some rebate sites now offer a browser plugin to alert you when the website you are shopping on offers their rebates.

4. **Find coupon codes** – Many retailers offer deals and discounts that are only available if you have the appropriate coupon code. Before checking out with your item, search the popular coupon code websites to see if there is a current code for

your retailer and copy and paste it into the "promo code" box on the checkout page. Search *"retailer* coupon code", for example "best buy coupon code".

5. **Buy and smile** – Now you can buy with confidence that you avoided paying full price and when your item comes, your smile will be even bigger

While you are using your strategies to save money, retailers are applying their bag of tricks to get the most money from you, even offering different prices to different people under different circumstances. Fight back with these tips. First turn on "private browsing" in your web browser to see if you get a lower price when the retailer can't read your web tracks (called cookies). If you don't need your purchase now, try abandoning your purchase in your shopping cart while logged into your retailer's account and see if you are emailed a coupon within a few days to entice you back.

Yes, there is some time and work involved to get that great deal, but that is part of the joy of the hunt and it's sure better than working overtime at your job to earn the extra money to pay full price. Even if you don't have time to make more money, you do have time to save money. There are times when it's nice to pay extra for convenience, but don't make that your default option.

The internet is great for helping you save big money by doing your own repairs on any number of items such as appliances, computers, homes, autos, and plenty more. In the "Buying a Home" chapter, I told you about several instances where I saved hundreds of dollars fixing a problem refrigerator myself after seeing "how to" videos on the web even though I had no prior experience. This really is *much* easier than you think. Search for the error code, brand, model, problem, etc. to read advice, watch YouTube repair videos, and buy a replacement part.

Practical tips for everyday spending

Books

You may think Amazon is the place to save money on books? Well, do even better with these.

- http://www.loyalbooks.com/ - Free audio and ebooks.
- http://www.gutenberg.org/ - Ebooks for free, especially the classics.
- http://www.digitalbook.io/ - Free audio and ebooks.

- www.paperbackswap.com – Swap your old books for someone else's for just the cost of shipping, usually less than $3.00 with USPS media mail rates.
- Your public library – Choose from thousands of books for FREE. Yes, you read that correctly – FREE. Can't find the book you want; most libraries will let you submit a request to hold a book or forward from another branch. Oh, and most also have DVDs, audio books, and even ebooks – usually searchable over the web. My library even started offering digital magazines thru *Zinio.com*.
- http://www.overdrive.com - Checkout free audio and ebooks thru an arrangement with your local library. I do a lot of walking which is much more fun when listening to a free audiobook from OverDrive.com.

Education

With college educations costs skyrocketing, it may be surprising to learn that nearly anyone can now take courses with some of the top professors for free. Now that I have your attention, here is the reality check. It may be quite a while before you can translate this easily into college credits or degrees. Nonetheless, these free online courses do offer more than just intellectual stimulation.

1. See if your college will offer credit for passing an exam and "testing out" of the course without actually taking it. If yes, use one of these free online courses to prepare yourself.
2. If you already have your degree and want to brush up or expand your skills, then some of these free online courses could be useful. Certain courses could look nice under the continuing education section of a resume.

Here are some to consider among a growing list (search for more with "mooc" – massive open online courses):

- https://www.coursera.org/
- https://www.edx.org/
- http://academicearth.org/
- http://www.saylor.org/

There are plenty of educational websites and apps for kids including PBS Kids, Mee-Genius, and iTouch. Here is one more that is fantastic for homework help and curiosity: https://www.khanacademy.org/ . Tell the kids that you don't mind them watching these videos after school.

Energy

There are numerous ways you can reduce your home energy costs -- some simple, some requiring an initial investment. Simple ones include turning off lights and electronics when not in use, replacing old light bulbs with fluorescents or LEDs, replacing old shower heads with new low flow models, replacing air-conditioning filters monthly, and closing your blinds to the sun in the summer.

Thermostats

The best way to control your home energy bill is thru your thermostat. For each degree you lower your winter thermostat, you can save up to 3% on your heating bill, while each degree you turn up your summer AC saves up to 7%. You know you are wasting money on heat when family members are wearing short sleeves during the winter.

Get real savings when you put your thermostat on autopilot. *Programmable thermostats* not only can save you 10-20% on your energy bill, but also makes your life simpler. You setup your thermostat to desired temperatures for certain times of the day and week. For instance, down to 60 degrees during the winter at night and during the day when no one is at home, and up to 67 during the morning when you get up and in the evening when you come home. Think about it – your heat will come on automatically before your alarm goes off and your feet touch that cold floor. But nearly half the people who have them don't use them. I have programmed many of them over the years and know that their complexity varies widely, but you only have to do it once and you can benefit indefinitely. If you don't want to take the 15 minutes to play with the buttons or even read the manual, then hire the neighbor kid to do it for twenty dollars. You'll soon wonder how you ever got along without it. It is an urban myth that you use more electricity to bring your temperature back up, than it does to maintain a constant level even when no one is home.

Comparison shop your supplier

You may have a choice of which energy company supplies your electricity and if so, you know that comparison shopping pays you in savings. Many electricity companies have split *distribution* of electricity from *supplying* it. Check your energy bill to see if you have a choice. If yes, start your comparison shopping at your company's website and search for the page that discusses your supplier options. It should lead you to a webpage that lists all the energy suppliers that supply electricity to your area. Check each of their webpages for the cost per kilowatt. Skip the ones that make your call in to find their prices. Read the fine-print of ones that offer special incentives. Be wary of companies that offer a very low teaser rate for a few months, before raising the rate to one higher than you had before. I recommend you take the options to lock in your rate for 1-2 years rather than fluctuate with a different price from month to month – you don't want to have to repeat your comparison too often. Many companies offer "green" energy for a few cents per kilowatt more.

You can generally sign-up directly on the new company's website for a no-hassle change and continue to get just one bill from your local company. You will never know the difference until you look at your bill and see the new lower amount. For example, lowering your rate even two cents per KW, say from $0.12 to $0.10 cents, equals a 17% lower bill from your *supplier* (your local company's *distribution* portion does not change.)

Vampires

Here I get to include a spooky tale in a personal finance book. We all have vampires all around us in our homes and offices – "vampire devices" that suck electricity even when they are turned off! Save ten dollars a month and unplug your chargers when not in use. Put your PCs, monitors, stereos, TVs, phone docks, and game consoles on power strips and turn them off when not in use – at least overnight or while at work and school.

Entertainment

There are plenty of ways to save on entertainment, especially in big cities. It's not hard to find local theater, concerts, and sports that are inexpensive – think local little theaters, colleges, high schools, and minor league sports. As always, big cities offer more options, but that doesn't have to mean expensive. Know where to go for great deals:

- https://www.goldstar.com/ - Partners make their tickets available to Goldstar's members at half-price as a way to introduce new audiences to theater, concerts, comedy, and sporting events. Free sign-up gets you a weekly email about half-price events in your area.

- http://www.fillaseat.com/ - I've become a big fan of this service. For one annual membership fee, you can get FREE tickets to entertainment events for a full year. Venues provide free tickets to *FillaSeat* when they have empty seats they want to fill with new customers. Most events include theater, concerts, comedy clubs, and dance, but you never know what may turn up now and then. Don't expect Broadway shows, but my wife and I have thoroughly enjoyed checking out many of the regional theaters. Date nights are a lot more often when they are FREE!
- http://www.smithsonianmag.com/museumday/ - The Smithsonian museums have to be the best collection of free museums anywhere, but they also sponsor a free museum day with participating museums throughout the country. Many cities have free museum days; search "free museum day …. *your city*".
- http://museums.bankofamerica.com/ - 150+ museums are free the first weekend of the month for BoA cardholders. Many other museums offer their own free admission on certain days of the week or month so check any time you are in a new town.
- http://www.nps.gov/findapark/feefreeparks.htm - Our country has decided that even most of our national parks must scramble for money, but some days are free.
- Get multi-packs of discounted movie tickets at many websites, warehouse clubs, recreation associations, and employer organizations.
- Tunes for free – Radio is free, but can be limited in some areas. Many free internet music websites are available with many more music options and customization of your favorites. Among my favorites are services that let you listen to real radio stations throughout the world.

When you have scored a free or half-priced show or concert, date night can easily include dinner, too – especially when dinner is also half price! You can find coupons for the national restaurant chains by subscribing to their email lists, on the web, and in local newspapers. It's also easy to get deals for local restaurants, starting with coupons in your mail from advertising flyers or coupon packets. But the easiest way to eat cheap is to get deals from one of the growing list of "local" deal sites including these:

- http://www.groupon.com/
- http://www.livingsocial.com/
- http://yipit.com/

http://www.restaurant.com/ may be the site with the biggest selection of discount restaurant certificates. It can be kind of a pain to use with its varying minimums, but it's easy to search by zip code or city so I often get a certificate before I go on vacation. It's extra nice when you use your AARP or other discount to get an even cheaper certificate.

Sorry, I couldn't find any half-price baby sitters for date-night and even if I did, you wouldn't necessarily want them.

Gifts

Birthday and holiday gift giving can be real budget busters, so agree upon a limit that will fit within the budget. Last minute shopping can limit opportunities to stay within budget and avoid paying full price. Our family keeps an eye open for gifts on sale throughout the year. When our children were younger, we would retrieve a few birthday and Christmas presents they had opened and bring them out later so they would have something new spread out over the next few months.

Gift cards make great gifts, so buy them for less than face value at warehouse clubs and gift card exchange websites; search "discount gift cards". You can also sell gift cards you don't want and turn that gift into real cash: Many retailers and restaurants offer bonus gift cards in December.

Groceries

Groceries can be one of a family's largest monthly expenses, but it is also the single easiest expense to save money. There are so many ways to save that you could easily cut your grocery bill by one third as we have.

- **Use coupons** – Coupons are probably the first thing people think about when saving on groceries, but it is probably the least important. My family are diligent (not extreme) couponers and probably average $5-$10 in coupons per week, more when our favorite store doubles coupons up to a two dollars or triples up to 99 cents. This can add up to several hundred dollars per year.
- **Use store brands** – Buying store brands instead of more expensive national brands probably saves my family more than coupons with much less effort. There are a few items that we prefer name brands and each family will have to decide those for themselves.

- **Stock up on what's on sale** – By far, the biggest saving strategy is to concentrate on sale items. Plan your shopping and meals by viewing the circulars to see what's on sale. If you don't subscribe to the newspaper so you can save money by getting coupons and sales circulars, then view sales online. After a while, you can get an idea of how often which items go on sale. Minimize the items you buy when not on sale, and stock up on enough sale items to last until the next sale. There are some items that we simply don't buy unless on sale, such as snack foods, soda, cereal, and many indulgences. It helps to have a big pantry to fill with sale items, but we use an overflow shelf in the laundry room.
- **Join store's loyalty program** – Many grocery and drug stores offer the best deals to members of their free loyalty program. These make sales even better.
- **Make a list** – Use paper or mobile phone apps and concentrate upon what's on sale, the fresh items you need every week, the things you are out of, and the meals you plan to prepare. Lists enable you to zero in on sale and coupon items and things you really need without wandering around the store being tempted on every isle. Keep a starter list on the refrigerator that family members can add items to as needed. Of course, there is also a smartphone/online app for that: *Ziplist* provides many cool and cost-saving features as well as lists accessible online and by smartphone including telling you where your items are on sale.
- **Don't shop hungry** – And take as few family members as possible so fewer un-planned extras are added to the cart.
- **Limit your impulse items** to a set amount, say three per week.
- **Compare unit costs** - Compare products, brands, sizes, and sale items by com-paring the "unit" price, for example, price per ounce, pound, serving, etc., rather than the overall price. Usually, the larger size is more economical per unit cost, but not if the smaller size is on sale.

The kinds of food you buy also make a big difference in your grocery bill. Conven-ience foods come at a cost. Carryout is easy when you are tired or busy, but meals from the freezer are just as easy, probably more healthy, and certainly more budget friendly. Keep some easy-to-microwave meals in the freezer for when you need them. Store bought frozen dinners are cheaper than carryout and home cooked meals from the freezer are cheaper than frozen dinners. Cook on Sunday and enjoy leftovers several times dur-ing the week. Or cook a big batch and freeze smaller portions.

I have saved my best grocery tip for last; stop going to the grocery store. Seriously, instead shop for your groceries online. There may be a small fee, but it is the best way to employ all the other savings methods in an organized, methodical process. A growing number of grocers have online shopping where you place your order online, then either pick it up at the store or have it delivered. Ordering online and employing the other savings methods outlined above have enabled our family to cut our grocery budget 1/3 to 2/5. Our grocery shopping now has an organized method:

1. Log on to the grocery website.
2. Review the sales circular to stock up on sale items.
3. Review the weekly email I get with special loyalty discounts and stock up.
4. Review my online "starter list" and add all items we use every week, such as milk, eggs, and produce, plus items my family wants that are on sale this week. Ignore non-essential items not on sale until they are.
5. Add items from the shopping list on the refrigerator that family members have added throughout the week. As much as possible, ignore non-essential items not on sale, stock up on those that are.
6. Go thru coupons. If this is double or triple coupon week, then indulge on items with big coupons even if not on sale.
7. See which items I need on savingstar.com that pays me a rebate, especially if I have a coupon.
8. At each step, use the search box to find items, click the filter that shows only "sale" items, then sort by either "lowest price" or "lowest unit price.".
9. Limit impulse items, anything not on sale, or for which I don't have a coupon or rebate.
10. Pay by credit card that gives 5 points for each grocery dollar spent.
11. Let someone else roam the isles to fill my order.

I urge everyone to try an organized, online shopping method for big savings. We use our shopping time to concentrate on savings rather than roaming the isles, and impulse items do not tempt us nearly as often. Occasionally, we do grocery shopping the old-fashioned way by going into a grocery store, and I always wince when I see the bill that results from this unorganized approach fraught with temptation, impulse purchases, and non-sale items.

Health care

Walk-in clinics

One of the most expensive ways to get health care is thru an emergency room. If your situation is not life threatening, a much more affordable way is at a walk-in clinic or urgent care center. Many are opening at drug stores and strip malls; search "urgent care centers" or "walk in clinics". Know where your closest urgent care clinic is in advance and which one is "in-network" for your insurance. They may also save time and have more convenient hours than a doctor's office.

Alert: Be wary of new stand-alone "emergency rooms" that look very similar to "urgent care clinics", but are MUCH MORE expensive! News stories abound about people being shocked to receive bills in the $1000s to take care of cuts and minor injuries. If time is not urgent, it's always best to ask about costs and insurance in *advance* to avoid shocks to your self and finances.

Drugs

Drug costs can be a big portion of health care costs. The simplest way to save significant money is always to ask for generic drugs whenever possible since they are like the name brand, only much cheaper. It may also pay to see if there are any less expensive alternative drugs. Drug prices can vary widely among pharmacies, so use this web search engine to find the cheapest option in your area, (many drugs are available at $4.00 for a 30 day supply): http://www.mcdtipster.com/. Mail order pharmacies may offer an even better deal, such as 30% - 60% less.

Health Savings Accounts

One way government contributes to your health care is by allowing you to make tax-free contributions to your own "health savings account" (HSAs). HSAs are not like "Flexible Spending Accounts" (FSAs) that require you to predict how sick you will be a year in advance, but do have many rules similar to an "Individual Retirement Account". You can contribute up to $3400 in 2017 ($6750 for families) and your unspent amount accumulates indefinitely. Unlike FSAs, where your unspent savings vaporize at the end of the year, your HSA savings can grow indefinitely. You can even use it to pay medical expenses in retirement. The catch is that your health insurance plan must have a deductible of at least $1300 which is probably why most people have not heard of HSAs. If you have one of these high-deductible health plans, it's extra important to watch your fees by haggling over medical fees, using walk-in care clinics, ensuring that every medical expense is credited towards your deductible, and verifying you are not erroneously being charged the "uninsured" full price rates.

Negotiate effectively

With the astonishing cost of medical bills rising faster than the rate of inflation, it's no surprise that health care is a prime area for negotiating fees. Several studies and polls reveal that more than half of patients who negotiated fees with doctors or hospitals succeeded in lowering their bills, with the best success at hospitals. Sometimes all you need to do is ask, other times you need to be prepared. Ask early rather than wait for the bill. You may be more successful if offering to pay cash up front or schedule at an off-peak time. If seeing an out-of-network specialist, offer a third less which is about what insurance would have reimbursed. Research typical costs for procedures in advance. Don't wear your jewelry and high end clothes when pleading for a reduction. Sometimes it pays to hire a professional to negotiate and review bills for you. Find one here: http://claims.org/ .

Comparison Shop

Medical costs can vary widely so it pays to shop around just like any other major expense. When your doctor orders a lab test or x-ray, you can get it at any facility just like a prescription – shop around for the least expensive. It's starting to get easier to get price information you can use for both negotiating and comparison shopping. Your health insurance website may also have cost information, doctor and hospital comparisons, and other tools.

- https://www.healthcarebluebook.com/ - Tools for web and mobile apps.
- http://www.opscost.com/ - Compare charges for common procedures at over 3,300 hospitals, sourced from government data and user reported bills.

Insurance

Rule number one for people with health insurance to save money is always to use providers, specialists, and facilities that are within your plan's network. This includes everyone involved in your medical procedure. Don't assume that all services at a hospital are "in network" for your insurance. Many people are shocked when they receive a bill to discover that the referral made by a hospital or physician is not covered by your insurance. Always verify in advance whether any medical provider, including referrals, are covered by your insurance. Additionally, ask if your doctor can do certain procedures, MRIs, or tests at an outpatient facility rather than a more expensive hospital.

The Department of Labor estimates that insurers reject one in seven health insurance claims. Most people just accept these rejections, but some studies show that nearly half of appeals are successful. So it's frequently worthwhile to research the rejection, fix any simple errors, get your doctor's assistance, do some research, follow your insurer's appeal process carefully, and file a written appeal. Give a clear reason why the appeal should be overturned, not just that you can't afford to pay it yourself. Your state's insurance regulator sometimes can help with certain types of appeals, providing names of non-profit advocates, or making inquiries to the insurer.

Let's conclude this topic with the reminder that healthy habits lead to less stress on both your life and budget. The best way to save on huge medical bills is healthy living, eating, and exercising.

Tech

Telephones

We haven't yet seen popular versions of that cool Dick Tracy watch phone or the Jetson's TV phone, but the humble telephone has changed dramatically over the past few decades with the breakup of the telephone monopoly, mobile phones, smartphones, internet calling, and VOIP phones. Smartphones can be expensive for both the phone and monthly plan, but you do have options to save with your landline phone that is still connected to those outside telephone poles. Some people save by bundling their telephone service with their TV and internet service from the same company. Others can save by switching to internet calling with *Skype* or "Voice over IP" (VOIP) calling that connects a device to your internet router and uses your internet connection rather than telephone lines to connect. Popular VOIP companies include *Magic Jack* and *Vonage,* but there are many others you can find and compare by searching "VOIP providers" to get telephone service for under $20 per month. A growing trend is to ditch your landline altogether and make your mobile phone your only phone. Speaking of mobile phones – it's hard to use that phrase and "savings" in the same sentence, but here is are a couple of tips. Did you know that many of the second tier wireless carriers use the same network and may even be owned by the big four, but cost much less money? (For example, Cricket and AT&T, Metro PCS and TMobile). Don't buy your accessories at your carrier's store or even website, save at least half by going online and search *"your phone model* accessories".

Free software

I never thought I would be talking about "tech" and "free" in the same section, but there is one tech area where you can get very nice free stuff – software. From the dawn of personal computers, there has actually been a lot of free software in practically every conceivable category and now of course it continues with free web browser add-ons and mobile apps. While advertisements are usually the worst thing to worry about with free mobile apps, free software has a few more worries including viruses, trialware, and bugs. The best defense is to download from a reputable website such as:

- http://www.pcworld.com/category/software/ and http://www.cnet.com/.

Let's spotlight just a few software categories that every computer user needs. New Windows PCs come with Microsoft *Defender* and *Security Essentials,* but you can find additional choices under the "security" categories of free software websites. You can only run one anti-virus software at a time, but ensure you have the full range of tools for anti-virus, firewall, and malware protection. I'm going to assert that it is also essential that everyone have an office suite that commonly includes a word processor, spreadsheet, and presentation program – and why not when there are so many very good free ones available. Many suites also include other software such as photo suites, drawing editors, databases, desktop publishers, or note takers. There are good reasons why people pay mega-bucks for the king-of-the-hill – *Microsoft Office* – including needing compatibility with work. Nevertheless, I think it is highly likely that most people will do very well with one of the FREE competitors including *Google Docs, LibreOffice, Open Office, Zoho*, and several others. There are also good free choices for your mobile device. It's also easy to get free photo and video editing software for all those photos you take including *Google Photos* and *Photoscape* among many others.

Speaking of free tech, download one of the many free Wi-Fi finders so you can find access while away from home. Best bets include libraries, inexpensive hotels, bookstores, McDonalds, Starbucks, and malls.

Tech problems

When you upgrade your tech, sell your used gadgets at places like gazelle.com, next-worth.com, many electronics retailers, and many others. To find places to recycle your electronics, search http://earth911.com/.

The downside to all those lovely tech toys we can't live without is that sooner or later they betray us with some kind of glitch, noise, crack, dead battery, or other annoyance. The good news is that while most of us aren't tech wizards, plenty of people are and are willing to share their expertise and advice, sometimes for free. There are plenty of specialized web forums where you can post a question and likely get a free answer to try with varying success. Start with websites that address plenty of common problems including http://www.ifixit.com/ and http://www.fixya.com/. Sometimes you may even be desperate enough to consult the user manual. Search for yours online, at the manufacturer's website, or at websites such as http://www.manualsonline.com/.

Printers

No doubt, you have discovered that replacement cartridges are soon more expensive than your printer, so print wisely. Pundits may talk paperless, but most people can't resist making a quick printout. Cut in half the amount of paper you use. Set your printer to double-sided printing. Don't recycle paper until you have used both sides. Reuse printouts with a blank side. Feed them back in to use the other side for less important printouts, namely those that don't leave the house or have long-term value. I use my printer's second tray to hold my reuse paper. To save on ink and toner, print in "draft/economy" mode for less important printouts. Don't print pages that are mostly covered with color or solid backgrounds – especially those Power Point handouts. When your *laser* printer reports that it is out of toner, take out the cartridge and shake it around to even out the remaining toner – at least a few times. Cartridges that use ink instead of toner can be refilled from ink refill kits that cost a tiny fraction of new cartridges. The first time takes a little longer and refills can sometimes be messy, but just wear rubber gloves and do it over the kitchen sink. Which would you rather do -- work two hours of overtime to pay for a new cartridge or take five minutes to refill?

Travel

Off-peak travel

Flexibility is one key to travel discounts. Traveling off-peak times and seasons is the best way to save. Families probably can't do this often, so next best is flexibility in days of the week. Experts say Tuesday or Wednesday are the cheapest days to fly. Studies vary on the best time to book domestic flights for non-holidays, tending to range from 21-49 days before your flight. When possible, use the "flexible dates" features of airline, hotel, and rental car booking websites. When really flexible, look for "last minute" deals and discounts. Most travel booking websites have them. Last minute airfare can be expensive, but a good way to find discounts is thru the airlines' twitter feeds. Finding literally last minute hotel discounts are useful with the mobile app, *"Hotel Tonight"*.

Websites

The internet has made it much easier to plan and book all types of travel – and most importantly, to avoid paying full price. There are so many good travel sites that most people know about, that I don't need to mention them here, but I note a few sites with special tools.

- http://www.kayak.com/more - This popular travel booking site has extra tools that help you save including price alerts, low fare tips, and fare histories.
- http://www.smartertravel.com/blogs/today-in-travel/airline-fees-the-ultimate-guide.html?id=2623262 – Don't just compare ticket prices, also compare all those pesky fees in this handy guide. Note for example that some airlines (Southwest and JetBlue) still offer free bags, which makes a huge difference when comparing total air travel deals.
- http://www.viator.com/ - Save big bucks by booking your cruise shore excursions directly rather than thru the cruise line.

Check these first for research, but add a stop at www.priceline.com where you specify general criteria for your booking, but not the exact brand or details. You have to bid, but can pay around 30% - 50% less for your flexibility. Many people know about Priceline, but the lesser-known "secret" to being successful is to first it www.biddingtraveler.com to see winning bids or http://biddingfortravel.yuku.com/ to get information about bidding strategies.

There are many good websites to compare prices and book hotels, airlines, rental cars, cruises, vacation homes, and house swapping. It's frequently worth your time to also check the hotel and airline websites directly because they may offer better deals than the travel booking sites. Additionally, some discount airlines may not be listed on travel sites at all, such as Southwest Airlines. Sometimes you can get a better deal by calling a hotel directly if they have many empty rooms they are trying to fill.

Hotels

Two features I usually search for to save money and time at hotels are free breakfast and internet. I always chuckle when I notice that expensive hotels usually charge more than ten dollars a day for internet access while inexpensive hotels usually offer it for free. But the most important feature I look for is the free breakfast buffet, especially when traveling with my family. Even if breakfast is the least expensive restaurant meal, it still saves good money as well as time. Another nice feature is that many of the hotels that provide free breakfast buffets also offer light snacks in the evening during the week and many times, I'm successful in convincing my family what a wonderful dinner it makes.

Top Travel Tips

Here are some travel tips I've discovered over the years from visiting 45 states and 27 countries. Airline consolidation in the United States has led to fewer choices and more fees for every little thing. In some parts of the world, the reverse is true, as new airlines have started to compete with traditional national airlines. Whenever possible, I take a non-American airline. They usually provide better service, lower prices, and get this – actual meals rather than a few peanuts. Moreover, many non-American airlines are members of frequent flyer programs with American airlines. If you do have to take an American airline and want more than a few mini-pretzels for lunch, be sure and bring your own snacks or sandwiches from home. When booking more than one passenger ticket, book them one at a time in case at least one of them is eligible for a discount fare. If you book four tickets at once for example and there are only 2 discount fares left, all four tickets will be charged the higher fare with no discount. Another travel secret: buy a hand travel-scale that enables you to weigh your bags before taking them to the airport. Don't find out too late that the really great souvenir you bought just cost you an extra $50 in airline baggage fees. If you are going to spend a week in a major city, investigate one of those city passes or multi-attraction discount cards from the local visitor's bureau that gives you discounts on many attractions for a lower price.

When you rent a car, you probably don't need the rental insurance if you already have it on your regular auto insurance or it's provided as a perk by your credit card company.

Avoid paying the rental car company to fill up your tank; they will probably charge you for a full tank at some unknown price even if your tank is still half full. Save a bundle and fill up the tank at a gas station near the rental car return – just remember to add enough time to your schedule to do this. Remember to bring your own GPS and EZ Pass/toll paying gadgets so you don't have to pay extra to rent them.

Save big bucks by booking your cruise shore excursions directly rather than thru the cruise line. Great Bed & Breakfast prices can be found on the deal sites like Groupon and LivingSocial.

Warranties

Save money by not buying those extended warranties that salesmen push right after selling you an appliance or electronic gadget that they assure you is very good. After that exhaustive research you did to find the best bargain, now are you going to throw your savings away on the extended warranty you likely are never going to use? Even if one time you do need to use it, can find it, figure out what to do with it, and do get some money back; you will still save big money over your lifetime by skipping them. Salespersons push these because they are a big profit item, since they are seldom used. I enjoy telling the salesperson, "It sounds like you don't have confidence in the product you just convinced me was so good." That's when my wife pretends she doesn't know me. Finally, remember my story from the "Buying a House" chapter where the home warranty company simply refused to pay when it was time.

As usual, there are exceptions to the general rule. We opted for the extended warranty when we purchased our minivan because we were determined that we were going to keep it as long as the kids were still at home – and who can tell how long that will be. We've got our money back just from the free car rentals while in the shop. My second exception is the extended warranties for our children's smartphones and tablets; they can't live without their smartphones, but is that reason enough not to lose, scratch, or water them? Yes, sometimes what you are really buying is peace of mind. Nonetheless, the real take away from this discussion should be not to buy insurance or warranties that you can afford to cover yourself.

With all these strategies and tips, you should be able to save thousands of dollars per year to make your budget easier. Just remember to turn most of those savings to debt payments and savings goals. Don't bust your credit card just because there is a sale.

Summary

- It is usually easier to save money than to earn more. Most of us have more control over reducing our spending than increasing our income. So rather than yearning for more money, spend more time learning to save.
- Spending wisely starts with the basic rule, "Avoid paying full price." Following this rule makes nearly any other financial situation easier. The more money you save when spending, the more you have for other purposes whether saving, spending, giving, or investing. It is both a mindset and a goal.
- Before you take a financial action, you should think "frugally". The two notions should go together. Save frugally. Invest frugally. Spend frugally. Even live frugally. Frugal should become a habit, a way of life. This doesn't mean no shopping, fun, or indulgences. Just do it economically, avoid paying full price, live within your means, and save for your goals. Thinking and acting frugally is the foundation for your other financial goals and security.
- Our frugal mindset reminds us always to look for savings opportunities and cheaper alternatives to full price products and services. Then we employ many strategies to accomplish this.
- The most important shopping strategies for practically any spending include comparison shopping, and looking for sales and deals, but there are also so many other ways to avoid paying full price. Using shopping strategies is worth your time and literally pays for your frugal endeavors.
- Since much of our shopping is now online shopping, it should frequently include all of these steps: research your item, comparison shop, look for sales, get cash back, hunt for coupon codes, and then buy and smile with the thrill of victory.
- The best way to save with grocery shopping is not coupons, but using a disciplined approach with sales, store brands, loyalty perks, lists, limited impulse buys, limited non-sale items, and double coupons. The best way to apply this strategic approach is with online shopping.
- Regardless of whether you think frugal is fun, there is no doubt that fun can be frugal with half-price entertainment, discount dining, vacation deals, used books and video games, refurbished electronics, and free internet radio tunes.

Chapter Twenty-three

Retirement

- Preparing for retirement
- Claiming Social Security Benefits
- Withdrawing savings
- Understanding annuities
- Earning and spending
- Reversing your mortgage

You have a lifetime to look forward to and prepare for retirement. Most people retire before age 65, some by choice and some by job lose or poor health. Now we are living longer in retirement than ever before, and a 65 year old has a better than 50% chance of living into their mid-eighties. How well we fare financially depends upon how well we have prepared for it, as well as how well we manage our income, savings, spending, and health in retirement.

Many of the same financial principles apply that we have discussed previously, but now we have extra issues because our income is harder to manage than just ensuring a paycheck every two weeks. Retirees should aim for income that is stable, beats inflation, and lasts for the rest of their lives – however long that might be. Investments should provide income, be available for emergencies, grow fast enough to beat inflation, weather market downturns, and perhaps be available for heirs. No one investment can meet all these goals, but the right combination can work nicely. Let's discuss our main options including Social Security, annuities, managing investments for income and growth, working, spending, and reverse mortgages.

Preparing for retirement

It should be no surprise that your retirement is more likely to be successful, if you plan for it in advance. I already covered the decades of saving huge amounts in *Part Two, Chapter 10 – Saving for Retirement*. As you approach retirement in your fifties and sixties, there are additional things you should do including saving more, shifting a portion of your investments from stocks to more conservative investments, ensuring debts are paid off, deciding how you will cover your health insurance, getting a better estimate of your retirement income and expenses, and preparing a retirement budget.

Test-drive your retirement budget

Isn't it interesting how often this budget topic keeps coming up? That should be no surprise because it is the basic tool to ensure you live within your means, and you should review it every time something major in your finances changes. Retirement certainly will change a lot. The best way to see if you are financially ready to retire is to calculate your budget in retirement. By this point, you should be well experienced in budgeting, but see *Chapter 7, Budgets* for the details. Consider these additional aspects of retirement finances.

Get an estimate of your Social Security benefits and decide when to begin collecting it. If you have a pension, talk to your HR department to get an estimate and discuss your health insurance, accrued leave, and what time of year the company match is deposited into your 401(k). See the coming section on "Withdrawing from savings" to calculate how much income you will use from your retirement savings. Don't forget that different income sources will have different income tax treatments. Discuss with your spouse their income, spending, and retirement plans.

Think about how your future income and expenses may change including health and drug costs, a mortgage and loans that may be paid off, kids or parents that may need support, and inflation. Some of your income may be fixed, but inflation will continue to increase most of your expenses – an average of 3% on most things, much more for health related expenses. Once you have a good budget estimate, consider test-driving it for a while to see whether you are ready to apply it indefinitely.

Plan your major expenses in retirement, especially the two biggest, housing and health care. If you will still be paying a mortgage, consider whether to pay it off early. If you will still be paying a mortgage or rent, consider whether you want to downsize to a smaller home, relocate to a different community, or have enough fixed income (SSA, pensions, or annuities) to cover it.

Plan for your insurance

Health insurance

Health care costs may be your next biggest expense after housing. . In fact, the health insurance issue could be the greatest challenge, especially if you retire before qualifying for Medicare at age 65 or you don't have retiree health benefits.

Retirees may find that getting health insurance on their own will be one of their biggest expenses as premiums and expenses double, triple, or worse, especially as they age or really need it. First, consider COBRA that allows you to continue your employer's coverage for 18 months even though you will pay the full premium. Apply for Medicare by your 65th birthday to avoid a 10% per year penalty when you do sign up. If you are still working at 65 and want to remain under your employer's play, note that you only have a limited period to sign up for Medicare once you stop working to avoid the penalty that lasts indefinitely. I strongly advise when you reach age 65, to review the Medicare rules regardless of your current health care options, so you aren't surprised later at the lifetime penalties, limited sign-up periods, and primary/secondary insurance payer rules. You will also need to analyze which Medicare options you want and whether you want any regular health insurance to supplement it.

- http://www.dol.gov/ebsa/faqs/faq-consumer-cobra.html - FAQs about COBRA temporary continuation of health insurance coverage.
- https://www.healthcare.gov/ - Review your options at the Affordable Care Act health insurance exchange website. If your state has its own exchange, you will be redirected there.
- http://medicare.gov/ - Get more information about Medicare.

Long term care insurance

A second insurance to consider is "long term care" (LTC) insurance to cover care when you no longer can live alone. Both the care and insurance are very expensive, especially for premiums the longer you wait. Some experts advise that you don't need LTC if you have small assets that will be depleted and make you eligible for Medicare coverage, or very large assets so you can cover the care yourself.

- http://longtermcare.gov/ - Get more information.
- http://www.aaltci.org/ - Find an agent who can sell LTC insurance from multiple insurers to get a more competitive rate.

Life insurance

You may not need life insurance once you no longer have kids at home, a mortgage, or a business. Before you just dump it, look into a "life settlement" in which you sell your life insurance to a third party who then pays the premiums and collects the insurance. You could get a nice sum, but there are requirements including age, amount of policy, and whether it's convertible to a universal or whole life policy. Get more information here: http://www.lisa.org/

Other insurance

Notify your auto and homeowners insurance when you retire and see if they offer discounts because you are home more and drive less.

Claiming Social Security Benefits

A Social Security benefit is one of the most important sources of retirement income for most retirees because it is guaranteed for life, increases with inflation, and includes benefits for spouses. For more than half of married retirees, SSA benefits provide more than half their income. But planning for SSA benefits can be complicated because your amount depends upon the amount earned by each spouse, the age you begin collecting, whether you are working in retirement, and how the primary, spousal, and survivor benefits relate to each other.

When to collect

When to claim Social Security is one of your most important decisions because the amount you receive increases each year you wait between ages 62-70 and married couples can opt between their own, a portion of their spouse's, or a survivor benefit after the primary beneficiary's death. The longer you wait to age 70, the greater your benefit. Your benefits increase around 6% each year you wait from age 62 to your "normal" retirement age (which for most people is 66-67 depending upon the year you were born), and around 8% from your normal retirement age until age 70. Flexibility about when to begin collecting benefits also includes other options. You can apply for benefits and immediately suspend them. Later, you can choose a lump sum of all your suspended benefits if you need money, or a higher monthly benefit based upon the later date you lift the suspension.

With both complexity and flexibility, it can be challenging to decide when to collect your benefits. Most planners aim for scenarios that hope to give you maximum lifetime benefits. But given that your lifetime is unknown, other points to consider include how much you need income early and how much you want to ensure high income in case you or your spouse lives a very long time and your savings runs out. Social Security rules, strategies, and scenarios are too many and complicated to explore in detail, but here are some guidelines to consider for your personal circumstances.

It may be useful to collect benefits early if:
- You really need the money.
- You expect your retirement savings to earn a nice rate of return and want to delay tapping them for income.
- You have poor health or your family does not have a record of life longevity.

It may pay to wait longer to begin collecting if:
- You plan to continue working and are subject to the "earnings test" before your normal retirement age. (See below.)
- You have family longevity genes and want to maximize your lifetime benefits by receiving the highest amount over a long lifespan.
- You want to provide the highest survivor benefits. (This could be particularly valuable to a much younger wife combined with the fact that women tend to live longer).

Married couples

If a single individual lives past 80, SSA benefits are designed to even out whether collecting less *early* or more *later*. It can get more complicated for married couples because they have more opportunities to mix and match benefits. So it's even more important that couples coordinate their retirement plans here. Spouses may collect half of the retiree's benefits or their own benefits, whichever is higher. Survivors may collect 100% of the deceased retiree's benefits or their own if higher. But all scenarios are affected by the age each spouse begins collecting. Therefore, there are plenty of scenarios, advice, and calculations to help decide which spouse should collect their own benefits, delay their benefits, apply for and suspend their benefits, or take a spousal benefit. You should investigate various scenarios about which spouse should take whose benefit when.

Let's discuss a few scenarios of many. The most recommended advice is for the highest earning spouse to delay benefits so the survivor's benefit will be as large as possible. The beneficiary can even apply for benefits, which would allow the spouse to start receiving spousal benefits, but immediately suspend their own benefits so the amount can continue to increase. Another scenario is for the lower earning spouse to apply for their own benefits earlier to get income while the higher earner waits, which would increase both the higher earner's benefit and the spouse's future survivor benefit. Note that dependent children under age 18 that are living with you can also receive benefits up to half your retirement benefit.

Even divorced ex-spouses may collect a benefit under certain eligibility requirements including ten years of marriage. Survivors must choose between their own benefits and a survivor's benefit based upon the deceased, but they can switch between the two and sometimes should. If the survivor is under their normal retirement age, they may receive more in the long run if they take the lower benefit first, and switch to the higher benefit at the normal retirement age. Survivors should also note that for people born after 1955, SSA has a slightly different "normal retirement age" for survivors versus retirees.

Thus there is plenty of incentive to hold off on collecting your Social Security benefits if you can and there are ways to do it. You can postpone collecting Social Security by retiring later, working part-time, withdrawing more from savings early, or collecting a benefit based upon your spouse's benefit while delaying your own. An obvious strategy is to delay SSA benefits while collecting more from your retirement savings early. Some studies show that this would break even in your early to mid-eighties depending upon rates of inflation and total returns.

Earnings test

If you work while collecting SSA benefits before normal retirement age, your benefits will be reduced $1 for each $2 of income over a certain amount. However, at your normal retirement age, SSA will increase your benefits as if you had delayed taking any benefits for the number of months equivalent to the amount you lost for working. It could take more than 14-15 years to get all the withheld funds back, but you get the increased benefit for life.

Taxes

A portion of your SSA benefits may be taxable depending upon your total income. See IRS Publication 915 for details.

In addition to all these complicating factors and scenarios, you may have your own circumstances so it's certainly worthwhile to discuss all of this with a Social Security representative or *knowledgeable* financial advisor. You also can find many books on this topic as well as organizations that will advise you for a fee. Start by getting more information here:

- For SSA benefits relating to spouses and ex-spouses, see *"Chapter 5 – Women"*.
- http://www.aarp.org/work/social-security/ - Of course AARP has a wealth of Social Security information, tools, and FAQs.
- http://www.ssa.gov/estimator/ - Get information and estimate your benefits at the Social Security website.
- http://www.socialsecurity.gov/planners/benefitcalculators.htm - Use many SSA calculators, tools, and charts including finding your "normal retirement age".

Withdrawing savings

Hopefully, you have saved a gigantic pile of money in your tax-advantaged retirement accounts before you are ready or have to retire. Once you retire, managing your retirement savings becomes even more challenging because you have to balance the need for immediate cash withdrawals versus your long-term need to make your savings last for as long as you *and your spouse* live. You have the challenge to make it last for up to 30 years while guarding against stock market crashes, failure to keep pace with inflation, and spending it too fast. You have options on what to do with your retirement accounts including leaving 401(k) accounts with your employers, rolling multiple accounts into a regular IRA, rolling into a ROTH IRA, taking a lump sum to buy an annuity, leaving some for heirs, and withdrawing regular installments to live on.

First, note that rules for withdrawing from your 401(k) and IRA retirement accounts can get complicated in some situations and costly if you make a mistake, so make sure you review current rules carefully. This is especially true if you withdraw before age 59 ½, have company stock in your 401(k), rollover from 401(k) to IRA accounts, or wait to withdraw until age 70 ½. For more information, see *"Part Two, Chapter 10 – Saving for Retirement",* review the IRS publications, and consult with your HR department or financial advisor.

I have previously discussed withdrawing your savings from retirement accounts before you retired, so now let's get to the real point of you saving all that money all those decades – withdrawing money from your retirement accounts so you will have income in retirement.

How much to withdraw

The first priority is to make whatever amount you have managed to save, last for the rest of your life, plus your spouse's. For many people, this could mean 30 years or more, especially if one spouse is much younger. Statistically, a male aged 65 at retirement could live another 19+ years and a female, 21+ years. Of course, this actually depends upon many factors such as health, genes, exercise, smoking, eating habits, etc., so many people will live much longer. This means that you will need to limit the amount you withdraw and spend, while continuing to manage your investments so they continue to grow. Therefore, the amount you can withdraw from your savings is NOT the amount you think you "need", but rather is based upon a calculation that increases the likelihood that your savings will last your lifetime plus your spouse's. You need a strategy to accomplish this and we will look at two: the 4% + inflation rule (4%+) and required minimum distribution (RMD). See my blog for additional discussion of this topic.

4% + inflation rule

The "4%" rule advises retirees to withdraw 4% of their retirement savings balance during their first year in retirement and even allows us to increase it each following year by the rate of inflation. Both academic research and widespread practice suggests that this withdrawal strategy makes it at least 90% likely that most people will have enough savings to last their lifetime. But it doesn't guarantee it since many factors can influence success including your actual life span, severity of market downturns, extent of low interest rate periods, how aggressively you invest your savings, and your withdrawal rate and strategy.

Calculating your first year's withdrawal is easy. Let's make it simple by using a retirement savings balance of $100,000 which you can extrapolate to your own level:

$100,000 x 0.04 = $4000 annually / 12 = $333 monthly.

In year two, you get to increase that by the rate of inflation, let's say 3%:

$4000 + ($4000 * .03 = $120) = $4120 annually / 12 = $343 monthly.

In year three, let's say inflation is 2.5%:

$4120 + ($4120 * .025 = $103) = $4223 annually / 12 = $351 monthly.

Required Minimum Distribution (RMD)

The IRS RMD rules (for people over age 70 ½ with 401(k)s and IRAs) are designed to recover the taxes that we deferred while saving. Once you reach age 70½, you should annually calculate your balances in these accounts to see whether you are required to take greater withdrawals. If you are required to take RMDs, do NOT neglect to do so. The IRS penalty is 50% of what you should have taken out and the company that administers your account reports the RMD amount to both you and the IRS.

But anyone can choose to follow this strategy at any age to determine how much you can or should withdraw each year. We saw that the 4%+ rule is based only upon your *initial* investment balance and subsequent annual inflation rates. The RMD is based upon life expectancy tables, amount of savings, and *current* market value of your investments. Retirees of any age can use this strategy by dividing their total year-end retirement savings balance by the relevant life-expectancy factor from the tables in *IRS Publication 590*. Therefore, you don't have a constant and increasing income amount based upon your first date of retirement as with the 4% plus inflation rule. However, the

RMD method won't run out of money because it is regularly fine-tuned based upon your age and remaining savings from recent market performance. It also takes into account your spouse's age and is designed to last past age 100.

A downside to this RMD strategy is that your year-to-year withdrawals will vary somewhat depending upon last year's market performance. To smooth out this variation, consider adjusting your actual withdrawals slightly by imposing a floor after bad years and a ceiling after good years. This means don't lower your spending as much as the RMD stipulates after poor years, and compensate by not raising your spending as much as allowed after great years.

4% vs RMD

The "4% +" strategy increases payouts based upon inflation, but ignores the reality check of how well your investments are performing. If you have many years of poor performance or low bond yields, your ever-increasing withdrawals could be unsustainable, while many years of good performance could require you to switch to the RMD to avoid a penalty. The RMD strategy adjusts based upon your age, spouse's age, and how well your investments are performing, but pays out much less at the beginning, especially before age 70. The "4%+" method provides a higher pay out than the RMD method at the beginning of the distribution period; then increases annually until it reaches its maximum when the retirement assets are fully used up which may or may not be before you and your spouse both die. During periods of prolonged inflation & market volatility, the RMD method can be expected to outperform the "4% +" distribution method. The RMD method always begins at a lower percentage than "4% +," reaches its maximum amount in midterm, often exceeds the "4% +" distribution during midterm, then declines but is *never* fully depleted during the owner's or spouse's lifetime.

Research suggests that the "4% +" method will *usually* last for the owner's lifetimes *depending* on Inflation rates and portfolio performance. If you want to be assured the investments and payouts will last throughout both your *and your spouse's* lifetime or you want to leave money to heirs, then consider the RMD distribution method which is designed to last past age 100. This is essential if your spouse is more than 10 years younger than you.

No matter what method you select, it is essential that you calculate the RMD each year after age 70 ½ to avoid the 50% penalty. Depending on annual Inflation rates and portfolio yields, the RMD withdrawal amount may exceed the "4% +" withdrawal amount at some point which would *require* you to use the RMD amount to avoid the IRS penalty.

Alternative withdrawal strategies

Alternative withdrawal options to the "4%+" and RMD rules include withdrawing less or more based upon need, age, and market performance or only withdrawing investment income.

Retirees living on their investment income from interest and dividends is a well-known goal. However, doing it exclusively while leaving your principle untouched can constrain your standard of living, make it difficult to increase your income with inflation, leave you at the mercy of market performance (especially during prolonged periods of interest rate declines), and tempt retirees to skew their investments too far towards income investments at the expense of growth. If you do try to live off your dividends, consider a strategy that selects stocks so that at least one pays their dividends each month of the year. It's a nice way to arrange for monthly income, even though it would fluctuate throughout the year.

TIP: Some REITS and Master Limited Partnerships pay over 10% dividends. Some telephone stocks pay over 5% in dividends. These can greatly boost dividend income, but you still have to remember to diversify your investments.

Regardless of the strategy you use to determine the amount of savings you can withdraw each year for income, you can add flexibility based upon your changing needs, market performance, and impending debt payoffs. But always keep in mind the need to make your savings last for both yours and your spouse's lifetime. You may need to withdraw more in certain years to pay for unusual expenses such as a vacation, new car, or new roof. Ideally, they can be timed with good market performance years. These expensive years should be balanced by lower withdrawals later or during bad market performance years. Therefore, the 4% + and RMS rules are useful guidelines that may need to be flexible based upon circumstances.

You may wish to use a "4% +" rule early in retirement to get higher pay outs for travel, active life style, or debts, but shift to an RMD strategy later to ensure your remaining assets account for investment performance and last for the lifetime of both spouses. If you use the 4%+ rule, consider reviewing your savings status every few years by using one of these calculators to match your age and savings balance against the odds of making your savings last. They can help you decide whether you should adjust your withdrawals up or down to stay on track. A periodic status check and adjustment can help guard against both running out of savings too soon, as well as keeping too much savings while living too frugally early in retirement.

- See this book's website for more detailed information about the 4% +, RMD and alternative withdrawal methods and tools. (For example, my father is sharing his wealth of spreadsheets and tools he uses to keep track of a variety of income, assets, expenses, and projections.)
- http://investor.gov/tools/calculators/required-minimum-distribution-calculator - 401(k) and IRA Required Minimum Distribution Calculator.
- http://www.irs.gov/Retirement-Plans/Plan-Participant,-Employee/Retirement-Topics---Required-Minimum-Distributions-%28RMDs%29 - See the IRS website to calculate withdrawal amounts based upon the RMD rules that match your life expectancy and savings balance. Get the life-expectancy factors from *IRS Publication 590*.
- Investment companies such as T Rowe Price, Fidelity.com and Vanguard.com have a variety of retirement planning tools. Note that many investment companies will give you investment and retirement planning advice when you have an IRA with them.
- http://retirementincomescenarios.blogspot.com/ - Professor William Sharpe's blog and free software to help analyze your scenarios.

How to withdraw

Once you have decided upon a strategy to calculate how *much* to withdraw, you can next decide *how* to do it. Your retirement savings may be in multiple types of accounts such as IRAs, 401(k)s, Roth accounts, and taxable, non-retirement investments. Each of those accounts may have multiple types of investments and you may even have multiple accounts of each type. So how do you juggle or manage all of these when cashing in your investments and withdrawing your money to live on? First, if you really do have many accounts, consider consolidating them into a manageable few. Let's discuss two aspects of withdrawing your money efficiently: tax strategies and making your savings last thru spending, inflation, and market downturns.

Tax strategies

Remember that you will owe taxes on savings withdrawn from any retirement accounts other than Roths, so you may need to file quarterly tax payments or bump up the tax withholding from any pensions or Social Security to cover your retirement account withdrawals. The most often quoted tax advice to retirees is to withdraw your savings in a tax-advantaged order, usually required minimum distributions (RMDs) when over age 70 ½, taxable accounts (non-retirement accounts), regular IRAs and 401(k)s, and then Roth accounts. RMDs, from 401(k)s and regular IRAs when you reach age 70 ½, have tax penalties if not done correctly. Taxable account will usually be taxed at the long-term capital gains rate of 15%. Regular IRAs and 401(k)s will generally be taxed at your regular tax rate. Roth withdrawals are tax free, can be passed to heirs tax free, and Roth IRAs do not require RMDs.

Of course, the U.S. tax code is based upon complexity, and individual's situations may differ. Therefore, many experts advocate keeping flexibility to withdraw from different accounts as needed, rather than exhausting each type of account completely in sequence. For example, circumstances may depend upon whether you foresee your highest earnings and tax brackets early or later in retirement, whether you want to maximize tax benefits for you or heirs, and what type and amount of assets you have in each type of account. Because of the complexity, amounts of money involved, and wide variety of personal circumstances; this is one of those areas where you may benefit from consulting with a tax professional, which is definitely not me.

Managing your drawdown

During the Great Recession and market crash, many recent retirees watched in dismay as their carefully accumulated retirement savings dwindled lower and lower just as they counted on it to last the rest of their lives. You can avoid this by planning ahead and having enough cash and safe bonds on hand to carry you thru a typical market downturn until your savings have recovered.

Whether you have many or few accounts and assets, you need a plan to manage the withdrawal of your assets, converting them to cash, and investing the rest for both income and growth. One strategy is to convert investments into the cash you need to live on for the next year at the time you rebalance your investments. (For more on "rebalancing," see *Part Three – Investing*.) Thus, when rebalancing your strong investments (whether stocks or bonds) into the under-performing investment type, you could convert a portion into the amount of cash you need for the next year. This would ensure your cash to live on is always coming from your growing investments and not from your shrinking investment type. If you don't need to rebalance, because for example you use target date funds that do it for you, then sell enough shares to replenish your cash. Do this 1-2 years in advance during the good times and see how long you can postpone during a downturn until your cash is gone or a market rebound is underway.

Bucket Strategy

A second strategy is known as the *bucket* or *basket* strategy. In *Chapter 16 – Investing Strategies*, I discussed an alternative asset allocation method based upon the time horizon of your saving goal. Now let's discuss that in more detail because it is most suited for managing your savings in retirement.

This bucket strategy divides your savings into multiple categories with your least volatile investments used for your soonest withdrawals and your most aggressive investments used for you latest withdrawals. This is designed to enable you to spend from safe investments without worrying when volatile investments are doing poorly, even for many years. In particular, you can avoid the prospect that faced retirees who retired right before the Great Recession who saw their retirement savings plunge right before they needed them. I recommend the bucket strategy that uses three buckets.

Bucket	Time horizon	Goal	Investments
Bucket One	0-2 years	Preserve savings and spend from this basket.	All in savings accounts, CDs, money market funds, or short-term bonds or Treasuries.
Bucket Two	3-5 years	Preserve savings, generate investment income, and refill basket one when basket three is underperform-	Safe income producing investments. Mostly short/intermediate bonds with some in higher yield bonds, high quality dividend

		ing.	paying stocks, balanced funds, or income/dividend funds.
Bucket Three	> 5 years	Invest for growth and refill buckets 1 and 2 when investment performance is doing well. Avoid using when investments are down.	Aggressive investments including growth and income. Asset allocation mostly in stocks and volatile bonds. For example, the classic 60/40 allocation has proven to provide nice growth with only half the volatility of all stocks. You can trim the stock portion as you grown older, but this bucket can always have a big percentage in stocks because you are already diversified with less risky investments in buckets 2 and 3.

Bucket 1 will contain enough cash to last you for the next year and emergencies. If you want to be cautious, it can include two years. We saw during the Great Recession that cash can earn practically nothing for extended periods, so some people choose to keep only one year of cash here or put the second year of cash in short term or government bonds.

Bucket 2 can contain your income producing assets. Leave it alone except to:
- Refill bucket 1 with its income from dividends and interest.
- Refill bucket 1 as needed by selling investments whenever bucket 3 is unavailable for use because its investments are doing poorly from a down market.
- Refill bucket 2 when bucket 3 investments are again doing well.

Bucket 3 contains your aggressive investments for both growth and income, especially stocks and volatile, high-yield bonds. Routinely refill bucket 1 with dividend and yield income from bucket 3. Whenever bucket 3 investments are doing well, refill buckets 1 and 2 by selling assets as needed. Whenever bucket 3 investments are doing poorly because of a down market, let bucket 3 recover by using bucket 2 assets instead. Don't forget to rebalance bucket 3 around once per year and follow the other investing principles covered in *Part Three - Investing*.

You have flexibility about how to refill your bucket 1 each year including:

- Using dividend and interest income from buckets 2 and 3 to automatically refill it. Note that this alone is unlikely to be enough, especially during extended periods of low interest rates as we saw after the Great Recession.
- Rebalancing within or between the other buckets and moving cash to bucket 1 by selling over-performing assets.
- Selling assets from bucket 3 when it's doing well or bucket 2 when you need to preserve an underperforming bucket 3.

The key to the three-bucket strategy is that you have at least 5 years of low-risk savings to live on regardless of what is happening to your aggressive investments in bucket 3. Even severe market downturns usually recover within 5 years so you rarely should need to touch your bucket 3 investments during a time when they are shrinking. This should give you the peace of mind to ride out any downturns without affecting your standard of living or panic-selling your stocks at a loss. Note that this could mean not refilling bucket 2 for up to five years if a down market lasted that long and prevented you from tapping bucket 3. During that five years you would be drawing down bucket 1, refilling from bucket 2, and letting bucket 3 recover.

You can find many variations of the bucket strategy, but I recommend this one because it provides the best combination of:

- **Safety** – You have up to five year of safe investments, enough to outlast most market downturns.
- **Returns** – Only 1-2 years of expenses are in super safe cash earning a pittance, while most of your 6+ year investments can remain in aggressive growth and income investments.
- **Flexibility** – You can use either bucket 2 or 3 to refill your cash coffers depending upon market conditions at the time, so you greatly increase the odds of selling growing assets rather than falling assets.

Putting it all together

This can all get complicated when you have to deal with multiple income sources, multiple savings and investment accounts, complicated tax strategies, and multiple buckets. Just how does all this actually fit together in a workable plan? Keeping in mind that different people's circumstances may be different, let's go over some general guidelines that should help you create a plan of your own.

You have complete control over your IRAs and taxable investments and can rebalance or sell whatever type of investment you want whenever you want. Thus, with these it's easy to follow either your "rebalance to get cash" or "buckets to cash" strategy.

On the other hand, 401(k)s may have lots of rules for getting your money out, but generally you tell the administrator how much you want each month and they sell the necessary percentage of each of your asset types equally to pay you. You may not be able to specify whether to sell stocks or bonds for example. It's easy to rebalance and diversify savings *within* a 401(k), but to move cash to an *external* account a year or more in advance will take some advance planning on your part. Thus, it is more difficult to fit a 401(k) into a bucket strategy.

You may want to simplify your planning by minimizing the number of accounts you have to juggle. If yes, start by converting your regular 401(k) accounts to one regular or ROTH IRA account so you can more easily rebalance assets and refill buckets with the flexibility of using the right asset from the right bucket at the right time.

Bucket 1 – Most people will want to fill this with cash from RMDs and taxable accounts that most tax strategies advise to use first.

Bucket 2 - Continue to use RMDs and taxable accounts if they are large to buy bonds, safe bond funds, and balanced funds. Then fill with 401(k) withdrawals and IRA holdings.

Bucket 3 – Hold your growth and aggressive income assets (stocks and volatile bond funds) in remaining 401(k) and IRA holdings, then your ROTH accounts.

If you keep multiple accounts, I suggest you use a spreadsheet or financial advisor to track which of your holdings from which account you have designated for which bucket. Let's do a hypothetical example using the 4% rule just to illustrate the ideas.

Savings of $500,000 in multiple accounts * 4% = $20,000 in first year's income. Let's assume 3% inflation for the first five years income. I have used exact dollar amounts so it's easier to see how the amounts, buckets, and accounts add up, but in real life feel free to use round numbers in your own accounting.

Bucket	Amount in bucket	Type of investments	Which of your many hypothetical investments to use to fill your bucket
Bucket 1	$40,600 = (yr. 1 = $20,000 + Yr. 2 = $20,600 @ 3% inflation) (2 year's income)	Half in savings account. Half in super safe bonds.	All funded from taxable accounts.
Bucket 2	$65,583 = ($21,218 + 3% $21,855 + 3% $22,510) (3 year's income)	Safe bond funds, retirement-income, and balanced funds.	First use remaining taxable accounts, say $10,000 from remaining taxable accounts. Next start filling bucket from retirement accounts: $55,583 in 401(k) or IRA accounts: - ABC retirement income fund - XYZ bond fund.
Bucket 3	$393,817 = ($500,000 less $40,600 in bucket 1 and $65,583 in bucket 2)	Diversified assets that match your asset allocation target such as: 60% stocks and stock funds 30% bond funds 5% REITs 5% commodity funds	$50,000 – Remaining IRA holdings: ABC Total Stock ETF XYZ REIT $200,000 - 401(k) holdings ABC S&P Index Fund ZYX Global ETF $143,817 - Roth accounts XYZ High yield bond fund REIT stocks ABC Commodities ETF

Rebalance and refill buckets annually or as market conditions permit. Note that having 60% of Bucket 3's assets in stocks equals only 47% of your total assets from all buckets in stocks, which is conservative investing.

Finally, remember to plan before you retire to get your cash for your first year or two in retirement to get your system rolling. Even better, if you are going to use the bucket strategy, put it in place several years before you might retire. The best way to avoid tapping your investments during an ill-timed downturn is to plan ahead and ensure you have 1-2 years of cash to cover living expenses before you need it. Consider diverting to a cash account for bucket 1, your last year of retirement savings you normally would have made to your IRA or 401(k). If you don't stash this cash in advance and the market nose-dives as you retire, then be prepared to cutback the amount you withdraw during the market downturn.

Cash flow

Regardless which withdrawal strategy you use, your cash flow method to ensure bills are paid on time is going to be more complicated than when you just depended upon a pay check to be directly deposited into your checking account. Ensure you have a plan, schedule, and method for getting money from your retirement accounts into your checking accounts to pay bills. You may need to coordinate multiple retirement accounts, Social Security, pensions, quarterly taxes, recurring bills, annual bills, emergency repairs, unplanned medical bills, and savings accounts. Now could be the time that you learn how to use a spreadsheet to forecast income and expenses for the coming yea. See my Dad's plan below and the book's website for more detailed cash flow information and tools.

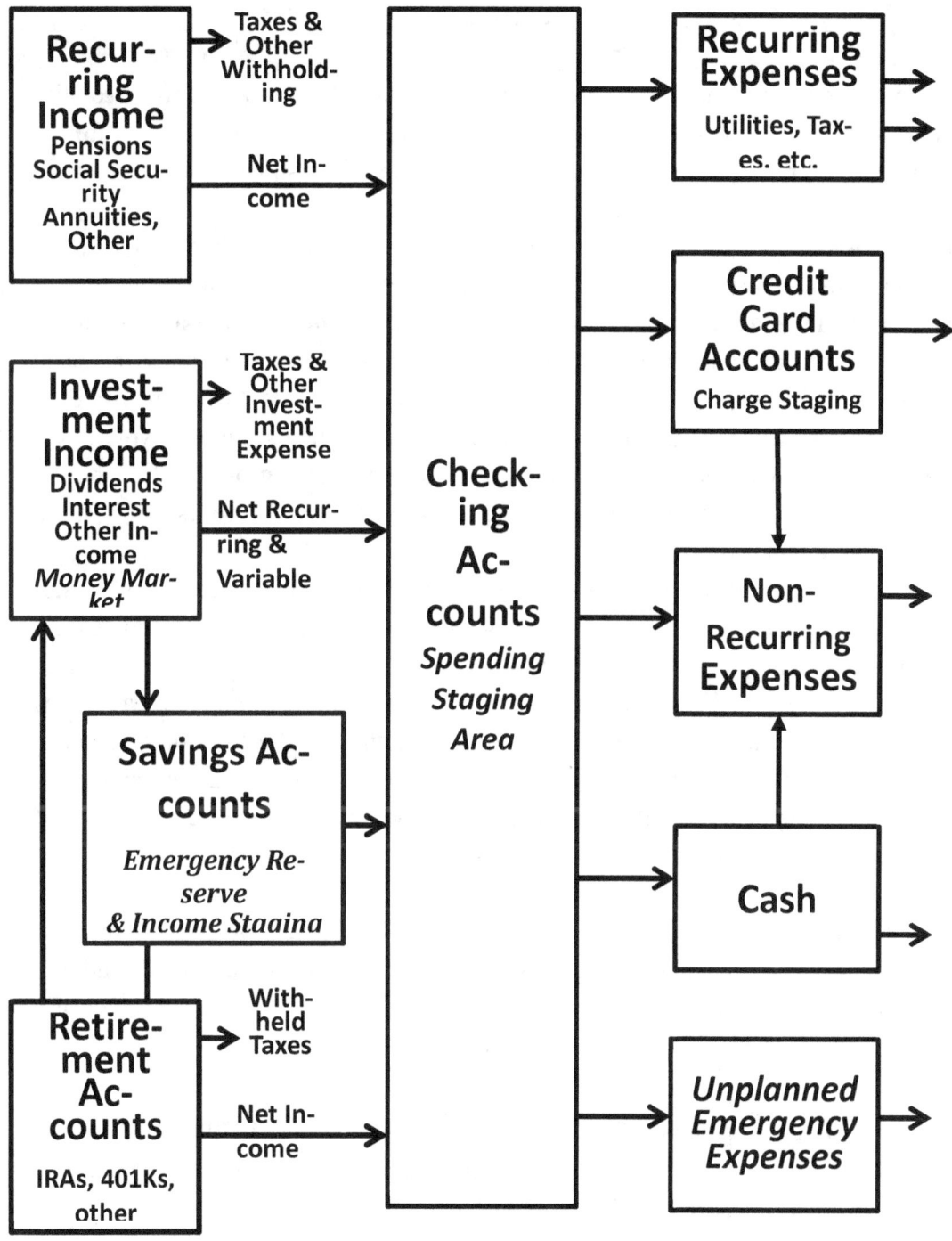

Investing

Even in retirement, you need to guard against the dual risks of crashes from volatile investments and failure to match inflation from safe investments. So continue to follow the basic investing principles even in retirement, including diversification and rebalancing of both stocks and less volatile investments. Yes, you still need stocks in your retirement as the best way to beat inflation and postpone the day you run out of savings. Moreover, moderate allocation in stocks also is the best way to keep your savings growing over decades in retirement, ensure asset diversification, and provide a cushion for emergencies. At age 65, most people should still have 55-65% of their savings in stocks, or adjust this a little depending upon how easily you could ride out a downturn with pensions, annuities, plentiful investments, or a bucket strategy. Then scale back your stock portion a few percentage points every few years when rebalancing or withdrawing investments. Growth becomes less important and preservation of your savings more important in your eighties.

As dividends and yield become even more important, review the section on "High yields and dividends" in the *Part Three* investing chapters. Note that relying too heavily on bonds at the expense of stocks leaves you vulnerable to the prevailing interest rate climate, which as we saw during the Great Recession and its aftermath, can leave rates extremely low for an extended time period – longer even than the time period that stocks crashed. Retirees may even consider a new type of mutual fund called "retirement income funds" that pay you a monthly check based upon how well your fund is doing. But if you want guaranteed income for life regardless of how well the market is doing, see the next section on annuities.

Remember that, while you cannot control market performance, you can control how much you pay in fees by picking investments with low fees such as index funds and Exchange Traded Funds (ETFs). Minimizing fees is especially important when you are investing for income, and yields and dividends are in a low rate climate.

More information on investing in retirement

- http://individual.troweprice.com/public/Retail/Retirement/Retirement-Planning - T Rowe Price's "Retirement Income Planner" makes it easy to see how your asset allocation can affect how much you may be able to spend each month while making your savings last.

- http://gosset.wharton.upenn.edu/mortality/perl/CalcForm.html - Wharton provides both detailed and simple calculators to estimate statistically how long you might live so you can get a general idea how long your retirement savings may need to last.

Understanding annuities

Managing your savings to last a lifetime is even more complicated than building up your savings. But, believe it or not, there is a way to ensure income for the rest of your life and that way leads to annuities. Anyone with enough money can buy an annuity, but you need to review your options carefully because there are several types, many options, and potentially hefty fees.

How much annuity?

The monthly amount you receive is based upon type of annuity (fixed or variable), when you begin receiving payments (immediate or deferred), amount invested, age, current interest rates, and various options you may choose. Consider getting an annuity amount to cover your fixed expenses such as housing, food, and medical expenses to ensure your basic needs are met for as long as you live. Total those expenses, subtract your Social Security and pension benefits, and buy an annuity to cover the remainder. Annuities, to at least cover your basic living expenses, can enable you to invest more aggressively for growth, ride out volatility in your investments, spend more savings early in retirement, and greatly increase the likelihood that you won't outlive your savings.

Keep a portion of your savings for more flexibility. You can always buy another annuity later if needed or interest rates rise which give a bigger payout. Use the remainder of your savings to cover less vital expenses, emergencies, medical bills, and income growth for as long as your money lasts. If you die before your money runs out, you can pass it to your heirs.

Types of annuities

Your choices include immediate annuities, deferred annuities, variable annuities, and equity indexed annuities. Basically, you can choose between immediate or deferred, fixed or variable, and combinations of these. Let's briefly review the types and options.

Immediate annuities

Immediate annuities are the most popular, least expensive, and easiest to understand. You pay a lump sum, called the premium, to an insurance or investment fund company and they promise to pay you a certain amount every month for the rest of your life. There aren't even a lot of fees with immediate annuities which might also be called an income annuity or single premium immediate annuity. These can pay during your lifetime, your survivor's, a fixed term, or a combination.

Two of the biggest reasons that more people do not take advantage of this path to guaranteed lifetime income are suspicion of high fees and fear they will die before getting their money back. First, note that the annuities with high fees are the variable and equity income annuities that we will discuss next while fees for immediate annuities can be very reasonable. Then consider that this is an insurance product and we rarely get our money back from insurance – but in this case, we are guaranteed to get financial security and peace of mind plus some of our money back.

Variable annuities

Payouts from variable annuities change based upon performance of a portfolio of funds. You invest in a choice of funds whose performance affects your payout and investment balance. You can buy a variable annuity with a lump sum or tax-deferred investments over time. Payouts can be immediate or deferred, for a specified period or lifetime.

With a fixed, immediate annuity, if you die before you have received all your premiums, the insurance company keeps your money and uses it to pay beneficiaries who live longer and receive more than their premiums. Variable annuities commonly come with a death benefit that will pay your heirs at least the amount you paid in, less anything you have received.

Variable annuities may offer guaranteed benefit options for a lower benefit or extra price. These guaranteed minimum options may include a minimum monthly income, investment account balance, or death benefit even if your fund investments decline.

These opportunities for investments to grow, combined with the guaranteed minimums are what make variable annuities attractive, especially after periods of market turbulence.

However, you should recognize by now that rewards aren't risk-free and benefits come with costs. When you hear criticism of annuities, it is usually about variable annuities being complicated and expensive with low returns compared to investing directly. Variable annuities have high fees, which may exceed 3% annually because you are paying administrative fees to the insurance company, fees of the underlying funds you invest in, and hefty commissions to the sales person. Therefore, even though you may be getting some investment growth, the returns will be much less than direct investments because of the high fees. (Remember that if you invest in low cost ETFs or index funds, you can pay fees less than 0.5% compared to variable annuity fees of greater than 3.0%.)

Deferred annuities

Deferred annuities don't begin paying until a future date. You can get deferred annuities for a variety of deferral dates. The two most common situations are to invest in a deferred annuity while working that begins after you retire, or to pay a lump sum when you retire for a fixed annuity deferred until your eighties. Unlike fixed immediate annuities, deferred annuities give you access to your money paid in. Deferred annuities do let you change your mind later and withdraw your money, but if you do it before a "surrender period" that is commonly 5-10 years, you will pay a hefty fee which is a common complaint about annuities versus investing on your own. Deferred annuities can be either fixed income or variable.

Fixed deferred or longevity annuities

Fixed deferred annuities are the simplest and are also called "longevity" annuities because you are insuring for a long life and, one of retirees' biggest concerns, running out of money before they die. In return for a small lump sum when you retire, you are buying a guaranteed income in your later years when you may need it most. You may have options about how long you want to defer payments, but the longer you do, the greater your payments will be, and deferring until your eighties is common. In return for deferring payouts, you get an annuity that is *much* less expensive than an immediate annuity. Deferred fixed annuities with a 15-20 year deferral may cost less than one fifth of a similar amount in an immediate annuity, or the same lump sum amount will buy a deferred annuity 4-5 times greater than an immediate annuity.

Deferred variable annuities

Deferred variable annuities have the same features described previously under variable annuities. Deferred annuities not only buys peace of mind now and financial security later; but also may let you spend more of your remaining savings in your early years since it won't need to last indefinitely. However, variable annuities are often criticized for complexity, high fees, and low returns compared to investing on your own.

Equity indexed annuities

Equity indexed annuities combine some features of fixed and variable annuities. They are variable because the payouts can increase based upon a market index doing well, but you are guaranteed a certain minimum amount even if the market index does poorly. Unlike variable annuities, you don't actually invest in index or mutual funds. Rather your payouts and guaranteed minimums are based upon a market index, frequently the S&P 500. However, your growth will always be less than the market index which is how the insurance company makes money. The attraction is that you can get guaranteed income while still participating in the market to try and get some growth. In reality, these will provide greater growth than many fixed income investments like CDs, but never as much as the stock index it tracks.

Of course, these guarantees come with a price. These annuities can be complicated with a variety of high fees, so make sure you understand what you may be buying as well as the fees. It is important to understand and ask plenty of questions about the pros and cons, fees, how payouts are calculated, any guaranteed minimums, death benefits, and how to get your money back if you choose.

Negative aspects

One of my favorite sayings is, "Everything has both pro's and con's". We have seen that annuities are one of the few ways to get *guaranteed* income that will last as long as your lifetime. Now let's review the con's. Critics have no shortage of complaints including complexity, high fees, low returns, losing access to your money, not being able to pass savings to your heirs, and the possibility of dying before you recoup your investment. Dealing with these issues is one reason why there are multiple types of annuities and options to choose from.

Immediate annuities pay out the most and are the most popular and least complicated. However, payouts don't normally rise with inflation, your investment won't grow with stocks, and you lose all access to your money just as you do with many other insurance products. Deferred fixed annuities are the least expensive and give the greatest payouts, but you will wait years for a benefit. Variable annuities can give you more access to your funds and a chance for growth, but are the most complicated and have the most fees. Equity index annuities aim to combine benefits from the other types of annuities, but growth will always be less than the market index because of growth caps and high fees.

Another problem with any annuity is that the amount they pay varies with the interest rate climate. During low interest rate periods, their monthly payments are low. One way to deal with this is to "ladder" your annuity purchases: for example, $50,000 - $100,000 every other year for several purchases at, hopefully, higher rates. In addition, the payouts will increase the longer you wait to purchase one, since they are partially based upon your age. Another option is to split your investment among more than one type of annuity; for example a basic immediate annuity for a nice payout now, plus a deferred variable annuity to get potential market growth in the future.

Annuity options

Most annuities have additional options that you can pay for that lessens some of the negative aspects of annuities. These include a *survivor annuity* for your spouse, *cost-of-living-adjustments* to protect against inflation eroding your income, or a *cash refund* payment to your heirs in case you die early. Any of these options will lower your monthly payout or increase your fees.

Where to buy them

You have choices when it comes to annuity types and options which means it really pays to comparison shop and see how much of a payout your investment will buy and how much each add-on option will lower that payout. Payouts can vary 10-15% between different insurance companies. You can compare and purchase annuities from many insurance and investment fund companies.

Annuities Summary

Annuities are best for retirees who need additional guaranteed income to cover their basic expenses because they have small or no pensions, expect to live a long time, don't have the time or expertise to manage their own savings, or just want the peace of mind and financial security of guaranteed income for life. Some studies have concluded that you will receive the most income by investing your savings in a well-diversified mix of stocks, bonds, and cash and then buying an immediate annuity when you are ready for income or a deferred fixed annuity to guarantee you won't outlive your money. However, you should still keep some of your savings free to cover future emergencies and invest for future growth to at least keep pace with inflation.

- Find online comparison tools at www.Vanguard.com and www.Fidelity.com .
- http://www.annuityshopper.com/ - View annuity information and get quotes.

Spending and earning

While saving and planning for retirement, you may have used calculators to help determine how much you should save. Many of those calculators are based upon your projected expenses in retirement but, twenty, ten, or even fire years out, those estimates are mostly guesses. Now that you are ready for retirement, you of course need to do a budget based upon *actual* income and expenses. Now that you know how much you can withdraw and spend from your savings (probably based upon the 4% or RMD rules) and how much savings you have, you can accurately calculate how much income you will get from savings. You will need to adjust your needs and wants accordingly based upon your latest retirement budget.

First, calculate your income by adding up the monthly amounts from the following: Social Security, Pensions, Annuities purchased, Savings (4% rule, RMD, dividends, etc). Once you have calculated your income, you can finalize your budget to ensure your spending is less than your income.

The spending side of pre-retirement estimates may need a reality check. All those assurances that retirees only spend 70-80% of what they do while working depends upon many things such as whether the kids have left, aging parents needing support, the mortgage is paid, your health is good, you want to travel, and a host of other things that may be unique to your situation. Nonetheless, for most people as they grow older, they become less active with fewer responsibilities and therefore spend less. Medical expenses are the big unknown, but will surely rise.

Fortunately, if your savings still fall short, there are other things you can do. Perhaps easier said than done, still your options include scaling back your lifestyle, pruning your budget, redoubling your efforts to become debt free, delaying and increasing Social Security, working longer, working part-time, moving to a smaller home, relocating to a lower cost area, and applying for a reverse mortgage.

Make your income go further by concentrating on all the ways we have discussed to save money, spend wisely, and avoid paying full price. Take advantage of senior discounts offered by restaurants, hotels, airlines, rental cars, movie theaters, entertainment venues, public transportation, and many more. Check out the discounts that come with www.AARP.com membership. Did you know that most states offer discounts in property taxes to seniors over 65? Use your new flexibility to get discounts by traveling off-peak, out-of-season, and last minute.

Website with jobs that are friendly for seniors:
- http://www.aarp.org/work/
- http://www.flexjobs.com/
- http://www.retirementjobs.com/
- http://seniors4hire.org/
- http://www.yourencore.com/

Reversing your mortgage

Regardless of how much or little you managed to save for your retirement, we have seen that you do have options for your retirement income. A quick recap includes:
- Preparing a retirement budget to ensure you are spending less than your income.
- Adjusting your lifestyle to fit your budget.
- Increasing your guaranteed income (waiting to take Social Security or buying an annuity).
- Withdrawing savings using a specific strategy (bucket, dividends, 4% rule, RMD)
- Continuing to invest a portion in stocks to ensure your savings grow faster than inflation and last a lifetime.

- Working longer or part-time.

Now let's turn to one of your biggest assets – your home. Retirement is much easier when you are not paying rent or a mortgage. Hopefully your home has a nice equity amount that you can use for emergencies or even living expenses if necessary. There are several ways you can tap it including a home equity loan, moving to a smaller home, and relocating to a less expensive location.

Many people have no intention of leaving their home, but they can still get their home to pay them. Reverse mortgages are just what they say; you get a mortgage on the equity in your home, but the bank pays you a lump sum, line of credit, monthly amount, or combination. You still get to live there as long as you continue to pay your taxes, insurance, and upkeep. To help ensure you can continue to pay these and do not default, applicant's income and credit history are reviewed. Additional requirements include:

- be age 62 or older,
- live in the home as your primary residence, and
- attend a counseling session to ensure you understand what you are getting into.

Many people use the monthly payments for income or line of credit for emergencies, but most people take a lump sum to pay off an existing mortgage or debts which frees up money for other things. The amount you receive is based upon the age of the youngest borrower (the older the more you get), current interest rate (the lower the more you get), home's value and equity, and FHA loan limits. Get an estimate of the amount you may qualify for: http://www.reversemortgage.org/About/ReverseMortgageCalculator.aspx .

Reverse mortgages are continuing to evolve, especially as the government changes rules, loan limits, and fees to reduce default risks under its program. The most popular are insured by the Federal Housing Administration (FHA). Its multiple HECM programs in the past have been replaced with new rules that calculate loan amounts, insurance fees, and potential set aside amounts based upon your financial risk assessment, age, and mortgage amount. Reverse mortgages are also available from private lenders and some states. Remember to comparison shop.

These may seem like easy money, but remember to review the negatives as well as the positives. Reverse mortgages can be an expensive way to get your equity as fees may include a large initial insurance premium to FHA, the usual mortgage origination fees and closing costs, and another FHA cumulative insurance fee when the home is sold. If you take one early in retirement, you not only get a smaller amount, but you may no longer have access to emergency funds later such as for medical bills. You could still lose your home if you fail to pay the taxes and homeowners insurance.

Don't fall prey to any salesman who suggests you get a reverse mortgage to pay for something he wants to sell to you including an annuity, life insurance, or other investment.

If you move, sell, die, or fail to pay your taxes and insurance, then you must repay the loan. If not, the bank can sell the home; pay the mortgage, cumulative insurance/service fees, and outstanding debts; and you or heirs would get anything that is left. Perhaps one of the best parts of a reverse mortgage is just knowing the option is available should you really need it. Find out more below.

- http://www.reversemortgage.org/ - Find information and a reputable lender.
- http://www.aarp.org – Search "reverse mortgage" for information and a calculator to see how much you might be eligible for.

More information about retirement finances

- http://www.aarp.org/money/money_tools/ - AARP provides many calculators helpful to retirees in a wide variety of topics.
- http://www.analyzenow.com/Free%20Programs/free_programs.htm - Many free spreadsheets for retirement, investing, and other financial issues including a Social Security Planner and Retirement Planner.
- http://www.bogleheads.org/wiki/Retirement_calculators_and_spending#Free_reti rement_calculators – The internet has many, free budget calculators, so this time I'm going to point you to a site that evaluates and links to some of the best.
- http://crr.bc.edu/booklets-brochures/ - Boston College's Center for Retirement Research has pamphlets that discuss *"Managing your Money in Retirement"* and *"The Social Security Claiming Guide"*.
- http://dinkytown.net/ - Calculators for insurance, annuities, retirement, savings, investing, and a whole lot more.
- http://senior.com/ - Living well in retirement.

Summary

- How well we fare financially in retirement depends upon how well we have prepared for it, as well as how well we manage our income, savings, and spending.
- Retirees should aim for income that is stable, beats inflation, and lasts for the rest of our lives – however long that might be. Investments should provide income, be available for emergencies, grow fast enough to beat inflation, weather market downturns, and perhaps be available for heirs.
- Prepare a retirement budget and test-drive it before retiring.
- A Social Security benefit is one of the most important sources of retirement income because it is guaranteed for life, increases with inflation, and includes benefits for spouses. But planning for SSA benefits can be complicated because your benefit depends upon the amount earned by each spouse, the age you begin collecting, whether you are working in retirement, and how the primary, spousal, and survivor benefits relate to each other.
- You should have a plan for converting your retirement savings into income such as the 4% rule, RMD, dividends income, or combination.
- A three bucket strategy for withdrawing savings based upon your time horizon is the best way to avoid spending your savings when the market is ravaging them.
- Even in retirement, you need to guard against both volatile investments declining and failure to match inflation from safe investments. You still need stocks in your retirement as the best way to beat inflation and prolong the day you run out of savings, but gradually shift your allocation more to safer investments as you get further into retirement.
- The best way to guarantee income for as long as you live is to buy an annuity to cover your basic expenses. Anyone with enough money can buy an annuity, but you need to review your options carefully because there are several types, many options, and potentially hefty fees.
- If your savings fall short, there are other things you can do, including scaling back your lifestyle, pruning your budget, redoubling your efforts to become debt free, delaying and increasing Social Security, working longer, working part-time, moving to a smaller home, relocating to a lower cost area, and applying for a reverse mortgage.

Part Five

Introduction to Part Five – Bonus Tips

We have covered a lot of topics and financial principles for managing, saving, investing, and spending your hard-earned money. It's never too late, no matter what your age or financial situation to start applying sound financial principles, but the earlier you start, the better your financial future will be. In Part Five, I want to cover a few topics in more detail that may improve your financial future even more.

Chapter Twenty-four

The Magic of Compound Interest

Albert Einstein is reputed to have said, "The most powerful force in the universe is *compound interest*. He who understands it, earns it. He who doesn't, pays it." Whether or not he actually said this, the idea of compound interest is important to understand for your financial future. Compound interest is the principle that even a small amount of initial savings can add up over time because you are earning interest, not only on your initial savings, but also on all that interest you previously earned. We have mentioned this many times, but it is so important that you understand how vital it is to start saving early and regularly, even if in small amounts at first, that I think it deserves more detail. Let's skim quickly over the mathematics, review some eye-opening examples, and discuss how this applies to real life.

The first point to understand is that *"compound"* interest is different from *"simple"* interest. You might think that if you saved $100 in a saving account paying 5% interest, you would earn $5 per year and at the end of five years, you would earn $25, plus your original $100 would give you $125 like this:

(principle * interest rate * term) + original principle = ending account balance
($100 * 0.05 interest * 5 years) = $25 + $100 = $125

This is "simple interest" -- you would actually earn more with "compound interest" because you would be earning interest on your interest. Here is the compound interest formula:

principle * (1 + interest rate)^{term} = ending account balance
$100 * (1 + 0.05)^5 = $127.63

Therefore, in this example, compound interest ($27.63) earns you more than 10% more than simple interest ($25.00). Let's move past the formulas to illustrate.

	Simple Interest	Compound Interest
Original principle	$100	$100
End of year 1	$105 = (100 * 0.05) + $100	$105 = (100 * 0.05) + $100
End of year 2	$110 = (100 * 0.05) + $105	$110.25 = (105 * 0.05) + $105
End of year 3	$115 = (100 * 0.05) + $110	$115.76 = (110.25 * 0.05) + $110.25
End of year 4	$120 = (100 * 0.05) + $115	$121.55 = (115.76 * 0.05) + $115.76
End of year 5	$125 = (100 * 0.05) + $120	$127.63 = (121.55 * 0.05) + $121.55

You may be thinking that an extra $2.63 isn't much, but envision what it could be if you saved more than $100 each month, increased the interest rate/yield, and let it compound for 20 or 30 years!

The internet has many compound interest calculators (search compound interest calculators) and they are fun – okay – eye-opening – to play around with. Here are some to try and when you return, I'll give you some eye-opening examples that illustrate why it is so costly to delay or minimize your saving.

- http://investor.gov/tools/calculators/compound-interest-calculator - Calculate your future amount based upon any starting amount, additional amount, interest rate, years to compound, and number of times per year it compounds.
- http://www.dinkytown.net/java/CompoundSavings.html - View compounding results on a graph as you change variables with slider bars.
- http://www.myarmyonesource.com/data/Calculators/Compound_Interest/CompoundInterest.html - Compare savings against a baseline as you move sliders to change your starting age and savings amounts.

Here is a table I created showing how $1000 would compound at various interest rates and over a different number of years.

Yrs	1%	2%	3%	4%	5%	6%	7%	8%	9%	10%
				$1000 at Interest rate / Investment yield						
1	1010	1020	1030	1040	1050	1060	1070	1080	1090	1100
2	1020	1040	1061	1082	1103	1124	1145	1166	1188	1210
3	1030	1061	1093	1125	1158	1191	1225	1260	1295	1331
4	1041	1082	1126	1170	1216	1262	1311	1360	1412	1464
5	1051	1104	1159	1217	1276	1338	1403	1469	1539	1611
6	1062	1126	1194	1265	1340	1419	1501	1587	1677	1772
7	1072	1149	1230	1316	1407	1504	1606	1714	1828	1949
8	1083	1172	1267	1369	1477	1594	1718	1851	1993	2144
9	1094	1195	1305	1423	1551	1689	1838	1999	2172	2358
10	1105	1219	1344	1480	1629	1791	1967	2159	2367	2594
11	1116	1243	1384	1539	1710	1898	2105	2332	2580	2853
12	1127	1268	1426	1601	1796	2012	2252	2518	2813	3138
13	1138	1294	1469	1665	1886	2133	2410	2720	3066	3452
14	1149	1319	1513	1732	1980	2261	2579	2937	3342	3797
15	1161	1346	1558	1801	2079	2397	2759	3172	3642	4177
16	1173	1373	1605	1873	2183	2540	2952	3426	3970	4595
17	1184	1400	1653	1948	2292	2693	3159	3700	4328	5054
18	1196	1428	1702	2026	2407	2854	3380	3996	4717	5560
19	1208	1457	1754	2107	2527	3026	3617	4316	5142	6116
20	1220	1486	1806	2191	2653	3207	3870	4661	5604	6727
21	1232	1516	1860	2279	2786	3400	4141	5034	6109	7400
22	1245	1546	1916	2370	2925	3604	4430	5437	6659	8140
23	1257	1577	1974	2465	3072	3820	4741	5871	7258	8954
24	1270	1608	2033	2563	3225	4049	5072	6341	7911	9850
25	1282	1641	2094	2666	3386	4292	5427	6848	8623	10835
26	1295	1673	2157	2772	3556	4549	5807	7396	9399	11918
27	1308	1707	2221	2883	3733	4822	6214	7988	10245	13110
28	1321	1741	2288	2999	3920	5112	6649	8627	11167	14421
29	1335	1776	2357	3119	4116	5418	7114	9317	12172	15863
30	1348	1811	2427	3243	4322	5743	7612	10063	13268	17449
31	1361	1848	2500	3373	4538	6088	8145	10868	14462	19194
32	1375	1885	2575	3508	4765	6453	8715	11737	15763	21114

33	1389	1922	2652	3648	5003	6841	9325	12676	17182	23225
34	1403	1961	2732	3794	5253	7251	9978	13690	18728	25548
35	1417	2000	2814	3946	5516	7686	10677	14785	20414	28102
36	1431	2040	2898	4104	5792	8147	11424	15968	22251	30913
37	1445	2081	2985	4268	6081	8636	12224	17246	24254	34004
38	1460	2122	3075	4439	6385	9154	13079	18625	26437	37404
39	1474	2165	3167	4616	6705	9704	13995	20115	28816	41145
40	1489	2208	3262	4801	7040	10286	14974	21725	31409	45259

Note the lessons we can learn from compound interest and savings strategies.

1. The greater the interest rate or investment yield, the greater our investment will grow. Review the chapters on "Investments" to remember which kind of investments may yield low rates or high rates. Remember that safe investments yield low rates and riskier investments yield higher rates. On average over an extended period of time, only stocks will yield high rates. Investing your *long*-term investments in *low* yielding investments will provide you much *less* growth, for example, retirement income or college savings.

2. The longer our savings can compound, the more our investment will grow. So the later we wait to invest, the less money we will get for our savings goals such as college and retirement.

3. Even small amounts can greatly compound over time. Note how $1000 invested at age 25 can grow forty years later to $14,974 at 7% in time for retirement at age 65. If we waited until age 35, our $1000 at 7% would only equal $7612 after thirty years at age 65. By waiting ten years to start saving, we would have to *double* our savings amount to get the same amount at retirement. This is why I stress how important it is to start saving at least a small amount for retirement from your very first day on your full-time job, and increase it with each raise.

4. The more money you save and invest, the faster it will compound and grow, especially in the later years.

Therefore, the most important lesson from this chapter is to see that the best way to grow your savings is to save and invest early, often, and at a reasonably high yield. Before we conclude this topic, let's note two remaining points about compound interest. Inflation, taxes, and investment expenses will reduce your yield. So if your investments are yielding a nice 7.00%, but your mutual fund expenses are 2.00% (instead of ETF's at

0.02%) and inflation is running 3.00%, your real gain is only 2.00% (7-2-3=2). Similarly if your savings are in bonds earning 1%, but inflation is running 2%, you are actually losing 1% in buying power (1-2=-1). In regards to taxes, note that with some investments you won't owe taxes until you sell (like stocks and bonds), while you will owe taxes every year on interest, dividends, and mutual fund distributions. Now we see why it is nice to have tax-favored savings plans like 529 college savings plans, 401(k) and IRA retirement accounts, and health savings accounts.

Finally, you should note that compound interest works against you for debts, so when you don't pay your credit card balances in full, you may OWE interest on your interest. Now it should be clear why paying only the minimum credit card payment takes so long to pay off the balance and why getting the lowest interest rate card you can is important. Let's close with the same quote we opened with, "The most powerful force in the universe is *compound interest*. He who understands it, *earns* it. He who doesn't, *pays* it."

Summary

- Compound interest is the principle that even a small amount of initial savings can add up over time because you are earning interest, not only on your initial savings, but also on all that interest you previously earned.
- The greater the interest rate/investment yield, the greater our investment will grow. See how investing your *long*-term investments in *low* yielding investments will provide you much *less* growth, for example, retirement income.
- The longer our savings can compound, the more our investment will grow. So the later we wait to save and invest, the less money we will get for our savings goals such as college and retirement.
- Even small amounts can greatly compound over time, so always save at least something towards your savings goals.
- The more money you save and invest, the faster it will compound and grow, especially in the later years.
- The best way to grow your savings is to save and invest early, often, and at a reasonably high yield with the lowest expenses.
- Tis better to receive the magic of compound interest than pay it.

Chapter Twenty-five

The Importance of Your Credit Rating

- Why is it important?
- What affects it?
- How to improve it?
- What will it get you?
- How to correct it?

I have mentioned credit scores many times in many different topics because it can affect you financial life in so many ways. Because so few people know what it does or is, in this chapter let's review it in more detail.

Why is it important?

Your credit score is a rating of your creditworthiness or the probability of you paying off future debts, based upon your past credit history of managing your credit and paying debts. Credit histories are maintained by three credit bureaus: Equifax, Experian, and TransUnion which provide credit reports and credit scores when requested by lenders. Your credit reports will show all your credit cards and loans, late payments, new credit inquiries, debt collections, and bankruptcies. The most used credit score is the FICO score which produces a numeric score from 300 to 850. VantageScore is used by some lenders and ranges from 501-990 based upon slightly different criteria.

Potential creditors use your credit score to determine how risky it would be to provide you credit and how likely you will pay your debts and on time. It is important because it is used by potential lenders to:

- grant you credit
- determine how good of an interest rate you will be charged
- set your credit limits
- offer credit card rewards and balance transfers

In addition to determining the credit you are offered, your credit rating may also affect a surprising number of other financial areas, such as auto insurance premiums, telephone contracts, rental applications, and job hunting. Yes, employers are increasingly reviewing applicants' credit reports (but not credit scores) especially for jobs dealing with finances, executive positions, or confidentiality. Employers must obtain applicant's written permission, but declining could mean being passed over.

Your credit rating can save you tens of thousands of dollars in interest over a lifetime and have a big impact on your financial future in a variety of ways, so it is important to handle your credit responsibly and maintain a good credit rating. A poor rating could mean paying higher interest rates and insurance premiums, making it harder to rent an apartment, and count against you in job hunting. Once you get your FICO rating above 760, there is no reason to obsess over it. Your credit scores will change from month to month since your credit history, balances, and payments change.

Your three VantageScore or FICO scores may differ slightly between the three credit bureaus because they may adjust the criteria the score is based upon and they may have different records reported to them by your creditors. Generally, creditors may use the middle of your three scores. If a couple is applying for a joint loan, both applicants' scores will be reviewed. If a lender does deny you credit or charge you a rate other than the best, they must tell you the credit score they used and what adversely affected their decision from the report.

What affects it?

Your credit score is based upon your credit and payment history. Note that the best scores do NOT come from being debt FREE, but from how well you manage debt over an extended period. Different scoring models differ in how they create your score, but all use the same factors. Here are the most important.

Credit card utilization – The percentage of your available credit limit that you are using. . Your score drops when balances (including current month charges) exceed 25 - 30% of your total available limit. To avoid problems, you can pay down your balances or increase your credit limit. Never using your credit cards also hurts because you don't show a record of responsibly using and managing credit. This may account for 30% of your FICO score.

Payment history – Payment history is one of the biggest components of your rating since it may account for 30-35% of your FICO score. Even one late payment can mean a big drop in your score and remain on your history for seven years. Consider using email, text, or calendar alerts to avoid late payments.

Average age of open credit lines – A longer credit history reflects more responsibility in managing good credit while a short history reflects more uncertainty. Opening a new card or closing an old card can therefore shorten your average and lower your score. This may be 15% of your FICO score.

Credit inquiries – Whenever you apply for a new loan or credit card, you drop a few points. The exception is when you apply for several auto or home loans to compare rates within a 30 day period. Checking your credit score does NOT affect your score. This may account for 10% of your FICO score.

Types of accounts – Many accounts show many creditors have approved your credit. It is useful to have several types of accounts, both revolving and installment. This may be 10-15% of your FICO score.

Debt problems – Debt collections, bankruptcies, liens, foreclosures, and even short sales of underwater homes will severely damage your credit rating and stay on for 7-10 years. Obviously, this is not the best way to show potential creditors that you are a good risk. However, bad financial situations happen and it is possible to recover from them by rebuilding a good credit history over time.

https://www.creditkarma.com/myfinances/simulator/index/ref/tools - The Credit Score Simulator lets you see how financial actions could affect your credit score over time.

Note that if you co-sign someone's loan or credit card, both signers' credit rating will be affected by the actions with the loan or card. This means that both names on a credit card will be affected by the actions on that card. Putting a child's name on your credit card is an effective way to build a good credit history for the child who can get their own card at age 21 with an established credit history.

How to improve it?

The best way to build a better credit rating is to use multiple credit cards once a month and pay ALL bills on time. Notice that this does not mean have a lot of debt, nor running a balance and paying interest. If you do carry a credit card balance, ensure it does not exceed 25-30% of your credit limit to keep the best score.

- Pay down your credit card debt to lower your utilization percentage.
- If you are a good customer with one late payment, call your creditor and ask them to remove the late payment report. Sometimes they will for good customers.
- Ask your credit card issuer for a higher credit limit. This increases your score by lowering your credit utilization percentage.
- Review your credit reports and dispute any errors.
- Transfer balances to a new card. Opening a new card lowers your score in the short term by lowering your account length average. However, it increases your number of accounts and available credit, and lowers your utilization percentage.

If you have poor or no credit history, the best way to develop a good one is to use a "secured" credit card. You pay a security deposit so it's easy to get approved for a secured card because the lender doesn't take any risk. Your credit limit is usually equal to your security deposit. If you fail to make payments, the secured credit card issuer uses your security deposit. Using your secured card responsibly and making ALL payments on time will gradually build up your credit rating. Once you have a good rating, you can use it to get regular credit cards and good rates on other loans.

It takes time to establish a record of responsible credit. If you are planning to take some of these steps to improve your rating before applying for a loan, allow several months at least before seeing significant improvement.

Beware of credit repair scams with guaranteed promises, extravagant claims, promises to remove negative but accurate information, unethical actions, and payment in advance. The Federal Trade Commission reports that they have never seen any of these extravagant claims work, but do receive plenty of complaints. For more information, see the FTC's webpage and free pamphlet: https://www.consumer.ftc.gov/articles/0058-credit-repair-how-help-yourself . Credit repair is something you can best do yourself for FREE with the steps listed here and some time to allow them to work.

There are many credit monitoring services that will alert you to problems for a monthly fee. Here is a cheaper, more effective alternative. For a small fee, you can request the three credit bureaus "freeze" your credit, which prevents anyone (including you) from opening new credit in your name. When you want to open new credit or loans, you would need to request your credit be unfrozen and pay a fee, but it's still cheaper than a monthly credit monitoring fee.

What will it get you?

The FICO score you need to get the best interest rate does fluctuate as lending standards are loosened or tightened, but you can use these general guidelines to get an idea where your credit score would place you. For years, *Fair Isaac,* which developed the FICO score, reported that the median score was around 720. This fluctuates, but gives you an idea where you stand.

Different types of loans require different ranges to get the best rates. To get the best mortgage rates, you usually need a FICO score of at least 730-760, but only 700-720 for auto loans. FICO scores in the 600s will mean paying higher interest rates, especially for autos and credit cards. Scores in the 500s will mean paying the highest rates for any loan – if you are able to get any. Let's illustrate a hypothetical example to show in dollars how different scores could affect your costs. Actual values change with the economic and lending climate, but the point is clear. Here is what borrowers with different FICO scores might pay for a $25,000 auto loan over four years.

FICO Score	Interest Rate	Monthly Payment	Total interest Paid
720	4%	$564.48	$2094.85
670	5%	$575.73	$2635.16
620	8%	$610.32	$4295.53
570	12%	$658.35	$6600.55

How to correct it?

A 2013 Federal Trade Commission study found that 20% of credit reports contained an error, and 5% were serious enough to affect someone's credit score significantly. Therefore, you should check your credit reports periodically or at least before you plan to get a new loan. You can request your credit report for free once per year from each of the three bureaus by going here: https://www.annualcreditreport.com/index.action. Some people are particularly diligent by rotating their annual requests to each of the three companies so they can monitor one report every four months. These reports show your loans and payment history. You will have to pay to get your actual credit scores, but see the websites below for free score estimates. Many credit card companies provide credit scores for free – check your statement or website.

The most common problem is that someone else's data was reported on someone else's record. If someone has a name or SSN close to yours, this could happen repeatedly. If you find an error, start with the creditor that reported it. A telephone call to customer service may resolve simple issues. If not, send written information and documentation to both the credit bureau and creditor or use the credit bureaus' online dispute webpage. The credit bureau is supposed to investigate your dispute within 30 days. Follow up if necessary. Request reconsideration if you have new information or the creditor used erroneous data.

Monitoring your credit reports is also the best way to monitor potential identity theft problems to see if anyone has opened accounts in your name. If you suspect an identity theft problem, you should report a fraud alert directly with each of the three credit bureaus thru the websites below as well as the creditor with the fraudulent account. You can get additional information and forms, such as the "ID Theft Affidavit" at www.ftc.gov/bcp/edu/microsites/idtheft/ or www.consumerfinance.gov/learnmore.

More information

- https://www.creditkarma.com/ - Get your credit score estimate for free based upon your history from TransUnion, plus other credit resources.
- http://www.credit.com/ - Get your credit score estimate for free based upon your history from Experian, plus other credit resources.
- https://www.quizzle.com/ - Get your free credit report and score from Experian combined with an analysis of which items in your report has affected your score.
- http://www.myfico.com/ - Purchase your actual credit scores.
- www.equifax.com - Equifax
- www.experian.com - Experian
- www.transunion.com – TransUnion

Summary

- Your credit rating is important because it is used by potential lenders to grant you credit, determine how good of an interest rate you will be charged, set your credit limits, and offer credit card rewards and balance transfers. It may also affect such things as auto insurance premiums, telephone contracts, rental applications, and job hunting.
- Most of your credit score comes from how much of your credit card limits you have used and how well you have paid bills on time.
- The best way to build a better credit rating is to use multiple credit cards once a month, pay ALL bills on time, and keep any balance under 25-30% of your credit limit.
- Manage your credit and debts responsibly to develop a high credit score and receive the best credit offers and loan rates. Pay all debts on time, every time.

Chapter Twenty-six

How to Become a Millionaire

- Start a business.
- Buy real estate.
- Invest in stocks.
- Improve your odds.

In 2016, more than 9 million American households had a net-worth, excluding their primary residence, above the magic million mark, which is about 8% of American households. Could one of us join that club without dreaming of becoming a sports legend, movie star, hit performing artist, CEO, or lottery ticket winner? Maybe it is not as crazy as you might think – especially if you start early enough. We have discussed dozens of financial principles that will get you pointed in the right direction. Now let's see what might take you to the next level.

The most important point is to not wait for a lucky break, but develop a plan with a goal. Skipping the lattes is not going to do it. You need to supercharge your income, assets, and investments. Here are three proven routes to success.

1. Start a Business.
2. Buy Real Estate.
3. Invest in Stocks.

Start a business

Rags to riches is part of the American dream, and plenty of people have turned an idea and hard work into a business and wealth. The Small Business Administration reports that there are 23 million small businesses in the U.S., so plenty of people are ready to try this route to financial success and fulfillment. However, know that it takes hard work, passion, and persistence – and still has a high failure rate. Most failures result from lack of experience, capital, and planning, so pay particular attention to these areas. Most businesses start with the same basics: a business plan, financing, online presence, and customers, so good organization helps. Of course, owning your own business provides more rewards than just wealth.

The problem, from the perspective of being a route to the millionaire club, is that more than 90% of small businesses have revenues less than $250,000. To get past that level, you will need more than just fantastic success. You will need to grow your business bigger, be bought out by a larger company, sell franchises, or license your product.

There are plenty of resources to help, including library shelves full of free books. Start with these:

- http://www.sba.gov/ - Small Business Administration has plenty of resources as well as financing.
- http://www.score.org/ - Workshops, tools, mentors, and local chapters.

Buy real estate

Real estate has long been the route to riches for many millionaires. You probably can't play in the same big league of commercial real estate, but residential real estate is cheap and easy enough for even novices to grow their expertise along with their fortune. Real estate takes money to get started, but the attraction of real estate is that "leverage" will enable a little money to control a lot of property. With leverage, you put down a relatively small down payment and borrow the rest to buy the property. Therefore, you need to be able to acquire cash, loans, and a growing level of expertise. With residential real estate, there are two methods to grow your fortune -- flipping and rentals.

Flipping

With "flipping", you buy a property cheaply, fix it up, and quickly sell it. The keys to flipping are to find "fixer-uppers" that you can buy *very* cheaply, do or contract the needed repairs affordably, sell the property quickly for a good profit, and develop the expertise to handle each of these steps. Many times different partners can bring the needed cash, real estate expertise, or renovation skills. You will need to estimate the eventual sale price you can get for a house; subtract the buying, selling, financing, and repair costs; factor in your profit margin; and then determine how much you can pay to buy a property. Buying foreclosed homes can be very profitable, but often requires all cash.

Renting

The easier, long-term real estate method is to buy and rent properties. Renting properties uses leverage (a small amount of your money to control much more expensive assets), other people's money (lenders and renters), and appreciation to increase your income and net worth (your assets minus debts). Owning 3-5 rental properties could give you a million dollar net worth in 30 -35 years when the mortgages are paid.

You need to buy properties cheaply enough that the rent will cover your mortgage, occasional repairs and vacancies, and hopefully a profit. This is much easier when you buy cheap houses and pay low interest rates. I discovered the attraction of being a landlord accidently when I moved from the suburbs to the big city so I could walk to work. I decided that it would be easier and faster to rent my first condo than it would be to sell it. I repeated this several times. I discovered that being a landlord doesn't require much more expertise than owning any other home and only occasional work to handle repairs or getting a new tenant. The beauty of rental properties is that someone else is paying your mortgage while you are enjoying the price appreciation and benefiting from the rising equity in your property. Here are landlord tips I've learned.

- To keep expenses low, look for rental properties with no or low homeowners association fees.
- Advertise for renters for free on craigslist.org.
- Owning a carpet cleaner saves money.
- Learning to use a paintbrush saves BIG bucks.

- Have a trusted contractor on speed dial that can take care of repair issues.
- Mortgage rates for investment properties are about a half to full point higher than for primary residences. But you can keep your low residential rate by living in a home for at least a year, then buying a new primary residence and renting your previous home.
- Own property that is nearby so you can easily get there.

Being a landlord is not for everyone, but you can turn over the management of your properties to a management company for around 10-15% of the rent. Some people rent vacation properties and make enough from weekly summer rentals to cover annual expenses and profits.

We sadly learned in 2007/09 that real estate prices do not always go up, but does that really matter to home owners and rental investment owners who own properties for years, even decades? Most of the time, homes appreciate a little more than the average rate of inflation, 2-4%. Remember that "averages" obscure the fact that some years will be much more or less and that different localities will differ. Just like certain stocks, sometimes real estate appreciates quickly. Nonetheless, real estate values are so large that a steady 2-4% adds up to big money over time. Example: a $300,000 house would nearly double in 20 years at 3.5% annual appreciation. Assuming you (and your renters) had paid off the mortgage in those twenty years, your equity and net worth would then be worth around $600,000! So owning a few investment properties would likely make you a millionaire in a certain period of time.

Therefore, the secret to being a millionaire is again to start small and scale up, just as with starting a business or investing. With real estate, this means expanding the number of properties you flip or rent. One you have a couple of rental properties, adding a few more is easier to manage and finance. This takes cash, and the beauty of rental real estate is that the more properties you have and the longer you own them, the more equity you have that can be used to invest in more properties, thru home equity loans or cash out refinancing. Getting your money out of real estate is not as easy as investments; nonetheless, they increase your net worth, eventually provide a steady income, usually appreciate steadily, and can be tapped in emergencies. Your library is filled with FREE books on how to become a successful real estate tycoon – or at least a successful landlord.

Invest in stocks

Starting a business and investing in real estate takes a special commitment and so is not for everyone, but investing in the stock market can and should be. Let's begin with an example that illustrates the key issues. Young people in particular, listen up. Here is the most straightforward method that does not take any special talents or lucky breaks. Invest $250 per month starting at age 24 (2 years after college to get you settled), earn 8.5% per year, enjoy the magic of compound interest, and be a millionaire at age 65. Use the "Dinkytown.net Cool Million" calculator to play with any of these variables and dream of the real world possibilities instead of the tery: http://www.dinkytown.net/java/Millionaire.html. Play with the levers on the calculator as we discuss the following principles. First, notice the key financial principles here that we have repeatedly discussed:

- Start saving early and steadily.
- Get a good rate of return, which can best be done with steady investing in stocks or low fee ETFs and index funds.
- Use the magic of compound interest over time rather than huge savings amounts to reach your goal.

Second, notice that while the **Dinkytown** calculator gives you many levers to play with, there are really three key factors that will determine how quickly you reach the millionaire club or other savings goals:

- How long you invest.
- The amount you save.
- The rate of return you earn.

Let's explore these key factors in more detail because they are closely intertwined. Changing one affects the others.

How long you invest

The longer you have to invest to reach your goal, the longer the magic of compound interest can work and correspondingly, the less you need to save and earn each year. The shorter the time until your goal, the more you need to save and earn each year. This is why it is so important to start saving early, even if it is a small amount. We saw in the chapter on compound interest that a small amount over a long time compounds more than a large amount over a short time. Move the levers on the Dinkytown calculator and see the effects for yourself.

Time also relates to the rate of return you should earn. The longer your time horizon, the less you need to earn each year to reach your goal. The shorter your time horizon, the more you have to earn each year to reach that goal. Also, consider this connection – the longer your time horizon, the *more* you can *afford* to take the volatility risks that aiming for a high yield will inevitably bring. This is because the longer time horizon enables you to smooth out the inevitable ups and downs in stock prices. Thus, a longer time horizon means you *need less* rate of return and risk to reach your goal, but can *afford more* risks that come from aiming for a higher rate of return and more savings faster. This is why I emphasize the importance of young and middle age savers investing mostly in stocks because they will best provide a high rate of return, and you have time to smooth out the inevitable ups and downs.

The **Dinkytown** calculator has a nice graph that shows your portfolio growing ever higher. Notice how it grows faster at the end of your time horizon – the more money you have invested, the more you earn. This shows why it's best if you can delay your goal, such as retirement, even a couple of years to really see your savings grow.

The rate of return you earn

We saw in our chapters on investing that you have many choices about how you want to invest. In our quest to get you to the millionaire's club, let's review one of those choices – how aggressively you invest to get the highest rate of return.

The "rule of 72" is a neat tip to amaze your friends and quickly calculate how long it will take to double your money. Just divide 72 by your investments' rate of return and the answer is the number of years it takes to double. Example: 72 divided by a rate of return of 8% equals 9 years to double. Playing with this rule, further illustrates that the higher your rate of return the faster your savings will grow. Increasing your rate of return does mean taking on more risk of volatility (stocks going down as well as up), but does NOT mean trying exotic investments, such as futures, forex, penny stocks, or your coworker's sure bet. Increasing your rate of return means adjusting your asset allocation to include a lower percentage of low yielding (but less volatile) investments, such as bonds and CDs, and get a larger percentage of higher yielding (but more volatile) investments such as stocks for your *long-term* investments. Note though, that many studies have found that increasing your stock allocation much above 70% stocks/30% bonds on average, only boosted yields a *few tenths* of a point per 10% shift over the long term.

Investing more aggressively means taking more risks, but an investment choice that guarantees a higher return is to *reduce your investing costs*. Changing from a mutual fund with 1.5% fees to an ETF with 0.5% in fees is the best way to boost your yield 1%. That 1% could mean an extra $160,000 after 20 years based upon a $200,000 portfolio yielding 8% instead of 7%. That 1% difference compounded annually could mean 3-4 fewer years to reach your savings quest such as becoming a millionaire or retiring early.

Whether your asset allocation is tilted toward an aggressive or balanced approach, the other investment principles still apply such as diversification, annual rebalancing, buy and hold, low fees, auto-pilot savings, don't panic during recession buying opportunities, etc. Review the chapters on investing.

The amount you save

In addition to the amount of **time** you invest and the **rate of return** you earn, your savings goal is affected by the **amount** you save. In fact, you have more control over your savings rate than your return rate, even if saving isn't always easy. We have covered "saving" in so many chapters, but here is one last quick review of ways you can increase your savings rate:

- Live within your means.
- Develop a budget that includes savings goals.
- Put your savings on autopilot.
- Take advantage of tax-deferred savings such as retirement, health, and college savings accounts.
- Ensure you get the full "company match" if your employer offers a 401(k) type retirement savings match.
- Increase your savings rate every time you get a raise.
- Live, spend, invest, and think frugally to decrease debt and increase savings.
- Avoid paying full price whenever possible.

Start saving early even if the amount is small, increase it every time your income grows, and really ramp it up during your peak earning years. Saving early, often, long, as much as possible, and at high rates of return is the more certain path to riches over time. Reaching the millionaire club is possible if you start early enough or steadily invest a large enough amount. No special expertise or hard work is necessary beyond the financial principles we have covered, especially in the section on investing.

Improve your odds

Earn more, save more

One way to boost your savings is to boost your income. That could mean a second job, side business, or advancing your career to more pay. Here are tips to consider:

- Manage your career rather than just waiting for openings or lucky breaks.
- Don't be just an average employee -- aim to excel, be known as an asset, and be considered for the next promotion. Put your efforts into what helps the customer, boss, and company. Solve problems. Suggest improvements and ways to grow the business.
- Managing other people is not for everyone, but it is a main way to earn more money, especially as you get higher up the ladder.
- Actively look for promotions and opportunities *outside* your company, state, or even country. Jumps in pay are often much greater when switching companies than getting promotions within.
- Diversify your skills just as you do your portfolio. Enhance your value to your current or another company by gaining many experiences outside your job, field, or comfort zone. Don't be stagnant – the world isn't.
- Enhance your value by getting training, education, and certifications even if you need to do it on your own. Many companies will help pay for outside training. Studies shows that more education leads to higher pay over a lifetime.
- Look for respected people who can mentor you with advice, information, and opportunities. Do the same for others.

Save big, compound big

Our previous investing examples assume you save the same amount every year, but in reality you should be increasing your savings periodically. In particular, many savers do most of their savings during their later peak earnings years and/or when their biggest expenses have ended: student loans, mortgage, and kids' college. Consider this scenario. Beginning at age 50 with $250,000 already in savings, ramp up new savings to $2000 per month, and reach your million dollars at age 62 with 7% rate of return. $2000 per month is roughly what over-age 50 savers can contribute to their 401(k) type accounts including "catch-up" contributions. Remember, couples get to divide this savings challenge between them so it doesn't seem so daunting. Regardless of how much you power-up your new savings or when you start, set a specific goal, whether a time period or dollar goal. Just setting a specific goal helps us work towards it. Remember to increase your savings whenever your income increases or you receive a bonus or windfall.

Poor health, poor wealth

Good health habits are more than just a health or happiness issue – they directly affect your finances in many ways. In lieu of subjecting you to a full chapter on this topic, just consider the basic facts from many recent studies.

- People with poor health habits tend to spend more on life insurance premiums, out-of-pocket expenses, and more ailments, hospital stays, doctor's visits, drugs, and other health care expenses.
- Smokers and overweight people often earn less than their colleagues from being passed over for training, promotions, plum assignments, and other unfair life travails.
- Poor health often makes it harder to participate completely in the full range of wealth-building opportunities.
- Medical bills and debt can be among the largest and most devastating hits to your finances and is the leading cause of bankruptcies.

What is your plan?

Regardless of your chosen route(s) to the millionaire club or any savings goal, research shows that you are more likely to succeed when you have a written and shared goal and a plan to reach it. Write down your goal and outline some details to reach it. Research the route you choose and then focus on it frequently. Share your ambitious goal. Research shows that sharing a goal increases the likelihood of achieving it. Reward yourself for successes. Of course there is a website for that:

- http://www.stickk.com/ .

You might have noticed that all these steps usually take a long time to accomplish, whether scaling up a business or real estate holdings, saving steadily, or waiting for compounding magic to work. But that is okay. More than 90% of millionaires are over 50. Patience is not just a virtue, it's one of the ingredients in whatever plan you choose to acquire wealth. The good news is that four-fifths of millionaires report they are self-made. Why shouldn't you be able to do it too, now that you know the keys to success?

Stories abound about sudden millionaires blowing thru their cash quickly, but surveys show that new millionaires who worked their way to the club don't feel rich. They know that a million dollars doesn't go as far as it used to, and it must last for the rest of their life. A significant portion of new millionaires still live, spend, and think frugally, especially if that helped get them there.

Summary

- Living below your means and saving the rest is the foundation to savings and financial security.
- Without special talents and breaks, there are only a few proven paths to the millionaire club: starting a business, buying real estate, and investing mostly in stocks.
- The earlier you start, the more likely your financial success.
- Reaching an investment goal depends upon the length of time, rate of return, and amount your save. You usually have some control over each of these intertwined factors.
- Actively endeavor to increase your income, savings, investments, and healthy habits.
- Don't wait for a lucky break. Set your goal, develop a plan, write it down, share it, and make it happen.

-

End Notes

Visit my website to get the latest blog posts, updated links, and extra tools. Leave me a comment, participate in the discussion, get the latest news, and see where your friends can buy their own copy of the book. Share the website with your family, friends, and anyone else who could use extra money, savings, financial security, and tips.

- http://www.FinancialGuideToLife.com
- https://www.facebook.com/FinancialGuideToLife/
- john@financialguidetolife.com